GETTING AHEAD

GETTING AHEAD

DEVELOPING COMPETENCIES
FOR STRATEGIC LEADERSHIP

ROZHAN OTHMAN

PARTRIDGE

To order additional copies of this book, contact
Toll Free 800 101 2657 (Singapore)
Toll Free 1 800 81 7340 (Malaysia)
orders.singapore@partridgepublishing.com

www.partridgepublishing.com/singapore

CONTENTS

TABLES AND FIGURES

Dedicated to my mother, who inculcated in me my reading habit; my wife for her support, devotion, and understanding; and my children, who always forced me to think strategically about how to deal with them.

Vision is not available for those who cannot "see" with their own eyes. Real strategists get their hands dirty digging for ideas, and real strategies are built from the occasional nuggets they uncover.

Henry Mintzberg

PREFACE

Writing this book was a journey of discovery. It began when I started researching how Malaysian companies were managing their talent management programs. The initiative started as a research project done in collaboration with Wardah Azimah Sumardi, who was my colleague when I was serving at Universiti Brunei Darussalam. I continued researching the subject with my students after returning to Malaysia.

A consistent theme of many talent management programs is developing leaders for strategic leadership position. However, there is a lack of knowledge on what this entails. This is one of the issues I had to address as I became involved in consulting work through the consulting firm Human Capital Development. There was the need to articulate and model what strategic leadership competencies is all about. We sometimes find that human resource (HR) managers are not able to explain how developing strategic leadership ability is different from the leadership programs they conducted for middle and junior managers.

This gap drove me to start researching what strategic leadership is all about and what competencies are needed to be an effective strategic leader. I had initially presented a paper on this topic at a conference in Geneva in 2014. In 2015, Human Capital Development asked me to conduct a training program on strategic leadership competencies. We received positive reaction from the program's participants. I decided that it was time that I write everything into a book.

I do not claim credit for everything that is written in this book. I benefited a lot from the work of other scholars. This book also benefited from the work done by my PhD students. Zumalia Norzailan's research on talent management was important in providing a deeper understanding of talent development. Shazlinda Md. Yusof's work provided insight on how Japanese managers exercise leadership. I also wish to thank Mr. Eddie Tie, group CEO of VitaLife, and Dato Jamaluddin Ibrahim, group CEO of Axiata, for agreeing to be interviewed for this book project.

I'd also like to thank Human Capital Development for sponsoring the publication of this book. The firm also provided me the opportunity to try the various ideas I've learned and discovered from my research in various consultancy projects. Many people shaped my thinking about leadership and strategy. Some are fellow academicians who shared with me their insights. Some were students in MBA and doctoral classes. Some are friends who were my peers when we were student activists. And some are leaders of business organisations as well as NGOs who shared with me their reflections and experiences. I'd like to thank everyone at Partridge Publishing who were involved publishing this book. Again, many people were involved in shepherding the manuscript to make it publishable. I thank you all

The list of people I should thank is long, and it is not possible to mention all the names I am indebted to. I believe they know who they are. I have done my best to avoid mistakes when writing this book. Any shortcomings in this book are mine.

ABBREVIATIONS

CPR: Collective psychological resilience
DVD: Digital video disc
IPR: Individual psychological resilience
KPI: Key performance indicator
LCM: Leadership competency model
LPS: Lean production system
MMC: Malaysia Mining Corporation
MNC: Multinational corporation
NGO: Non-governmental organisation.
Petronas: Petroliam Nasional Berhad (Malaysia's national petroleum company)
QCC: Quality control circle
TM: Telekom Malaysia
TNB: Tenaga Nasional Berhad (a national electricity company)

CHAPTER 1

From Operational Leadership to Strategic Leadership

Introduction

B reakthrough happens because someone, usually a leader, decides the status quo is unacceptable or unsatisfactory. Typically, this spurs the search for new ideas and innovation. As a result, we see changes and transformations. But not all leaders create such a change. Many would simply loiter around where they currently are. Contentment with the status quo leads them to continue to do more of the same.

The ability to recognise that the status quo is not sustainable or that it will soon become unsustainable and then take the steps to spur the organisation to greater heights is a hallmark of a strategic leader. However, it takes more than just giving speeches about vision and mission to create a strategic shift. It takes more than just having a PR exercise and launching ceremonies to create strategic realignment. Many leaders get lost in doing just that. They spend time in PR exercises and giving noble speeches without understanding how to actually create impact. Strategic leadership effectiveness is about delivering result by creating a leap in performance.

Even though the term 'strategy' is often used in business and military planning, there are many examples of good strategies put in place in the public sector, in schools, and even in NGOs. The public sector in many countries has seen significant improvements in their service delivery as a result of adopting new technologies to improve their services. NGOs like Greenpeace have created a significant impact on our awareness of environmental issues. The Alliance for Climate Protection has had a major impact in generating public awareness and activism on climate change.

In business, we see many breakthrough products that have redefined market, competition, and even the way we lead our lives. Smartphones give us computing power in our palms. Green technologies make it possible to not treat the destruction of the environment as an inevitable aspect of modernisation. Hybrid cars make it possible to achieve a high level of fuel efficiency and reduce emissions. The Internet democratised access to information and broke the monopolies of media moguls and governments in the control over information. In addition, it also enabled consumers to perform business transactions from the comfort of their homes. Sites like eBay and mudah.my enable buyers and sellers to transact in virtual markets. In the service industry, discount airlines like Air Asia operate on an innovative business and operational model that makes air travel affordable to more people. Air travel is no longer a privilege of the well to do.

In military strategy, the "winning hearts and minds" approach in fighting the insurgency in Malaysia proved critical in defeating the communist threat. Civilian population living near jungles were moved to new villages to cut off material support to the Communist Party of Malaya. This, along with military operations, starved the communist fighters and forced them to retreat deep into the jungle. This made them less effective and forced them to focus on their basic survival instead of conducting attacks. Winning the hearts and mind of those who used to support the communist insurgents, whether willingly or reluctantly, was also important in getting high-quality intelligence that is critical is any war. The Americans, however, did not do as well in Vietnam. They were confident that their air power and conventional warfare capabilities would ensure victory. It was the communists who won the hearts and minds of the people, especially in rural areas of Vietnam.

In the sixteenth century, the ability to think strategically proved critical in the war between England and Spain. The English fleet was able to defeat the Spanish Armada in 1588 by building smaller and more manoeuvrable ships to defeat the Spanish armada which relied on bigger but less manoeuvrable ships. The English navy also used canons that had a longer range than the ones used by the Spanish armada. This enabled them to bombard the Spanish ships from a safe distance. The English were also innovative in using 'hell burners', burning ships to ram into the Spanish fleet waiting near Calais. It broke up the Spanish formation and made it easier for the smaller but more manoeuvrable British ships to attack. This is another case of addressing a challenge strategically by creatively thinking of new solutions and changing the rules of the game.

On the other hand, there is also a long history of failures in both business and warfare due to a lack of strategic thinking. There are businesses that can't seem to adapt to their environments. Nokia has exited the cellular phone market even though it once held the biggest market share. Zaitun Industries, recognised as a pioneer in halal cosmetics and consumer goods, is no longer around. Merlin hotels used to be a key landmark in major Malaysian cities but has also faded away. TWA, Pan Am, and Pelangi Air (a regional airline in Malaysia) were key players in their respective markets but no longer fly. Mega TV was one of earliest subscription TV service in Malaysia. It, too, closed up shop.

In warfare, the British failed to defend Malaya from the Japanese invasion because it made all the wrong assumptions and was rigid in the various defensive measures it took. The British assumed that any Japanese invasion would come from the sea. As a result, many fixed fortifications built by the British had their artillery pointed to the east towards the South China Sea. In the end, the Japanese attacked from the south through Thailand.

The Israelis were caught by surprise during the 1973 October War because they had been lulled by repeated Egyptian military exercises across the Sinai and thought that the final troop movement to launch the attack was just another exercise. The Israelis were also overconfident in believing that the Bar Lev line, a long fortification made of sand, was impenetrable. The Egyptian army simply hosed down the sand wall with water pumped from the Suez Canal.

Behind every story of success and failure were leaders. The successful stories were made by leaders who read the situation before them correctly and made the commitment to pursue the course of action that led to their success. On the other hand, failures are partly due to leaders misreading the situation and became victims of the changing environment. In some cases, they read the situation correctly but could not execute the necessary actions. And in some cases, failures happened because leaders were so contented, so disconnected from reality, and so insular that they never bothered to read the situation before them.

In today's fast-changing world, leaders have to be even more alert of unexpected competitors and unanticipated moves. Nobody in early 2000 would have expected Apple to become a major player in the mobile-phone business. Likewise, nobody would have expected Air Asia, an ailing airline formed by DRB-HICOM in 2001 and then bought over by Tune Air for RM1, to become a major competitor in the region, posing a serious challenge to Malaysia Airlines. Dunkin Donuts would not have imagined that the biggest challenger to its donut business in the Malaysian market would come from Big Apple Donut and Coffee, a local start-up established in 2007. Even Japanese consumer electronics and electrical goods companies are finding their once-dominant positions are now seriously undermined by new players from Korea and China.

Not all leaders are good strategists. Some rose up the ranks after long careers at the operational level. They continue to think and behave like operational leaders. These leaders are not able to refocus their attention on the big picture. Instead of understanding the shape of the forest and how it is changing, they continue to be preoccupied with looking at the trees. Some are precedence-based in their outlook. They act based on what they have grown accustomed to doing in the past. Suggest something new to them, and a typical retort they will give is, "We've always done it this way", or "We've never tried this new idea before." Instead of shaping history, these leaders are trapped in history. Instead of leading others forward, they keep people in the past.

A study this author conducted on leaders of Malaysian finance companies during the Asian financial crisis in 1997 illustrates how the ability to think strategically can make a difference in the behaviour of firms. The leaders of these firms were asked whether they had anticipated the crisis or whether it came as a complete surprise. Half of the respondents said they knew the crisis was going to happen even before it started. The other half reported that it came as a surprise. Those who anticipated the crisis took remedial steps immediately. On the other hand, those who did not anticipate the crisis took remedial steps only about two months later.

What contributed to these differences in perception? They all were in the midst of the same conditions. Two things stood out as the differences between these two groups. First, the anticipators knew the crisis was long term. Those who did not anticipate the crisis thought it was just a short-term problem. Second, the anticipators monitored their environments by also examining the regional and global economic environments. Those who did not anticipate the crisis just monitored what their competitors were doing. In other words, the anticipators were looking at the macro-environment and understood that the crisis was going to be a protracted one. On the other hand, those who failed to anticipate the crisis were focused on the micro-environment and did not fully comprehend the dynamics behind the crisis. They might have also accepted the mantra from some politicians that the crisis would be over in two months. It is very obvious here who were the strategic leaders and who had a less strategic outlook.

Among the key competencies needed at the senior level are strategic leadership competencies. These are distinct from the leadership competencies needed at the lower and middle levels. Lower-level leadership is more about supervisory skills and the leadership of teams. Middle-level leadership is about leading operational and tactical issues. Often, they involve dealing with functional-level problems, though it can sometimes involve managing cross-functional collaboration.

Strategic leadership competencies are distinct because they involve the exercise of leadership within a top management team. While members of top management may represent their functional areas, their effectiveness depends on their abilities to act in an integrated manner. As for those leading at the top, they need to have a bird's-eye view of the organisation and of their competitive environment. The time horizon for their plan is long term, and the problems they have to deal with are often ambiguous, novel, poorly defined, and require a lot of sense making.

Axiata is a Malaysian telecommunication company with presence in many Asian countries and employs 25,000 people across the region. It has a diverse workforce from many countries and has to ensure that it has a sufficient crop of future leaders to lead its operations. Dato Seri Jamaluddin Ibrahim, the group CEO of Axiata, points out that a strategic leader is expected to "push the needle." This means that the performance level that is expected from a strategic leader is more than just small incremental improvements. He or she is expected to take the company to the next level. If the company is currently earning RM1 billion, the strategic leader needs to figure out how to make it a RM2 billion a year company. Like a race car driver, the strategic leader needs to boost performance and press on the accelerator to push the company's speedometer to a higher performance level. This will require going beyond doing more of what the organisation is currently doing. The strategic leader will have to think of the capabilities his or her organisation will need to reach the next level.

Strategic decisions often require coordination across functional areas. A decision on a new product requires coordination between the R&D, marketing, and production functions. The R&D function has to develop the product. Marketing needs to study the market, identify what customers want, and ultimately, how to distribute and sell the product. The production department needs to assess what it will need to produce the new product and the cost to produce it. Even the financial controller needs to assess the budget for the whole initiative and decide how to fund it. The HRM department needs to support the decision by making sure the right people with the right skills are available. All these require considerable coordination across functional boundaries and to develop a common mechanism such as the establishment of cross-functional teams to ensure effective execution. Managing such cross-functional collaboration is part of the responsibility of leaders at the senior level.

In addition, because of the higher ambiguity and novelty of problems at the strategic level, dealing with strategic problems requires more creativity. There are often no precedence or standard procedures on how to deal with these problems. When a competitor introduces a disruptive innovation by using a new technology, it redefines the rules of competition. Sometime it even makes the company's technologies obsolete. Responding to these moves is much more difficult because it requires more than just incremental changes. There is no recipe or playbook on how to deal with such a situation. This is why Nokia and Research in Motion (makers of BlackBerry) experienced considerable difficulty responding to the emergence of smartphones. In the case of Air Asia's entry into the airline industry, it changed the way consumers view air travel. Discount airlines like Air Asia basically make air travel a commodity that is price sensitive. Full-service airlines like Malaysia Airlines were not designed to compete as a low-cost service provider and found their once near monopoly position in the domestic market affected. They cannot ignore the appeal of low airfare to customers and cannot price their fare too high.

The search for a solution to these challenges requires considerable creative thinking. Doing what competitors are already doing will, at best, create parity but will not ensure sustainable competitive advantage and success. JetBlue

Operational leadership	Strategic leadership
• Low ambiguity	• High ambiguity
• Low novelty	• High novelty
• Procedural based	• Imagination based
• Short term	• Long-term
• Productive output	• Creative output
• Scorekeeping	• Strategizing
• Functional focus	• Cross-functional
• Internal orientation	• External oriented

Table 1.1: Differences between Operational Leadership and Strategic Leadership

Airways in the United States and Malindo Air in Malaysia position themselves as low-cost airlines that come with more comfort and frills. This differentiating move may well help them create a profitable niche. Resourcefulness in seeking new ways to compete is important for strategic leadership.

On the other hand, problems at the operational level are usually more clearly defined. As such, problems are usually not novel. Many of the problems faced are short and medium term. There are often rules and procedures to guide the problem solving. Operational problems are usually dealt at the functional level. Occasionally, cross-functional collaboration is necessary. Operational leadership is about executing well once a strategy has been decided. It involves finding optimum use of resources. Operational managers are often held accountable to short-term outcomes and cost-based control. Productivity is key to operational execution. This does not mean that creativity is totally unnecessary. At the operational level, creative effort is more focused on process innovation to improve efficiency. However, as Corson and Miyagawa point out, as operational leaders move upwards in their organisations, they have to shift from being scorekeepers to strategists. This involves redirecting their focus and ways of thinking.

Dato Seri Jamaluddin Ibrahim explains that managers at the operational level have to think about the immediate impact of their work. For some, this can come in the form meeting their sales or production targets. For other operational managers, this can be whether they've been able to meet cost-cutting targets. However, managers at the strategic level have to think about the impact of their decisions and their business on the environment the business inhabit. They have to think about the impact on society, the environment, the economy, and population. It's no longer just thinking about immediate targets.

Two key adjustments operational leaders have to make as they move to the strategic level positions are to recognise that their thinking has to be more externally oriented and that leadership at this level is no longer just about leading their respective functions. Even though they continue to represent a function, they have to see themselves as organisational leaders. Their effectiveness at this level involves their abilities to understand the external environment and steer the whole organisation to make it more competitive. Beatty and Hughes report that a survey about the job of chief financial officers show that even in a specialised function like finance, chief financial officers spend between 65 and 75 percent of their time on strategic issues. Table 1 summarises the difference between operational and strategic leadership.

Unlearning Old Habits

The different competencies needed by operational leaders as they move up the hierarchy means that they will have to unlearn some of their old competencies and habits and learn new ones. Unfortunately, this does not always happen. Even when managers try to do it, they do not find it easy. Management researchers recognise that human behaviour at work is often shaped by behavioural momentum. Greave explains this essentially means that the influence of past behaviours and habits is so strong that people tend to behave the way they always did even when they accept the need to change. Past habits create a strong momentum that keeps people trapped in their old behaviours. In the case of managers advancing in their careers, some still think and behave like operational leaders even when they are on the top management team.

Some jobs expect people to be microfocused. Typically, this involves extensive use of specialised technical knowledge. This is especially the case in the professional disciplines like accounting, engineering, and medicine. Managers who are technical specialists may have more difficulties in the transition into a strategic role. One vice president complained to this author about her boss, who came from a technical background and had very little management experience. In spite of being in the number-one position in the organisation, he still spends a lot of time scrutinizing travel claims of his subordinates. This is a job best left to lower-level subordinates. The organisation didn't pay the number one a five-figure monthly salary for him to spend his time doing the job of a clerk.

There are also situations where people do not develop strategic leadership competencies because they were not allowed to think and behave strategically. This sometimes happens when the number-one leader circles himself or herself with "yes men" and "yes women" whose roles are to make him or her feel good and provide political support. Even though they are all a part of the top management team, the culture that prevails is one that does not encourage diversity and critical discussion of ideas. People who have been conditioned to behave like brainless dolts cannot suddenly be expected to show courage, competence, and creativity when they ascend to the number-one position. That's why we sometimes see leaders who were in the number-two position being criticised for their incompetence by their former boss after they ascend to the number-one position. They got to their current position by being yes men and women to their then bosses.

Management writers Laurence Peter and Raymond Hull introduced the term "Peter Principle" to describe the phenomenon where competent people are promoted into incompetence. This is basically a situation where someone who is competent in a current position is promoted because of his or her outstanding performance to a higher position. However, the higher position requires a totally different set of competencies, and the person's performance declines after promotion. Examples include good teachers who are promoted to become principals who find themselves ill-equipped for the leadership and administrative role expected in their new position. A good surgeon promoted to an administrative position can also encounter similar difficulties. A professor who excels in research who is promoted to an administrative position may also perform poorly in the new position. Earlier doctoral training and experience in teaching and research did not involve developing leadership and administrative abilities.

But What Is Strategy?

Before we discuss strategic leadership competencies further, it is important that we are clear what strategy is all about. Ask this simple question to a group, and you will typically get about a dozen different answers. What exactly is strategy? Before we answer this question, let us be clear first what strategy is not.

1. A strategy is not just about having a long-term plan. There are many long-term plans that do not have any strategic value. In fact, some long-term plans are nothing more than just a calendar of activities that were prepared without any strategic thinking involved. Many of these activities are just a repeat of past activities.

2. Strategizing is not just about having a vision or goals or objectives or creating vision and mission statements. The lazy ones can always search through Google for vision and mission statements and copy and paste it. Likewise, goal setting can be a pretty arbitrary process with someone or a group of people deciding on the goals without any appreciation of the reality in the external environment. In the end, all these vision and mission statements, as well as goals, are just wish lists. A good strategy is one that articulates the goals as a causal model. This causal model defines what are the desired outcomes and what has to happen to create the outcome. Addressing the issue of what has to happen to create the outcome forces planners to think about their organisation's internal capabilities and to what extent their goals are realistic and attainable. A good swimmer can set the vision or goal of becoming a world tennis champion. But it is probably not a realistic goal if he is already in his forties and never played tennis before.

3. A good strategy is not just about doing what others do. Imitation is easy, but it is not always a sustainable strategic move. If the strengths of a market leader are easily imitated, chances are that there will be many other imitators. In the end, there will be many similar competitors with no one really having a competitive edge. Imitation does not help differentiate between competitors.

4. Adopting best practices is usually not the best strategy. The so-called best practices of market leaders were usually developed within their specific context. This context includes the influence of many intangibles, including their organisational culture and history. Many

best practices also include tacit knowledge that may not be understood by others. In fact, even the market leaders themselves may not be aware of the tacit aspects of their practices. When what is thought to be a best practice is adopted by an organisation with a different internal environment, these practices usually do not yield the same benefits. For instance, quality control circle initiatives are very successfully used in Japan. However, attempts to adopt it in other countries, including Malaysia, has not yielded the same outcomes as in Japan.

5. Managing strategies is not about monitoring key performance indicators (KPIs). Some planners focus a considerable amount of their effort monitoring key performance indicators. KPIs are the laggard measures of the intended outcomes. Knowing whether the KPIs have been achieved does little to help leaders manage their strategies. Managing strategy should be focused on managing the performance drivers that are supposed to deliver the KPIs. Performance drivers are the antecedents to the outcomes. Thus, leaders should focus on measuring the performance drivers in order to ensure the attainment of the KPIs. There is no point monitoring the KPIs if the performance drivers are neglected. Those who are responsible for the KPIs will be unfairly judged. The failure to put in place the performance drivers can come in many forms. It can be in the form of the failure to develop the necessary capabilities, unwilling to make the necessary investment, not executing important activities well, relying on ineffective processes, or the failure to acquire the necessary expertise or technologies. These are the things that should be monitored and managed to ensure the attainment of the KPIs.

Having explained what is not strategy, let us now explain a number of key ideas about strategy.

1. Strategy is the primary responsibility of top management. However, the process of strategizing varies between organisations. In many organisations, it is top management's prerogative. However, Nonaka describes the strategizing process in many Japanese organisations as middle-up-bottom. This is mainly because it is at the middle level that information from the market converges to form a picture of the external environment. In addition, middle-level managers are still

quite close to the market to have a good understanding what the data collected means. Thus, the input to strategy and strategic change usually comes from middle management. It is then considered by top management. Once the decision on the strategic options has been made, implementation involves everyone and goes all the way to the bottom.

2. Kenichi Ohmae points out that the key issue in strategizing is deciding on how to develop competitive advantage. This is the primary concern in strategic thinking. This understanding is the basis for creating competitive distance from competitors. A plan that does not define clearly the competitive advantage that an organisation intends to rely on is not a strategic plan. One of the classic ideas on competitive advantage is by Michael Porter, who presents three basic options for creating competitive advantage. Organisations can create competitive advantage through differentiation, become a low-cost producer, or focus on serving a specific market well. Miles and Snow conceptualise competitive advantage in terms of seizing first-mover advantage or second-mover actions or by defending a defined niche. All these strategic options can be successful and profitable. Deciding on the competitive advantage that an organisation wants to rely on requires the ability to read the competitive situation correctly. Once a decision has been made on how to compete, the next step is executing the chosen option flawlessly.

3. Mintzberg points out that strategizing involves creativity. It involves exploring and searching for insights and ideas. There is the tendency for planners to be preoccupied with plans and key performance indicators that they ignore the more fundamental aspect of thinking creatively about their strategies. Unfortunately, in some organisations, strategizing has become bureaucratised and involves a lot of paperwork and filling of forms. In fact, some managers complain that they are so bogged down with filling forms and preparing reports that they are detracted from their work.

4. Strategy is more about synthesis. Many planners are too focused on the analytical aspect of strategizing. Analysis is simply a process of breaking

down a problem. It helps planners understand the components of a system or problem and how they interact. However, analysis alone is not enough to strategise. The planner has to synthesise all the information to form the big picture. Analysis is about looking at the trees. Synthesis is about inferring about the forest after having examined the trees. It's a bit like when a sick person with high temperature sees a doctor. The doctor will take his or her temperature, check the throat and ears, take a blood pressure, and listen to the person's chest. This is analysis. This is necessary but not enough to treat the patient. The doctor must make an inference from his or her analysis about the illness. Is it throat infection? Is it ear infection? Is it dengue fever? Is it a flu? Or is it some exotic viral infection? This inference is the product of synthesizing a conclusion from the insights gained from the analysis.

5. Strategy is equifinal. The notion of equifinality simply means that a given outcome or goal can be potentially reached through many ways. For instance, two competitors competing in the same market may rely on different capabilities to achieve their goals. Both Apple and Samsung are vying to be the leader in smartphones. But their approaches to achieving their goals are different. Apple competes by offering a very limited range of iPhone models targeted at the high-end price range. Samsung, on the other hand, offers many products with different levels of functionality targeted to multiple price segments. They compete in the same product category but use different approaches. Another example of equifinality is in how automotive companies create efficiencies. American car manufacturers used to create efficiencies through economies of scale. They built big assembly plants and went for vertical integration. Japanese car manufacturers could not use the same formula because of limited capital (in the early days), and they had little control over needed natural resources. Almost all raw material had to be imported, and this made the price higher. Instead of creating economies of scale, Toyota developed the lean production system (LPS) that focused on waste reduction in every activity to achieve efficiency. Though using a different approach than the Americans, Toyota was able to achieve a high level of efficiency. Creative strategists leverage on equifinality by

developing novel competitive approaches. Uncreative strategic planners will just try to imitate others or do more of what they've always done.

6. Related to developing competitive advantage is having a clear idea of the value the organisation is creating. Businesses must understand what customers consider valuable. Success depends on delivering what customers want. For instance, is the company selling a product or a service? The answer to this question has important implications for how the company competes. For instance, is a restaurant selling products or services? If it sees the value it is creating as products, it will focus on preparing food. On the other hand, if it defines its business as service, it will treat food as just a component of its service. A restaurant that defines its business as a service will consider the ambience, quality of waiter service, cleanliness, speed, and food quality as the different dimensions of its value creation. It will consciously manage all these components.

7. Strategic leaders also need to develop internal capabilities that are aligned with the challenges they are facing. They sometimes have to adapt the organisation to face the changing situation. These capabilities need to be developed to support the competitive approach an organisation relies on. This includes developing the human resources of the organisation. One important aspect of this effort is developing future leaders. Many organisations recognise the importance of preparing their managers for advancement into senior leadership positions. Among the issues that Christoph Mueller had to address in his turnaround effort at Malaysia Airlines Berhad is developing future leaders. He recognises that a strong company needs capable leaders, especially at the higher levels. The typical approach in developing future strategic leaders is by introducing talent management programs.

8. Good strategies are simple and focused. A strategy needs to be understandable for it to be useful. Thick strategy documents are usually difficult to understand. In fact, one can argue that the thickness of a strategy document is inversely related to its successful implementation. Complex and lengthy strategies often have too many unnecessary details. When a strategy document is too detailed, it

limits discretion and creativity at lower levels. As a result, the strategy becomes a straitjacket of KPIs that overwhelm people. Having too many elements in the strategy also makes it difficult to stay focused on the important issues. The consulting firm McKinsey & Company observes the rule of three. They will only have three objectives, three priorities, and so on. You know an organisation has lost its focus when its strategy has more than ten priorities or seeks to pursue fifteen outcomes. In fact, when a strategy document is thick or when it discusses many detailed issues and yet leaves those involved unclear of what are the key strategic issues, it is usually because the planners were never clear of the difference between strategic and nonstrategic issues.

9. A strategic idea has to be executed well. A good strategy will lead to nothing if it is not implemented properly. However, implementing a strategy is not always a straightforward matter. Some strategies require incremental improvement of current capabilities. However, some strategies require a transformation of the organisation. This may involve changing its internal capabilities, technology base, and market. Making all these changes requires upsetting the current internal structure, power balance, and priorities. Some members of the organisation have made investments in the current capabilities and commitments to current market. Asking them to let go of all these is never easy. It often becomes a political process. A good strategist needs to have the influence to manage the internal dynamics of the organisation when planning strategy implementation. Some strategic management techniques, like the Balanced Scorecard and Management by Objectives, offer some tools for implementing strategy but do not address the complexity of organisational politics in strategy implementation.

Closing

As more organisations recognise the value of developing a concerted and proactive approach to competition, they also recognise the importance of developing leaders with strategic leadership competencies. Competing effectively requires the ability to read the evolving environment. Strategic leaders also need to develop internal capabilities that are aligned with the challenges they face. They sometimes have to adapt the organisation to face changing situations. These abilities need to be developed. Prior work experience at the lower and middle levels of a firm are usually not sufficient to develop these competencies.

Many organisations recognise the importance of preparing their managers for advancement into senior leadership positions. The typical approach is by introducing talent management programs. It takes more than just a training program to develop strategic leadership competencies. Managers need to acquire new knowledge, learn new skills, and above all, change their thinking and work habits. Many talent management programs have development activities that span over a period of a few years to develop the leadership competencies to lead at the senior level. The time and resources commitment organisations make to develop their futures reflect both the difficulty of the process and the importance of doing it.

It is important that all these talent management and leadership development initiatives understand the distinct characteristics of strategic leadership competencies. Otherwise, they may end up focusing mainly on developing leadership competencies for current roles and positions instead of developing future senior managers who are supposed to lead at the strategic level. These managers may become better at what they are currently doing. But they are not necessarily better equipped for a strategic leadership role. This book hopes to make a contribution by discussing strategic leadership competencies. It discusses what it takes to develop strategic leadership competencies.

CHAPTER 2

Strategic Leadership
Competency Model

Introduction

A typical feature of many talent management programs is to anchor the leadership development to a leadership competency model. Likewise, the development of strategic leadership competencies has to begin with defining clearly a model of strategic leadership competencies. A strategic leadership competency model provides a basis for planning the mix of development activities needed to shape operational leaders into strategic leaders.

A simple way to understand this is to imagine the task of transforming a group of golfers into an effective hockey team. Merely bringing the golfers to play hockey together will not be enough to turn them into an effective team. Transforming a group of golfers into a hockey team requires that the coach has a clear idea of the competencies the team needs to be an effective hockey team. The skills, rules and mindset needed to be an effective hockey team is different from playing golf. Hockey requires teamwork. Hockey players require considerable dexterity because they have to dribble and pass the ball to their team members. Playing hockey also involves speed and requires a lot of running and sprinting. Stamina, endurance, and strength are important. Because hockey is a team game, players play for the glory of the team, and this involves a lot of coordination between them. Winning against another team involves a lot of planning and intelligence collection. A hockey team needs to understand their opponent's strengths and weaknesses. Each match requires decisions on the formation the team will use and how team members will be deployed. This includes understanding the roles and skills of the different positions. Only when clear of the competency requirements can the coach develop a training program to build the golfers into an effective hockey team.

The same applies in the development of strategic leadership competencies. One cannot expect to create strategic leaders from a training program that focuses on skills relevant to operational leadership or supervisory skills. Major companies use leadership competency models as the basis for their leadership development programs. Colgate-Palmolive's leadership competency model defines "providing a strategic perspective" as one of the competencies the company's leaders need to develop. This competency is developed through developing three subcompetencies termed as having a "business and global perspective", "strategic vision", and being "customer focused". Tenaga Nasional uses the Leadership Potential Inventory as its leadership competency model. It makes an implicit reference to strategic leadership competencies under the mastery of complexity dimension. This dimension has three components – adaptability, conceptual thinking, and able to navigate complexity and ambiguity. 3M differentiates between its basic leadership competencies, what it calls fundamental and essential leadership competencies, and the strategic leadership competencies which the company terms as visionary leadership competencies. Alldredge and Nilan explain that the latter includes competencies that are needed to develop leaders who are able to see beyond their own immediate areas of responsibility.

Admittedly, models are a simplification of reality. Models can make a complex phenomenon appear simple. Some management researchers, such as Hollenbeck, criticise the use of competency models. Hollenbeck's criticisms include the fact it is unlikely that a single set of characteristics adequately describes what is needed to be an effective leader. He argues that leadership is complex and that reducing it to a model of a set of competencies ignores these complexities. Hollenbeck also argues that leadership competency models tend to present the competencies as though they are independent of each other. These models do not explain how these competencies interact with each other. He also points out that some competencies can easily become liabilities. It depends a lot on how the competencies are understood and used. For instance, communication skills, which is an important aspect of charisma, can be used for motivating others, but they can also be used to manipulate them.

A counterargument to Hollenbeck's criticism is that education has for the most part been based on some model of the knowledge that students should acquire. As mentioned earlier, models are simplifications and do not explain everything. But a good model should describe important aspects of the phenomenon examined. For instance, drivers face many varied conditions when driving. But this does not mean student drivers have to be taught every single conceivable condition they may face in the future. This is unrealistic, and merely attempting to list all the possible conditions will be endless. Instead, student drivers need to be taught driving skills that can be used in different conditions. Driving school curriculums are designed to impart the important skills. In the end, the driver needs to use his or her judgment on how to use the skills when dealing with the different driving conditions. The skills included in the driving curriculum reflect a competency model of the abilities one must have to be a safe driver. Consider what will happen if we allow driving lessons to be random and not guided by some model of what is needed to drive safely.

A competency model must be able to differentiate between the competencies of low-performing individuals and the competencies of high-performance individuals. Competence is not just about having skills, knowledge, and abilities. Competence is about being good at performing the tasks relevant to a job. Lawler states that it is about a person's mastery of the skills needed to do well in her or his job. A competency model needs to identify those skills that drive performance in the job.

Competency models are useful not because there are exact models of reality. Nor are they useful because they are complete and sacred. It is important for strategists to recognise that all models are works in progress. As we understand a model better, we will be better able to decide the important variables that should be included in the model. The important thing to recognise is that models, including competency models, are not supposed to be rigid and static. For instance, our model of the weather becomes more complex as more powerful information processing capabilities that enable us to process more weather-related data exist. Likewise, the sophistication of models in engineering has increased considerably with the availability of computer-aided design technologies. Models must be able to describe the phenomenon of interest. Goods models must be able to also explain how the system being modelled works. A great model can also be used to predict. Statistical analysis and mathematical models enable us to do this.

Alldredge and Nilan's description of how 3M formulated its leadership competency model shows how their leadership competency model evolves over time to reflect changes in the company's focus and strategy. No leadership competency model, including the strategic leadership competency model to be presented in this book, is final. The model can be refined and changed as we understand more about strategic leadership.

Leadership Competencies Model

A model of leadership competencies can incorporate many elements. The formulation of a leadership competency model should be based on the organisation's understanding of the qualities of effective leadership. These qualities can differ considerably across organisations. This is because of the differences in competitive requirements across industries and businesses and the competitive approach of the organisation. An organisation like 3M that relies on product innovation requires a different set of competencies than a contract manufacturer like Foxconn that depends on efficiency. Likewise, the competencies needed for effective leadership in these organisations differ in some respects.

However, the basic ability to think and lead strategically has some general characteristics. These characteristics form the basis of a strategic leadership competency model. This discussion about strategic leadership competencies by no means nullifies the value of leadership competencies used in leadership development at the lower and middle levels. Competencies such as developing teamwork, managing performance, and delegation skills will continue to be important as a manager advances to senior-level positions. In fact, Beatty and Hughes report that studies show that most strategic decisions are made in teams. The teamwork competencies developed earlier in a manager's career will continue to be important. These basic leadership competencies are still necessary, but they are not sufficient at the top management level. They must be complemented by strategic leadership competencies.

Before we can discuss strategic leadership competencies, it is important to understand what is a strategy and what strategists do. Unfortunately, the word "strategy" is so extensively used for many things that its actual meaning becomes confusing. Dan Schendel, the editor-in-chief of *Strategic Management Journal*, laments that everything has become "strategic" in business. The word "strategy" has its origin in Greek and comes from the word *strategos*. The word "strategos" is synonymous with leadership and is usually used to refer to top military leaders such as generals and admirals. In modern Greece, the word

---

Insight Box 2.1

Strategic Capabilities Building

In addition to assessing the environment, a strategist needs to have a holistic understanding of the resources and capabilities of the organisation. This understanding will help a strategist decide on how to develop a competitive advantage and on what competitive advantage the organisation will be able to build. Dell competes as a low-cost producer of personal computers by making good use of the efficiencies created by its supply chain management capabilities. Air Asia dealt with the fuel price increase in 2008 by making better use of its assets. Among other things, it generated ancillary income by selling advertisement space on the fuselage of its aircraft. Canon has been able to diversify its business into many different products – including scanners, digital cameras, printers, and photocopiers – because of its basic strengths in areas like imaging, precision mechanics, and optics.

"strategos" refers to the highest ranking officer of the army. These are leaders who are supposed to come up with a plan to win the war.

Two things stand out from this understanding. First, strategizing is top-management responsibility. It is synonymous with the leadership role at the apex of the organisation. Failure to strategise is failure in the exercise of leadership. Second, the planning the leader does must be about how to win. As mentioned in the previous chapter, the essence of strategizing is about deciding on the organisation's competitive advantage. This is because to win a war, a general must formulate a plan that can outmanoeuvre the opponent. Every military planner knows that formulating a winning plan requires intelligence to understand the enemy, the climate, and combat terrain, and an accurate and realistic assessment of the capabilities of one's own force. Ultimately, the plan has to be executed flawlessly. Doing this requires coordination and communication. Each plan must also be novel and unanticipated to create an element of surprise for the enemy.

A strategy is more than just a long-term plan. At the most fundamental level, a strategy must clearly identify the competitive advantage an organisation should develop and rely on. Mintzberg explains this succinctly when he argued that there is a difference between strategy formulation and strategic planning. Planning is about scheduling a sequence of activities to achieve a goal. It requires analytical skills. Strategy formulation, however, is about creativity; it is about imagining and involves the ability to synthesise ideas. A strategic plan can be quite meaningless if it is used to execute an idea or pursue a goal that has no strategic value, that is, does not create competitive advantage. This understanding of the competitive advantage an organisation wants to develop is the basis for formulating the organisation's value creation logic.

Michael Porter defines a strategist as the one whose job is to understand and cope with competition. A strategist uses this understanding to conceptualise the logic behind the plan he or she is formulating. This requires a certain level of abstract thinking. It involves thinking of issues at the organisational level and not just the functional level. One has to be able to see the forest and not just the trees. The strategist has to be future oriented and look at what Gavetti terms as

---

Insight Box 2.2

Strategizing Based on Asymmetry

In military strategy, the Vietcong managed to defeat the French, and later the Americans, in Vietnam not by building the same strengths and capabilities as their enemies but by using tactics that leveraged on its strength as a force fighting in its own territory and dependent on the support of the local population. Likewise, in 2006, Hezbollah managed to strike a crushing blow on the Israeli army by relying on ambushes. It made good use of its knowledge of the terrain in southern Lebanon to conduct attacks. It created tank killer units to ambush and destroy Israeli tanks. The successes of the Vietcong and Hezbollah gave rise to the term "asymmetric warfare" to refer to the war between foes that have seemingly opposite capabilities.

"cognitively distant opportunities." These are ideas about opportunities that most people do not easily recognise. It requires a certain perceptiveness to notice these opportunities. Schoemaker and colleagues point out that a strategist must also be able to engage in sense making when facing ambiguity and decide on a plan. This often involves making sense of ambiguous signals and incomplete information to form inferences about threats and opportunities.

Once a decision on competitive advantage has been made, the strategic leader must also be able to execute the ideas related to creating the advantage. Quite often, a strategic decision requires a shift in approach from the current one. An organisation that is shifting its competitive approach cannot be competing using internal capabilities designed for the competitive approach it relied on in the past. The organisation may need to acquire new resources, develop new products and capabilities, as well as enter new markets. All these require change. As such, strategic leaders need to initiate and manage change successful. Many writers argue that strategic leaders need to have execution skills to implement their strategies. This is indeed true. However, at the strategic leadership level, execution skill is more about executing change. The change can be in the form of incremental improvements or transformational change. This depends on the challenges perceived by the organisation and the response it selects.

A key element in leading change is having a leadership team to lead the process. Leading strategic change is not a task that can be carried out by one person. A strategic leader needs to surround himself or herself with capable leaders who can help realise the strategy. Selecting the right persons for the leadership team is critical. A bad selection decision will create liabilities in the leadership team. It ends up with people who are either a burden or an impediment to the changes needed to ensure the success in implementing a strategy.

Introducing something new is not easy. Thus, a strategic leader needs to win over support for the idea from peers and the rest of the organisation. Gaining such support requires building alliances and support for the change. And the leader must be able to do all this while being guided by his or her moral compass. All these have to be done with a long-term view of the interest of the organisation.

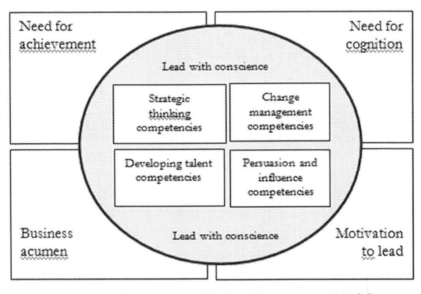

Figure 2.1: Strategic Leadership Competency Model

All these can be surmised as indicating that developing strategic leadership competencies involves developing strategic thinking skills, changing management skills, developing persuasion and influence skills, developing talented people for the leadership team, and leading with conscience.

Strategic Leadership Competency Model

At the outer layer of the strategic leadership competency models are characteristics that make someone suited for the strategic leadership role. These are not competencies, per se, but are a combination of personal characteristics and prior experience. The first is achievement orientation. Individuals with high achievement orientation are driven by the need to achieve something greater. They are not easily contented with the status quo. A sure way to fail in developing strategic leadership competencies is choosing participants who are happy with merely maintaining the status quo. They are not going to be motivated to "push the needle" but would be content with doing the minimum.

The second characteristic of the managers who are suited for developing strategic leadership competencies are those who have high need for cognition. Cacoppio and Petty define need for cognition as a person's tendency to engage and enjoy thinking effort. Individuals with high need for cognition are more likely to search for new information, enjoy purposeful thinking, and are more likely to form judgements based on rational arguments. They are also more likely to remember information gathered. On the other hand, low need for cognition individuals are less likely to search for new information and more likely to rely on subjective judgment. They are also more likely to judge based on stereotypes and their assessment of the source of information rather than the merit of the information. As a result, they are less likely to explore new possibilities and options. Instead, they tend to be more content with the status quo. Leadership at the strategic level requires people with high need for cognition who are willing to visualise new possibilities. On the other hand, training someone with low need for cognition strategic leadership competencies is akin to teaching someone who is aquaphobic how to swim.

Achievement Orientation	
Low	High
• Content with taking things easy • Satisfied with small achievements • Exerts minimal effort • Prefers to maintain status quo	• Strives to reach the next level • Sets high goals • Goes the extra mile • Restless with status quo • Motivated by new challenges • Plans ahead to go beyond current attainments

Table 2a: Comparison of Characteristics of Those with Low and High Levels of Achievement Orientation

Willingness to Lead	
Low	High
• Prefers to be led • Unable to visualise new purpose and vision • Dependent on leader to structure task • Uncomfortable dealing with novel problems • Have preference for routinised tasks • Lacks self-confidence and possibly has low self-esteem	• Willing to take charge and lead • Comfortable with having to think about new vision and purpose • Able to plan and manage own task • Feels challenged and stimulated with novel problems • Self-confident and have high self-esteem

Table 2b: Comparison of Characteristics of Those with Low and High Levels of Self-Efficacy to Lead

Related to high need for achievement, strategic leaders need to be individuals who have the motivation to lead. Chan and Drasgow define motivation to lead as an individual's willingness to assume leadership. Individuals with high motivation to lead are more willing to participate in leadership training and make intense efforts in exercising leadership. Two key qualities shape this confidence. The first is a person's self-assessment of his or her ability to lead at the higher level. This positive self-assessment can be the product of actual abilities or the belief that one has the ability to learn the needed competencies to lead. This perception of one's abilities is the result of learning as well as prior leadership experience. The second is motivation to lead. De Vries points out that some individuals have a preference to be led, to have their work structured by a leader. Individuals with low motivation to lead will not make good strategic leaders simply because as strategic leaders, they are expected to be independent and self-reliant in discharging their responsibilities.

Finally, to be effective as a strategic leader requires that the manager possess business acumen. This is related to the understanding the nature of the organisation's business, how the organisation competes, the competitive environment, the industry the organisation operates in, and possess the skills to understand business data and reports. Tables 2a, 2b, 2c, and 2d show the comparisons between individuals who are high and low on these four qualities.

This model shows the four qualities needed by candidates to undergo development programs to become a strategic leader. Once the candidates for this program are chosen, they need to develop these strategic leadership competencies. These are needed to ensure that those who undergo strategic leadership competency development are suited for the role. Figure 2.1 depicts this relationship. The inner components of this model are the strategic leadership competencies.

At the core of leading strategically is leading with conscience. Developing leaders with conscience is important to ensuring that all the other competencies in this model are used for greater good. Conscience is the foundation of good leadership. Strategic thinking competencies, change management competencies, talent development competencies, and persuasion and influence competencies should be anchored to conscience. These competencies will stick together in

Need for Cognition	
Low	High
• Content with current understanding and knowledge • Satisfied with merely knowing something but not interested in "why" or "how" • Prefers to do things the way they've always been done • Considers thinking a burdensome effort • Only learns what is needed for immediate job	• Driven by curiosity and excited about new knowledge and experience • Seeks to always question why and how something is done the way it is done • Has a habit of questioning the status quo and always seeks improvement • Finds thinking and creative effort stimulating and a source of joy • Have a broad interest and knowledgeable about many things

Table 2c: Comparison of Characteristics of Those with Low and High Levels of Need for Cognition

Business Acumen	
Low	High
• Sees operational issues as technical issues • Inward looking and insulated from market and industry • Unable to assess financial implications of decisions and actions • Works in silo and uninterested in what happens outside functional area	• Able to frame technical issues in the context of business issues • Externally oriented and understands dynamics of market and industry • Able to assess financial implications of decisions and actions • Willing to collaborate with those in other functional areas

Table 2d: Comparison of Characteristics of Those Who Are Low and High on Business Acumen

creating greater good when applied by leaders with conscience. Without conscience, these competencies can end up being used opportunistically and exploitatively.

Strategic Thinking

Moon defines strategic thinking as the ability to think of alternative ways to compete and create value for customers. Graetz explains that the purpose of strategic thinking is to seek innovation and explore new futures that are a departure from the present. It involves solving strategic problems utilizing a rational and convergent approach as well as a creative and divergent thinking. In some situations, it may involve redefining the organisation's core strategies. Schoemaker, Krupp, and Howland point out that strategic thinking also requires a high level of vigilance of the threats and opportunities in the environment and the ability to scan the environment and anticipate change.

Fundamental to strategic thinking is the ability to conceptualise strategic issues and to translate these ideas into actions. All the complex information gathered has to be simplified into a set of coherent ideas that can be translated into an action plan. Reaching this end requires considerable mental effort to form inferences from the information gathered. As Mintzberg points out, strategic thinking must precede strategic planning. Developing a strategic plan without undergoing strategic thinking first is akin to buying ingredients before deciding on the dish to cook. However, it is important to understand that strategic thinking is not a step or a sequence of activities. Instead, strategic thinking is a continuous process that involves continuous learning and monitoring of the environment. Like a general monitoring the battlefield, the strategic leader must not let his or her guard down and retreat into complacency. While formulating ideas about competitive advantage has to begin at the beginning of the strategizing process, constant monitoring and learning are needed to assess the effectiveness of the idea and to adapt to new insights gained.

It is important for all strategic leaders to remember that their decisions on how to compete are basically business hypotheses. This hypothesis is the educated guess on how to serve the market well and outperform competitors. However, all business decisions have some uncertainties and imperfections, and there is always a chance it may not work. The business hypotheses need to be validated by data. This data will be generated as a strategy is implemented. Quite often, some of the initial plan has to be refined to improve its implementation. Sometime changes may nullify earlier assumptions and require a rethinking of the chosen strategy. As such, being vigilant and keeping track of the outcomes are important. The strategic leader has to have his or her ears on the ground to see how the strategy is turning out.

Even though strategic thinking is often described as being concerned with conceptualizing high-level ideas, this does not mean that strategic leaders need not have an understanding of operational issues. On the contrary, Hammer argues that operations are the foundation of strategies. Scholes, the director of the consulting firm Strategos, points out that successful companies are good at defining a strategic direction and implementing the strategy. The latter is basically the process of operationalizing a strategic idea. This is why effective strategic thinking requires that the leader have a good grasp of operational issues, especially the organisation's internal capabilities. Ohmae terms this, "keeping details in perspective." Japanese leaders are very aware of this. Examples of successful Japanese corporate leaders highlight their emphasis on *gemba* leadership. The word "gemba" simply means the place where action is happening. Gemba leadership is about leading from the front and solving problems where they happen as they happen. Leaders who are in touch with their gemba have a good grasp of operational issues. As such, they are better able to gauge the viability of the strategic options they are considering and seek a good fit between external conditions and internal capabilities.

Quite often we see leaders who are in strategic positions but are not able to think strategically. Some are too precedence oriented, preferring to do only what they are already familiar with. There are also those who are just petty and micro-oriented, not able to let go of their operational focuses. They get bogged down with micro issues that are better left to operational-level leaders. And there are also those who see strategizing as a bureaucratic process. They become obsessed with demanding and generating reports and documents. They expect their subordinates to comply with all kinds of rules and standards. Some think that managing strategy is about setting KPIs. A lot of time is spent formulating detailed KPIs, and merely providing the information on these indicators becomes a nightmare. These KPIs are often formulated without deciding, first and foremost, what competitive advantage the organisation wants to rely on. This becomes a case of strategic planning without strategic thinking. Instead of KPIs becoming a motivator, they become shackles that force managers to think of short-term attainments at the expense of long-term interests.

Change Management Competencies

When the captain of ship sees another ship heading straight towards his or her ship, the captain has to act decisively to steer the ship towards a safer course. Fortunately, a mechanical system, such as a ship, can be easily steered. Organisations are a lot more complex. Organisations are not mechanical systems that can be manipulated at will. Steering an organisation towards a new course is more like shepherding a large herd of cattle than steering a ship.

Steering an organisation to adopt a new idea is a challenge in more than one way. New ideas, unlike mould, do not grow on their own. An idea grows when it is shared, discussed, and debated. A strategic idea may begin as an epiphany. The process of scanning the environment and examining trends may lead to the discovery of an opportunity or insight on how to do something better. The idea may emerge as an intuitive response to stimuli in the environment.

Quite often there is some uncertainty about the soundness of an idea. Strategic leaders have to test their ideas by discussing them with their colleagues. This process is termed by Crossan as the "interpretation stage of organisational learning." An idea deemed viable at this stage will then be shared with others in the organisation. Once it is accepted across various parts of the organization, it is integrated into the organisation. Finally, the new idea is institutionalised by the organisation when it creates policies and procedures that formalise the adoption of these ideas. These four stages – intuition, interpretation, integration, and institutionalisation – constitute the model of organisational learning proposed by Crossan. The discovery of an idea is only useful when

---

Insight Box 2.3

Reinventing MMC

There are situations where a strategy shift can be substantial and require a major transformation. Malaysian Mining Corporation, MMC, was initially established as the Malayan Tin Dredging Company in London in 1911. Its core business was tin mining. In 1981, the company was renamed MMC and was the largest fully integrated tin mining company in the world. However, the fall of tin prices in 1983 led the company to exit the tin-mining business and to divest all its mining activities. It has since become a utilities and infrastructure company. This is an example of changes in the environment that presented a shock to the Malaysian economy and a major company. The whole tin-mining industry in Malaysia practically collapsed, and this forced MMC to reinvent itself. The transformation MMC underwent was a major one, with many people laid off.

The present MMC operates in three core business areas: port and logistical services, energy and utilities, and engineering and construction. A new competency pool had to be developed to reposition the company in its new markets. Had MMC continued to operate based on the old competency set, it would have certainly failed.

---

the learning at the individual level translates into adaptation at the organisational level. The process can be time consuming because the journey that an idea has to travel to migrate from personal learning to organisational learning can take time. This understanding highlights the need for strategy leaders to shepherd their ideas to gain ownership and commitment.

Inevitably, a new strategic idea will create a shift in the strategic focus and direction of an organisation. In some cases, this shift can be small and incremental. From time to time, we hear of new iPhone models being launched by Apple. Other industry players also try to launch new models to persuade consumers that their products are better. These are incremental responses to competitive pressure that do not require major transformation.

At times, the shift may require more substantial adjustments. Research in Motion, the maker of BlackBerry, had to engage in considerable rethinking about its offerings and technology base. The OS- and Android-based smartphones offer many capabilities that BlackBerry phones offer, but they are offered free, are more flexible, and can run with many applications. Some of these applications undermined the fee-based revenue BlackBerry relied on for the use of email and other data service on its phones. BlackBerry had to rethink its business and offerings.

An effective strategic leader understands the extent of change needed to support a new strategic idea. In addition, he or she has the ability to initiate the change needed to support the new idea. A strategic leader does not do something just to follow the flavour of the day. A strategic leader is selective and calculative in the changes he or she initiates. The ability to plan and execute this transformation is critical for a strategic leader. The strategic leader needs to make sure the organisation has the capabilities to compete and shape the future. A sure way to fail is by trying to create a new future while relying on capabilities designed to support the competitive approach used in the past.

Execution skill at the strategic level is often about making the necessary changes when adopting a new strategic idea. It demands more than the execution skills at the operational level. Execution at the operational level is often about executing actions based on standard operating procedures and well-defined rules. Execution of new strategic ideas cannot rely on existing procedures simply because there are no established procedures. Quite often it involves managing change across many functional areas. Making these changes requires change management skills. As a start, managing change requires that strategic leaders have a clear idea of what should be changed, how much they should be changed, and what has to be preserved. The strategic leader also has to be able to win support for the change, gain buy-in and ownership for the change, and initiate a sustainable change. This has to be carefully planned to ensure that the disruption created by the change is temporary and that it will ultimately lead to improvements.

Developing Talent Competencies

When Bill Gates was asked about the best decisions he had made, he said it was selecting people to work with. Leaders need to circle themselves with competent, trustworthy, and smart people who share their vision. Thinking strategically and managing the change process that is periodically required are not tasks that can be done by one person. This leadership activity needs a team. Effective leaders recognise that they need to surround themselves with people who can cross-check, caution, and question them. Oprah Winfrey said that the best situation for her as a leader is when she is surrounded by people who are smarter than she is. It creates a situation where she can learn something from those around her. Steve Jobs expressed the same sentiment when he said that great things in business are not done by one person; they are done by a team of people.

To ensure that the organisation has the pool of smart leaders, strategic leaders invest their time and energy in developing talented managers to become future leaders. One company that is recognised as a leader in talent development is General Electric. When Jack Welch was its CEO, he spent 60 percent of his time on human resource issues. This includes spending time training the company's next generation of leaders. He considers attending meetings and discussions on human resource issues as opportunities to evaluate talent.

A mistake some leaders make is to surround themselves with people who make them feel good. As discussed earlier, these are yes men and women who bring little added value from their presence on the leadership team. Such leaders see the ideal members of his or leadership team as being those who do not question, who are there to massage his or her ego, and who rose up the hierarchy by being conformists and rule followers. When faced with discontinuity in the environment, they are not able to sense it and even less able to respond to it.

The effect of not having talented people on the management team can be debilitating. The CEO of an organisation this author came to know about lamented about the poor quality of members of his top management team, labelling most of them as useless and incompetent. He came from outside the organisation and found the strategic realignment he had initiated was impeded by the indifference of members of his own management team. The relationship between members of top management was so bad that they didn't even bother to reply each other's emails. Instead, there was intense politicking between members of the management team. In such a situation, the organisation is pulled in many directions by the different political factions. This is the price of not developing talent for senior leadership positions.

Persuasion and Influence Competencies

The introduction of a new idea, especially one that requires strategic shifts in an organisation, would naturally stir controversies and debates about the idea. Some in the organisation may not be convinced of the merits of the idea. Selling a new idea requires considerable persuasion.

In addition, a new idea can be seen as disruptive to the existing arrangements in the organisation. It can affect the organisation's order of priority. Some ideas may require reallocation of resources. This can affect current activities and commitments. Many people who have invested their efforts and commitments in the current activities would be hesitant to simply abandon these commitments. New ideas and the change it sometime entails can also be disruptive to current power equilibrium in the organisation. A decision to introduce a new product can mean phasing out an existing one or attaching less importance to certain products. This will mean less resource allocation to these existing products. Lower resource allocation signifies lower importance and status to the people involved with the existing products.

Mintzberg's seminal work on strategy implementation highlights that the realised strategy is not always the same as the intended strategy. His study of Volkswagen and the US war in Vietnam shows that as a strategy is implemented, many forces interact to shape and reshape it. He used the term "emergent strategy" to describe the strategy that is finally created by the interaction of these forces. Inertia can frustrate the desire to initiate change. Political manoeuvring takes place as leaders try to protect their interests, power, and resources. Resistance can develop as people try to remain within their comfort zones or perceive the change as a threat to their interests.

As such, getting a new strategic idea accepted and implemented requires persuasion and influence competencies. Resolving the conflict that emerges requires the ability to manage disputes. Winning over support requires building alliances with other leaders. Leaders behind a new strategic idea often need to rely on informal processes and informal communications to win support for new ideas. The formal procedures and processes are an imperfect system of rules. They are more suited for governing the expected and routinised activities and are often based on precedence. However, such rules do not exist to help resolve new and novel issues. To be effective, strategic leaders need to have persuasion and influence competencies.

Leaders often have to use persuasion and influence to win over support from others. In Japanese organisations, issues and decisions are often discussed and negotiated outside meetings. When meetings are held, they are used to formalise decisions that have been made earlier. Western observers tend to misunderstand this and think that the consensus-oriented behaviours of Japanese are indicative of high pressure to conform. Quite often, issues are discussed during their *nomikai* sessions; that is, after work hours' drinking sessions.

In addition, Japanese companies use open office design that enables people to interact with each other on a direct and regular basis. They often engage in *uchiawase,* or informal small discussions, on issues that have to be decided on. These uchiawase discussions are often used to sell ideas, negotiate resources, and examine alternatives. Quite often these discussions lead to decisions or agreements on key options with the formal meetings used to finalise the decisions. All these mechanisms are informal and outside the organisation's formal rules and procedures. These are examples of persuasion and influence that can help win support for an idea and reduce open conflict. Strategic leaders need to develop the ability to also rely on such informal means as a part of their skills in winning support for their ideas.

In many Western societies, people feel comfortable confronting issues and each other in meetings. This is not the case everywhere. In some Eastern societies, people tend to not express disagreements openly, especially disagreements with the leader. Quite often, leaders mistakenly treat silence as indicating agreement. In reality, the silence indicates that people have reservations about the decision.

One way to overcome this reluctance to disagree openly is by having informal discussions before the meeting. Unfortunately, managers are not taught to use informal communication to aid decision-making. Jack Welch recognised this and made it a point to create an informal climate to encourage discussions and debates over ideas when he was the CEO of General Electric. This is all the more important in Eastern societies.

Because strategic change inevitably involves a departure from the status quo, it can be difficult to get everyone to agree with the change initiative. As such, it takes considerable persuasion skills to sell an idea. Leaders need to build bridges and network with other leaders to engage them and win over their support. These often require relying on informal communication and negotiation with their peers. This is the form of persuasion and influence skills that strategic leaders need to develop.

Leading with Conscience

We expect our leaders, whether they are political leaders or business leaders, to act in a way that serves common interest. We expect our political leaders to serve a cause and higher sense of purpose. We expect them to improve our well-being, provide us safety and security, and act with integrity and in an honest manner. We expect our political leaders to regulate the conduct of business and protect our common interests. We want our business leaders to be socially responsible, protect the environment, and not to exploit the public. Businesses should make profit to create wealth and create employment opportunities but not at the expenses of consumers and society. Unfortunately, more often than not, we see politicians who are more concerned with improving their well-being than the people's well-being. We also see corporate leaders who betray the trust given to them and become embroiled in scandals and exploitation. When political leaders and corporate leaders start jumping into bed together, we get a toxic mix. We see this in the many scandals that have surfaced over the last few decades. We are justified in feeling disappointed when we see both political leaders and business leaders caught with their hands in the cookie jar.

Insight Box 2.4

Profit through Purpose

Steve Jobs define Apple's goal as being about making the best personal computers in the world and to make products that Apple employees would be proud to sell and recommend to their family and friends. Bill Gates used the wealth he generated from the success of Microsoft to establish a foundation. A key focus of this foundation is to provide vaccines to poor people. Soichiro Honda, the founder of Honda, wrote, "If I had been a spiritual leader I would have focused not on mysterious ideals, but on helping people understand and resolve the issues they face in their daily lives, urging a philosophy of reason and common sense." He considers the job of a leader is to help others and improve their lives. Panasonic defines its business philosophy as being about creating a better life and a better world. Eddie Tie, the group CEO of VitaLife, the company that owns and sells the VitaLife brand of products, is motivated by a determination to do well and enjoys turning around companies. He describes himself as a "playful non-conformist". He had spent the earlier part of his career in various companies in Malaysia before being recruited to run and turn around VitaLife at its head office in Sydney. He explained that there were times in his earlier career when he switched jobs and ended with lower pay just because of the challenge presented by the new job. He has since brought VitaLife back into the black, and the company has expanded into many ASEAN countries. All these leaders see profit as a reward for achieving greater good. This can be in the form of helping the less privileged or turning around a failed business and, in the course of doing so, protects value and the livelihood of many people.

Interesting enough, many corporate leaders who have become icons of business success typically define their businesses in terms of a higher-order purpose. It is not just about money. Richard Branson, the maverick British entrepreneur, explains his motive for getting into business as being driven by the bad experience he had with other businesses. He said, "The reason I went into business originally was not because I thought that I could make a lot of money, but because experiences I had personally with businesses were dire and I wanted to create an experience that I and my friends could enjoy."

John Mackey, the founder of Whole Foods Market, a retail chain selling organic food, said, "Most people want more transcendent values. They want to believe and understand how their work is contributing to helping other people making the world a better place." Great CEOs make creating value as the core of what they do. They are not just in business to make money by hook or by crook. On a good day, one can get lucky and make quick money on the stock market. This does not require managerial or entrepreneurial skills. All one needs are information and a certain amount of luck.

Some may describe the above leaders as being driven by idealism. Both Richard Branson and Eddie Tie have a nagging dislike of the status quo. They believe things can be better and seek to make things better. John Mackey wanted to bring healthy food and improve the health of customers. Steve Jobs was concerned about doing something new that could be a source of pride. The late Anita Roddick, who founded Body Shop, argued that businesses need to have a moral agenda. Profit should not be the end and sole focus of business. While profit is important for a business, it is not everything. These leaders want to contribute to more than just enriching shareholders. There is something within them, their consciences, that motivates them to think of more than just profit.

Conscience can be broadly defined as human knowledge of right and wrong and includes our moral consciousness that influences our decision-making. Conscience is also regarded as "an authority", a warning signal that demarcates between appropriate and inappropriate behaviours. It is our moral faculty or feeling that prompts us to see that certain actions are morally right or wrong. Individuals who are guided by their consciences have the ability to integrate moral reasoning into action and thinking.

In business, it is always possible to see conflicts and priorities pulling organisations in different directions. The CFO wants to see better revenue to improve cash flow in the short-term and may prefer decisions that deliver quick results. The R&D function may want more time to fine-tune and improve an innovation. The marketing function may prefer to have more new products, even if they still have imperfections, to push sales revenue. The company may also find itself being asked to pay kickbacks to politicians for contracts. Or the company's purchasing manager may be persuaded to accept substandard products by a vendor in return for under-the-counter payment. A banker may request that the company raise the amount of a loan it applied for in return for loan approval. The difference between the amount the company initially applied for and the new amount is to be transferred into the banker's account in the Caymans. All these can easily pull companies apart and derail their commitments to integrity. This is where having a leader with conscience is important to ensure that the company remains committed to quality and delivers fair and honest value to its customers.

A former student of mine related his experience working for an American chemical company. This was way back in the 1970s, and he had just graduated. The company moved into a new office in Kuala Lumpur, and he was asked to help get the facilities ready. Among other things, he had to arrange for utilities and phone connection. To his surprise, the personnel processing one the applications he submitted requested under-the-counter payment to approve his application. He mentioned this to his superior. The company has a firm policy of not paying bribes. His superior decided that they would not entertain the demand but just operate with whatever facilities they could get without paying bribes. This is an example of a leader with conscience, a clear sense of right and wrong, and setting clear boundaries.

If management is firm in upholding integrity and ethical standards, those lower in the organisation will follow suit. Leaders at the strategic level set the tone in every organisation. The same is the case in politics. Whenever there is widespread corruption in a country, we can be assured it is because of corruption at the top of the political leadership. As a Chinese proverb says, "The fish rots from the head." Look at the head when we see rot at other parts of the body. That's why having leaders with conscience at the strategic level is very important.

Conscience is important in developing strategic leadership competencies for a number of reasons. First, leaders who lead with conscience are more ethically responsible. Second, leaders with conscience possess the qualities that help endear others to them. This is an asset in developing their influence skills and building alliances during time of change. Third, seen from the point of view of followers, leaders with conscience are considerate, and all of us will agree that working under such a leader is highly desirable. Fourth, leaders with conscience ensure that when they engage in strategic thinking, they are guided by a higher purpose and a commitment to a moral agenda. When these leaders manage change and engage in politics, they do so in ethical, just, and functional manners.

There is a Malay parable that describes giving something valuable to a bad person is akin to "giving flower to a monkey." Teaching strategic thinking, change management techniques, and persuasion skills to a corrupt or toxic leader will very likely lead to abuse. There is no shortage of toxic leaders who use all their skills and abilities to embezzle, abuse, manipulate, and mistreat others. We see this in business, politics, and even in non-profit organisations. If we do not lay the right foundation when developing strategic leadership competencies, we will be building a house of cards. This foundation is leadership with conscience. Only when this foundation is in place will the other competencies bring greater good to society.

Closing

It is imperative that organisations understand the distinct characteristics of strategic leadership competencies. It is also important to recognise that not all high performers have the potential to become strategic leaders. Organisations need to invest in developing more strategic leaders to ensure it has a pool of managers to progress into senior leadership position. A well-designed strategic leadership competency program will be needed to do this. This has to begin with a clear understanding what strategic leadership competencies are all about. The strategic leadership competency model presented in this chapter can serve as the framework for developing better leaders and better corporations for the present and future. This model presents the key competencies that managers need to develop as they advance to senior-level leadership.

CHAPTER 3

Strategic Thinking: Thinking Ahead to Get Ahead

Introduction

When Malaysia-based Air Asia's Group CEO Tony Fernandes was asked about opportunities in Southeast Asia and whether the region has political stability to support economic growth, his response was simple: "Look, I've been through everything—SARS, bird flu, tsunami, earthquakes, red shirts, yellow shirts, army shirts. You name it, I've had it. But there's always business, right?" His view is a remarkable departure from the conventional view that argues that investors should be concerned about political stability in the market they are about to enter. Fernandes' unconventional view marks the way strategic leaders think. They look for opportunities where others see risks, they identify the common where others see differences, they seek to be different when others choose to be similar, they exit a market when too many people have entered it, and they enter a market that others may not even know exists.

Netflix is a company offering Internet TV services to subscription-based members. The company was started by Reed Hastings in 1997 after he became embarrassed at having to pay a penalty for returning a video cassette he rented late. He decided to innovate by providing a subscription-based service instead of a per unit rental. He also saw an opportunity in a new technology that was just being commercialised at that time; that is, the DVD. Since members pay a subscription fee, there are no rentals or late return fines. And it did not start with just providing DVD to its subscribers. Hastings was at that time already looking ahead to see the future of technologies. He recognised that the Internet was going to be next delivery channel for entertainment. Even though video streaming was still new then and had imperfections, Hastings knew that it was going to be the future and positioned Netflix to tap into the new opportunity. By 2002, Netflix went for public listing and had 600,000 members in the United States. By 2005, its membership rose to 4.2 million. In 2007, it introduced its video streaming service. Today, Netflix is the leader in subscription-based Internet TV services with more than 57 million members and services in fifty countries.

Netflix was started as a result of dissatisfaction with the status quo. This dissatisfaction led to the search for a new business model, new technologies, and new delivery channels. The ability to see convergence of these three – a subscription-based membership, the use of DVDs and later on video streaming, and a new delivery channel through the Internet – created a new potential. Netflix did not try to be like the dominant players at that time. Netflix bucked the trend and demolished the dominant business model that existed before which had relied on retail-based video cassette rental. At the centre of Hasting's thinking was simply how to serve the customer better than the other players present then. Again, he was not trying to do what others were already doing. In creating a new way to deliver value, Hastings redefined competition in the business. This is what strategic thinking entails. This helped Netflix define and develop its competitive advantage.

The same mindset could be seen in the establishment of Grameen Bank in 1983 in Bangladesh. When its founder, Professor Muhammad Yunus, started the effort to lend to the poor, conventional bankers told him that his idea wouldn't work. His scheme, which involves lending small amounts to poor people to help them start small businesses, was unprecedented. His approach came to be known as micro-credit. It is now a showcase of success in eradicating poverty and has been adopted in many countries. By 2006, the bank had outstanding loans to seven million poor people and enjoyed a repayment rate of 99 percent. The high repayment rate shows that poor people can be good credit risks. Muhammad Yunus's actions reflect his dissatisfaction with the status quo. He decided to defy convention by lending to a segment that the typical bank considers not creditworthy. He did not choose to be just a follower of the pack. Grameen Bank broke away from the pack when it decided to focus on the poor. This is another case of strategic thinking in action.

Strategizing and Creativity

Strategies are not the products of imposing more rules and standards that constrain creativity. Neither will strategies emerge from a mindset that is fixated with doing things the way they have always been done. A strategist is always alert for the new and different. The obvious and known do not excite a strategist as much as the new and novel. A strategist is able to differentiate between chaff and wheat when presented with information. Gavetti terms this as the ability to see "cognitively distant opportunities". The opportunity is there, but no one saw it because no one was looking for it. A strategist is someone who looks at what others are not looking for.

Mintzberg points out that the key point to recognise is that strategizing is first and foremost about creative thinking. Many organisations and business students develop a preference for specific analytical tools. Some would use the SWOT analysis, some prefer the TOWS matrix, others rely on Design Thinking, and some use the various tools associated with the Blue Ocean Strategy. Yet, the use of these various tools do not always yield sound strategies. This author's observation from participating in strategy workshops and teaching strategy to MBA students is that many participants experience difficulties identifying strategic issues. As a result, they may generate a lot of information but are still not clear which ones have strategic value. In some cases, the use of these tools becomes more about filling in forms and matrices without much creative thinking taking place and without much willingness to ask difficult questions.

One strategy discussion I facilitated saw a manager from an oil company state that his company's strength was that it had a lot of money. I then asked him if the company had so much money, why did it have to borrow money? Is merely having a lot of money a strength? Or should the strength be the ability to generate higher return on the money compared to competitors? Knowing that one's organisation has a lot of money is merely saying the obvious, what is already known. Having the ability to generate high return on the money is a strength and has strategic value. It is not difficult to see that some of the more developed economies, like Japan and Singapore, are actually resource poor but are technologically advanced and economically rich because of their resourcefulness. On the other hand, resource-rich and resource-dependent economies can be rich but lack resourcefulness and are dependent on others for technologies.

It is important to recognise that tools do not substitute for thinking. Strategic analysis tools aid and assist analysis. But such tools in the hands of rigid bureaucrats, uninformed planners, and unimaginative leaders will not get anywhere. These leaders are more likely to use these tools in a mechanistic manner without infusing into it much creative thinking.

A strategic mindset is built around a number of foundations. The following sections elaborate on these foundations and their components.

1. Ability to conceptualise strategic issues

A key ability that strategic thinkers need to be able to do is to conceptualise strategic issues. This involves the ability to reduce complex ideas into a simpler set of ideas. Organisations usually perform strategic assessments either as a reaction or in anticipation of changes and new challenges. Quite often, there is considerable ambiguity in the information available on the unfolding situation. Strategic thinkers have to make sense of this ambiguity. Indeed, competitive advantage depends largely on the ability to sense, read, and interpret this ambiguous information. The clear and explicit information is usually evident to everyone. Facts about government spending, inflation, and population size are easily known to all. However, the understanding of how all these interact and shape the future is not always clear to everyone. A strategic thinker needs to be able to summarise this understanding into a conceptual model of the future and how the organisation should adapt to it. This model simplifies complex information into a more manageable set of information. Having this model helps strategic thinkers understand the key issues and aids in communicating the strategic intent to others more effectively. In order to do this, strategic leaders need to be able to do a number of things.

a. Detect trends from events and discontinuities in a trend. Some people have to be told of the changes happening around them in order to recognise these changes. Strategists, on the other hand, are quick to see connections between events and form a bigger picture of what is happening. They are able to see trends where others perceive random events. This ability is usually the product of the breadth of knowledge that they have and their abilities to engage in scientific reasoning. This involves the ability to see how sequences of events may be connected and the ability to seek and use evidence to help shape understanding. The opposite of this ability is superstitious learning, where a person believes in something in spite of the lack of evidence. Rita McGrath describes that as a result of superstitious learning, we attribute the wrong causes to events. In primitive society, this can be in the form of

---

Insight Box 3.1

Intel's Aggressive Initiative

Ohmae describes how Intel successfully pursued aggressive initiative as its competitive approach. Prior to the invention of PCs, one major market for processor chips was the automotive industry. The market then was dominated by Motorola. Intel, which was established in 1968, decided to enter the market and embarked on a "Conquer Ford" strategy. Motorola had long sold processor chips to car manufacturers. Its customer then had to figure how to use the chips. Intel took a different approach. It sold its chips as a part of a solution package. The company also provided its expertise on how its customers could best make use of the chips. In doing this, it redefined the rules of the game and the critical factors for success. Intel was able to replace Motorola as the supplier of chips to Ford. This then opened the way for Intel to win other markets in the US automotive industry.

---

beliefs that illnesses are caused by evil spirits. In modern society, people can also develop wrong understanding of the causes of a problem because of flawed diagnosis, perceptual bias, and incomplete information.

b. Mumford points out that strategic leaders need to assess the "downstream consequences" of their actions and decisions. They have to be mindful of the consequences of the strategic choices that they make. This would involve assessing carefully the full range of outcomes created by their actions or decisions. This is especially important in strategic decision-making because decisions made at this level often affect the whole organisation. A simple decision such as a budget cut and reallocation of resources can have far-reaching consequences. Quite often strategic decisions create a series of consequences that can affect employees at the furthest end of the organisation and customers as well as suppliers. Once these decisions are executed, they are difficult or costly to reverse. There is no shortage of examples of organisations that decide to initiate a cost-cutting and downsizing exercise without thinking fully how the initiative affects workload and morale at lower levels of the organisation. One toll highway operator in Malaysia found that morale and effectiveness suffered after it downsized and ended up having to upsize again. Since those who left included the most talented, their departures undermined the operation of the highway. The company had to upsize again, but since the new recruits were not as experienced as those who left, they were not as effective in their work. One year after the downsizing exercise, the workforce was bigger than before the downsizing. In one telco that this author studied, a downsizing exercise led to an erosion of trust and undermined morale among those who remained in the organisation. The remaining employees felt betrayed, with many reporting that they would be reluctant to go the extra mile for the company. Top management often sees workforce reduction as a cost-cutting exercise without understanding the behavioural consequences of their actions. Strategic leaders need to think through thoroughly the ramifications of their decisions.

c. Identify key issues that are going to shape the future. Strategizing is a future-oriented activity. The quality of a strategy depends on how much it prepares an organisation to face the future. Anticipating the future is not an exact science, and different people seeing the same information may come to different conclusions about the future. Some organisations wait and respond to changes as they happen. Some organisations position themselves to shape the future. These are strategic choices that are affected by the risk appetite of leaders. Strategic leaders can enhance their abilities to anticipate the future by understanding who the trendsetters are, the technology drivers who can shape the future, possible directions in the innovation taking place in their industries, changes in customer preferences and behaviours, the regulatory environment and expected changes in regulations, and new competitors that may enter the market. In addition, they need to assess the internal capabilities of their organisations. This includes understanding their core competencies, the degree of flexibility they have in recombining their competencies, and their knowledge stock.

d. Identify the basis for competitive advantage in the environment the organisation competes in. Ohmae points out that the key to developing competitive advantage is understanding the key factors for success in a business. These are factors that must be present to compete successfully in a business. It is an important starting point in deciding how to compete. Once this is clear, organisations need to ensure that they develop the key factors for success. However, developing the key factors for success alone may not be sufficient to ensure success. In an environment where competitors are similarly good in the key factors for success, Ohmae argues that strategic leaders need to differentiate by developing relative advantages. Ohmae points out that organisations can also compete by pursuing aggressive initiatives. This approach essentially involves redefining the rules of the game to the advantage of the organisation.

2. Ability to perform competitive assessment

The strategic leadership role requires a leader who is able to assess the competitive challenges the organisation is facing and subsequently lead his or her organisation in competing based on this understanding. At the heart of competitive assessment is understanding the customer. Competitors exist only because they are competing for the same customer. Companies that are not clear of their customers will not be able to assess their competitors. Likewise, companies that do not understand what their customers want can be easily outmanoeuvred by more customer-centric competitors. Not all players in the same industry are competitors. BMW, Porsche, and Kia are in the same industry. But BMW and Porsche do not compete with Kia. Companies need to examine how customer preferences can change, possible new moves by current competitors, new entrants, and how changes in the environment can affect the market. Strategic thinkers need to monitor competitors and be vigilant of possible new entrants. It is important that in making competitive assessment, strategic thinkers ask the following questions: (a) Who are our customers, and what are their current and future expectations? (b) How many ways are there to deliver value to our customers? (c) Who is also trying to win these customers? (d) Who else has the internal capabilities that can appeal to our customers in the future? (e) Are our own internal capabilities in line with the expectations of our customer?

3. Ability to develop system thinking

Leading at the strategic level requires that leaders develop a bird's-eye view of the organisation. Strategic leaders have to get out of their functional focus which only sees the splintered parts of the organisation. Moon argues that strategic leaders need to see the totality of the organisation. Liedtka explains that strategic leaders also need to have an end-to-end perspective of the value chain of activities in the organisation. They need to understand the interconnectedness and synergy created by the various functions and activities in their organisations. Every organisation consists of highly interdependent components. Value is created when these components interact in a synergistic manner. An organisation is very much like an orchestra.

Insight Box 3.2

New Entrants Changing Competitive Landscape

Who'd imagine Apple would become a major player in the cell phone market fifteen years ago, or that very few US-based PC companies would still be around? Nokia probably never imagined fifteen years ago that it would be competing with Apple in the mobile phone market. Most of the major players in the PC market today (Acer, Asus, Lenovo, Toshiba, Sony, BenQ, etc.) are Asian. Who'd imagine just five years ago that key players in the smartphone market would today be challenged by new arrivals like Oppo and Xiaomei from China? A strategic leader in Microsoft should now be predicting which company has the technologies and capabilities to threaten its dominance with its Windows operating system. It may not be too long before an alternative appears. Microsoft better keep Android on its radar screen.

The quality of music played by the orchestra depends on the coordination of all the instruments involved. In many ways, the skills that a strategic thinker needs to develop are like the skills of a composer of an orchestra. The composer has to understand each instrument and how they can be arranged to interact to create a wonderful music. An operational leader is like an individual musician who has to be good at playing an instrument. However, performance alone is not enough to ensure the performance of the orchestra. An effective strategic thinker recognises this and understands that the ability to enhance performance and competitiveness depends on the coordinated actions of all parts of an organisation. There are three key elements in developing system thinking. The first is understanding the components and boundaries of the system. Understanding the components involves understanding the value of each component. The second is understanding how the components interact to create value. This understanding will enable strategic thinkers to understand where and how value is created. Third, Sirmon, Hitt, and Ireland point out that understanding how value is created and can be enhanced involves the ability to visualise how the components can be enriched, recombined, and reconfigured to create better value. Management researchers like Kogut and Zander term this ability "combinative ability". Adaptive organisations are those that are quick to adapt to threats and opportunities. This ability to adapt involves changing the internal arrangements of the organisation. Sometimes this also involves changing the boundaries of the system. Many organisations spin off certain functions into independent entities that then operate as their vendors. Petronas, Malaysia's national petroleum company, did this when it spun off its IT function and formed the company iPerintis. This process redrew the company's boundary. However, it later brought back iPerintis into the company to become its IT division.

4. Equifinal thinking

Equifinality is the recognition that there is often more than one way to reach a goal. Strategic thinkers who understand this are more likely to explore alternative ways to create an outcome. They are less likely to succumb to the temptation to just imitate others. An example of equifinal thinking can be seen in the automotive industry. The rise in fuel price and concerns about environmental issues has led automotive companies

Insight Box 3.3

Equifinality and Combinative Ability

Canon is a company that is known for the broad range of products it offers. Canon's range of products includes digital cameras, scanners, photocopy machines, printers, and fax machine. A casual observer may wonder why Canon is in such a disparate range of products. However, closer examination shows that all these products share the same core technologies that include imaging, optics, and precision mechanics. These are also the same technologies that are the core technologies of companies like Xerox. Canon's ability to venture into these different products is the outcome of its combinative ability. It was able to imagine the equifinal ways these technologies could be combined. Xerox, on the other hand, is focused on a more limited range of products.

to compete by offering highly efficient vehicles. However, the route used differs considerably. Toyota and Honda leverage on hybrid technologies to produce fuel efficient cars. Nissan and Renault rely on electric vehicles. Mazda went back to the drawing board and designed more efficient engines. Its Skyactive engines improve efficiency by improving compression ratio. Sometimes equifinality can also mean that an approach can lead to more than one possible outcome. Apple's journey into the smartphone business is one such example. The initiative started as an attempt to develop a palm-sized Macintosh computer. Apple decided to also include telephony capabilities in the computer. It ended up with the iPhone. Pfizer's Viagra started as a research to develop vassal dilators for treating heart problems. Instead, it ended up being used to treat some other condition. Equifinal thinkers are more likely to rely on creativity to identify alternative ways to compete. This ability helps leaders discover unique approaches that can provide sources of competitive advantage that are difficult for others to imitate.

5. Creative thinking

Amabile defines creativity simply as the production of novel and useful ideas. It is the basic ingredient in innovation. In strategic thinking, creative thinking is necessary to get strategist to think outside the box. Merely imitating another does not involve much creativity and does not confer much competitive advantage. Creativity can be found in many situations. Fine art involves a lot of creativity. The same is true in the performing arts. Even cooking can involve the use of creativity. However, creativity in strategic thinking has a different focus. Its main concern is looking for new and unique ways to compete. Some of the behaviours that can help foster creative thinking include the following.:

a. Willingness to question assumptions

The dissatisfaction with the status quo lead many strategic leaders to question assumptions. Strategic thinkers take their dissatisfaction with the status quo a step further by questioning conventional assumptions. In doing so, they discover opportunities others do not even realise exist. It helps them enter untapped markets. As Ohmae points out, assumptions often impose constraints on what can and cannot be done. Muhammad Yunus questioned the assumption held among bankers that the poor are not credit worthy. Steve Jobs questioned the assumption about computing. He believed that computing did not have to be difficult, dull, and intimidating and came up with the notion of user-friendly computing by using user graphic interface. Starting an airline is, by itself, not new. But coming up with the idea of a low-cost airline that makes air travel affordable for more people requires thinking differently. Whereas conventional airlines promise a pampered and luxurious experience and along with it a high fare, Southwest's Herb Kelleher and Air Asia's Tony Fernandes decided to offer no-frills, low-cost air travel. The move made air travel a commodity that is within the reach of those who had otherwise not considered flying a viable option. This is a departure from the way conventional airlines position their services. Strategic thinkers take their dissatisfaction with the status quo a step further by questioning conventional assumptions. In doing so, they discover opportunities others do not even realise exist. It helps them enter untapped markets.

b. Divergent thinking

Rigid thinkers prefer to do what they have always done. They gain comfort from the familiar. Strategic thinkers are divergent thinkers. They explore many possible options. This often involves going outside the obvious and familiar. Divergent thinkers actively and persistently seek the new and always try to be different. Because of this, they are more likely to discover the rare forms of value creation and new sources of competitive advantage. Divergent thinking and the willingness to question assumptions work in tandem to help thinkers look for novel ideas. This enables them to tap into unserved markets and serve current markets better. One barrier to divergent thinking is target fixation. Slywotzky

---

Insight Box 3.4

Strategizing by Defying Convention

When Sony was developing the Walkman in the 1980s, its own market research found that the product was not viable. The company's marketing division said, among other things, that the use of earphones to listen to music would not be well received by Japanese consumers. Yet, Akio Morita, who was then Sony's chairman, insisted on continuing with the project. The Walkman became an instant success, and the rest is history. The group CEO of VitaLife, Eddie Tie, is another example of a leader who did not let current models constrain their thinking. VitaLife sells vitamins and supplements in many markets. These products are usually marketed through pharmacies. Unfortunately, the terms imposed by pharmacy chains are usually not favourable to suppliers like VitaLife, often squeezing the profit margin of its products. Eddie decided to question the assumption that pharmacy chains are a necessity for his company. By doing this, he came up with a different approach. He decided that a better strategy was to sell VitaLife products through independent pharmacies located near major pharmacy chains. These pharmacies are usually operated by their owners and are more flexible with their terms. Their proximity to the branch of a pharmacy chain means that they will have a similar location advantage. This enabled VitaLife to come up with a win-win approach in accessing markets.

describes how target fixation can lead to tragic consequences for dive bomber pilots during the Second World War. Some of these pilots became so fixated on diving to their targets to drop their bombs that they ignored important information such as altitude. As a result, they pulled up from the dive too late and ended up slamming to the ground. The same situation can happen in business. Companies can continue to serve customer segments that are no longer profitable, invest in technologies that are no longer in demand, or rely on internal capabilities that are not aligned to customer expectations. Such a behaviour can be especially fatal when the market has reached maturity or is experiencing decline.

c. Able to see convergence of ideas

Opportunities do not simply appear from a vacuum. Quite often, new opportunities are created by innovation. Most innovation is the product of a combination of ideas. For instance, smartphones are not 100 percent new in terms of the technologies used. Instead, a smartphone is the combination of many existing technologies into one gadget. At the turn of the millennium, consumers had to use the personal digital assistant as their electronic organiser and a cellphone to make phone calls. Many used MP3 players or the Walkman for portable entertainment. And they'd need a computer to browse the Internet. Today, all these functions and many more are integrated into the smartphone. Strategic thinkers are able to create new value by looking ahead and understanding how ideas, technologies, and demands converge. Dato Jamaluddin Ibrahim, group CEO of Axiata, points out that taking a business to the next level is not just about small and incremental improvements. It often involves looking at the new technologies that can create new opportunities. This understanding helps strategic leaders predict discontinuities and points of inflection in their businesses. Air Asia is able to attain high efficiency by relying on the Internet for ticket sales and check-in. It also able to leverage on outsourcing, a trend and business model that emerged in the new millennium, to keep its maintenance cost and cost of food services low. Air Asia also relies on a network form of organisation to create multiple subsidiaries as national airlines in different Asian countries to enable it to operate from multiple regional hubs. Likewise, innovations

---

Insight Box 3.5

Divergent Thinking and Search for competitive Advantage

An example of a company that relied on divergent thinking to enhance its competitiveness is Coca-Cola. Pepsi and Coca-Cola had always been competing neck to neck in the cola drink market. Both spent an enormous amount of resources on advertising to protect and expand their markets. Slywotzky mentions that Coca-Cola later did an assessment of the behaviour of profit margins in the sale of cola drinks. They discovered that soda drinks are sold through three main channels – grocery stores, soda fountains like the ones used in many fast food outlets, and vending machines. They discovered that the profit margin is highest from sales through vending machines. Sales through grocery stores delivered ten cents per ounce margin, soda fountains were generating ten cents per ounce, but vending machines were delivering eight cents per ounce. This led them to focus on expanding their vending machine sales, and this helped improve their performance. This discovery was made possible by continuously searching for new alternatives and new ideas and by not being over-reliant on doing more of what is currently done.

---

in management practice can also converge with technological changes to create strategic opportunities. The adoption of a LPS and supply chain management practices in the automotive industry as well as advancements in ICT have created opportunities for logistics service companies. Instead of just delivering goods from one point to another, some logistics companies also provide just-in-sequence services. These companies will collect parts from multiple suppliers and then arrange these parts according to their sequence of use on the production line. They are then delivered straight to the manufacturer's workstations where they will be used. Again, recognizing this opportunity involves understanding how technologies are converging. Proponents of design thinking called this process of seeing the connection between ideas as finding patterns from observations and data collected. Other cognitive researchers call this ability to connect ideas synthesis thinking.

d. Able to assess limits and discontinuities

Opportunities come and go. A good strategist understands that opportunities generally have a limited life. Some opportunities can become a liability when market conditions change. Likewise, technological changes can also reduce the attractiveness of an opportunity. One example is the decision by a Malaysian company to diversify its business by acquiring a money-losing payphone business in 2006. It thought it could turn the payphone business around. Unfortunately, a high mobile phone penetration rate in Malaysia made payphones unnecessary. The low cost of owning and using mobile phones changed market conditions and rendered entering the payphone business a liability. This company experienced loss for the first time in more than fifteen years after making the acquisition. Strategists must understand the limits of an opportunity and anticipate discontinuities to decide when to exit a market. IBM saw the dwindling profit margin from its PC business. The PC market was becoming crowded with competitors offering fairly similar products. Consumers saw PCs as a commodity and had little brand loyalty. IBM decided to exit the PC business because it was no longer meeting its profit targets. When the company reinvented itself into a solutions company, it sold off its PC business to Lenovo in 2005. Companies can also respond to potential discontinuities by innovating to either protect against threats or gain entry into new markets. During the 2008 rise in oil price, Air Asia found that its profit margin was under pressure. Many airlines imposed a fuel surcharge. However, Air Asia started looking for ancillary income to supplement the income from passenger fares. This came in the form of in-flight sales of souvenirs, baggage fees, and cargo services to generate more income. Such an innovation enabled the airline to deal with a threat that had the potential to undermine its low-cost model. By 2010, ancillary income contributed almost 15 percent of Air Asia's income. The ability to understand the limitations of the current business model and anticipate discontinuities is important in helping organisations take measures to avert a crisis and decline. This, in turn, will help them plan the development of new capabilities to compete in the future.

e.   Keeping details in perspective

For strategists to make effective decisions, they need to understand their businesses. Macro-level decisions such as strategy, policy, and vision have ramifications for micro-level issues such as employees' attitudes, motivations, and work behaviours. Likewise, micro-level realities can enable or impede macro-level decisions if they are in conflict. As such, it is necessary to have a sense of the details when making decisions. Ohmae explains that this involves understanding the internal capabilities of the organisation and how these capabilities are developed. This often includes knowing the personalities and key actors in the organisation. Some strategic leaders do this by staying

---

Insight Box 3.6

Staying Close to the Ground to Keep Details in Perspective

When Jack Welch was the CEO of General Electric, he made it a point to meet low-level employees whenever he visited any of General Electric's subsidiaries. This gave him the opportunity to listen directly from people on the front line, are often dealing with the customers, or involved in making the products. The input from these workers enabled him to have an unsanitised view of the issues and problems facing the subsidiary. This way, by the time he met the management team of the subsidiary, there was little he did not know, and it discouraged the subsidiary's managers from filtering bad news when they communicated with Welch.

---

connected with the lowest level of the organisation. They recognise that information that flows up the organisational hierarchy is often filtered. One way for CEOs to obtain more accurate information is connecting those at the bottom. The insight gained helps them keep detailed issues in perspective. Equally important in keeping details in perspective is in understanding the external environment. Some CEOs make it a point to spend a high proportion of their time outside the organisation. John Chambers, the CEO of Cisco, spends about half of his time meeting clients in order to understand the market better. Honda does a similar thing. An example was when the company wanted to develop the Honda Fit (in Malaysia it is known as Honda Jazz). The car was intended as a compact model for the European market. Many European cities are old and have narrow streets. The company sent its R&D engineers to Europe to understand how consumers use their cars, the road conditions there, and even the shopping habits of Europeans. In all these examples, these leaders do not rely on just formal reports to form their judgements. Keeping details in perspective is important because it enables a strategic leader to have a better grasp of reality. This helps her or him to understand issues thoroughly and quickly. The search for better ideas becomes more in tune with reality and is more likely to succeed.

6. Causal thinking

Strategies are more than just about setting goals and formulating visions and missions. A strategic thinker needs to formulate a causal model of the outcomes the organisation is pursuing. This means having a clear model of the outcomes and the drivers that will create the outcome. The causal thinking in formulating a strategy has to be at two levels. First, what are the desired outcomes and the sources of competitive advantage needed to create these outcomes? Second, given the competitive advantage an organisation intends to rely on, a strategic leader needs to assess the internal capabilities that should be in place to create the advantage. Without a causal model of a strategy, goals may end up being just a wish list of nice to do ideas. A clear causal model of the strategy enables the strategist to understand the resource commitment necessary to create the outcomes desired.

A study conducted by this author on strategy implementation among Malaysian firms found that the failure to develop an understanding of the strategy's causal model can lead to problems in its implementation. Managers develop different interpretations of what needs to be done. These different interpretations then spill over into conflict during resource allocation decisions. In addition, understanding the causal model of the strategy provides managers with a clear idea of the drivers of the outcome. As far as managing strategy implementation is concerned, the drivers should be managed given that they are instrumental in creating the outcome. One flaw in the way some companies manage their strategies is

---

Insight Box 3.7

Staying Close to Customers to Keep Details in Perspective

Another example of how a detailed understanding of external conditions can create strategic impact is Eisai Pharmaceuticals. Eisai is a Japanese pharmaceutical company that sought to develop its competitive advantage by understanding patients better. Pharmaceutical salespeople usually deal with doctors and pharmacists. Even though the end users are patients, they do not deal with them. Eisai decided to deal with hospital patients directly and sought patients' feedback on how they used medications and their needs. This step proved very insightful to Eisai and helped it shape their product development activities. For instance, they discovered that medication for treating migraines usually takes about thirty minutes to take effect. The problem is a migraine is usually extremely painful, and thirty minutes is a long time to suffer. Eisai went back to the drawing board and managed to develop a painkiller for migraines that takes effect in just five minutes. This helped Eisai differentiate its products from its competitors.

---

their focus on the outcomes, usually measured by their KPIs, but without understanding clearly the drivers of theses outcomes. KPIs are laggard indicators. By the time it is known whether these KPIs are achieved, it is too late to take remedial steps. Remedial steps can only be taken by monitoring the lead indicators which measure the performance drivers. Managing the drivers will help improve the attainment of the final outcomes.

7. Intent-focused

Being intent-focused is the seventh foundation in strategic thinking. Liedtka explains that being intent-focused is about being goal-driven and anchoring the organisation's decisions to superordinate goals. It provides managers with constancy of purpose in facing the changes in the environment. When strategists are intent-focused, they will be able to explore the equifinal possibilities that can be creatively generated without losing focus of their ultimate aims. A leader who is intent-focused also creates a sense of stability for his or her followers when facing a dynamic environment. It enables leaders to understand the ultimate outcomes desired while exercising their autonomy and creativity in performing their jobs. Being intent-focused requires that strategists understand their hierarchies of objectives. Managers need to recognise that objectives are often pursued to attain a higher-level objective. Understanding this will help leaders understand their ultimate aims and recognise that there may be different options that can help them reach the final objectives. Sometime planners are so focused on the immediate and short-term objectives that they lose track of their ultimate goals. A good example is Kodak. The company has a long history and a solid reputation in film-based photography. Kodak researchers were the pioneers in developing digital photography. When their researchers developed the digital camera, it was met with opposition from those involved in Kodak's film business. As a result, the company never pursued the opportunities offered by digital photography. Unfortunately, its competitors jumped on the opportunity, and when film-based photography became obsolete, Kodak was hit hard. This failure happened because many in Kodak were too invested in the status quo and failed to see that their ultimate objectives should be about sustaining good performance. They pursued sentimental short-term objectives that were at the expense of the ultimate and long-term objectives of the business.

8. Intelligent opportunism

The eighth foundation of strategic thinking is intelligent opportunism. Liedtka argues that the constancy of purpose generated by strategic intent has to be balanced with the flexibility to adapt to opportunities in the environment. This ensures that the firm does not become too rigid in pursuing a course of action. Eisenhardt and Sull argue that strategic advantage comes from the ability to seize fleeting opportunities. Strategic leaders need to be quick in identifying emerging threats and opportunities and respond to them. This flexibility includes the willingness to even re-examine intent and adapt the strategy to changing situations. Intelligent opportunism is the product of cognition, informed risk taking, and speed in execution. Cognition is about seeking information and understanding changes in the environment to identify opportunities. Informed risk taking is about understanding the risks associated with the opportunities and makes the choice that is consistent with the organisation's risk appetite.

For leaders who are more willing to take risk, this may involve being the first mover in seizing opportunities. For the more risk averse, it can be by being the second mover. Both options can lead to improved performance, though perhaps with different levels of profitability. Speed in execution is about taking decisive steps to seize an opportunity. This involves understanding the key factors for success in the choice made. Both a first-mover and second-mover approach needs to be executed well. Unfortunately, leaders sometimes develop mental barriers that prevent them from taking advantage of opportunities. One example is Xerox. It is the company that first developed the personal computer but failed to exploit the technology to its advantage. Xerox was too absorbed with its photocopying business that it ignored the potential from the personal computer invented by its researchers. Xerox researchers were also the ones that developed the word processor we now know as Word. The potential of the software, then known as Bravo, was not appreciated by Xerox. It was then bought by Microsoft and is now a part of Microsoft Office. Like Kodak, Xerox's competitors exploited the new technologies it discovered.

The preceding discussion highlights the fact that developing strategic thinking competencies goes beyond teaching about techniques and tools. Even though the field of strategic management has seen the emergence of many tools and techniques to help managers formulate and implement strategies, the success in using these techniques and tools is mixed. There are many situations where uncreative and rigid-minded people use tools that are supposed to help with strategic analysis and still end up nowhere. Often, the use of these tools becomes more like a form-filling exercise. It cannot be overemphasised that the key to becoming a strategist is thinking skills. It is the critical and creative thinking that goes with the use of these tools and techniques that is crucial. The mind must be in gear before the techniques and tools are used. Developing this mindset involves changing habits, perspectives, expanding the knowledge base, and cultivating a curious attitude.

It is also important to recognise that strategic thinking is not an event. It is not something that is done once a year during a strategy retreat. The mind of a strategic leader is always vigilant and looking for threats as well as opportunities. The strategic leader is always restless and questioning how things can and should be improved. The strategic leader is satisfied with his or her achievements only briefly and will then look for newer mountains to climb. The strategic leader is slightly paranoid about how things can go wrong. On the surface, he or she appears confident and sometimes a bit arrogant. But in reality, the strategic leader always has a healthy level of doubt. Because of this doubt, he or she is never complacent. As Bill Gates puts it, he is always asking, "whether there is a junction just after the next bend."

As mentioned in the previous chapter, strategic thinkers are people with a high need for cognition. A strategic thinker is an active learner who seeks to learn continuously. Strategic thinking does not end at the end of strategy retreats. Nor does it reside in thick documents. A strategy is an idea that is alive and always growing and morphing with every new lesson and insight that the strategic leader gains. Look at any strategic leader, and you will see someone who reads more than the average person, who is curious, and who continuously seeks to understand what he or she does not yet know. On the other hand, those who are less curious, read less, and prefer to remain within their comfort zones are less likely to be able to think strategically. To such individuals, strategic thinking is about mechanistically following a series of steps on how to strategise that they learned from a training program or read in a book. The process is often devoid of much deep thinking. Strategic thinking to such individuals is an episode in their calendar of activities. Quite often, when they do discuss strategy it is because they were instructed to do so or because they have to submit a strategic planning document.

Creating Competitive Distance

Strategic thinking should enable leaders to make inferences about a number of issues. First is how an organisation should develop competitive advantage. A strategy is not just a long-term plan or calendar of activities. An organisation can develop a long list of activities that still does not confer any competitive advantage. In fact, the organisation can be busy and consumed, executing these activities as competitors overtake them. The case of Kodak is a good example of a company that was basically busy doing more with their film-based business at a time when digital photography was making films obsolete.

Second, creating competitive distance involves ensuring that the advantage is enduring, sustainable, and cannot be easily replicated by others. Management researchers argue that a competitive advantage needs to be sustainable to ensure long-term profitability. For instance, reducing price is not a sustainable competitive advantage if competitors can also react by cutting their prices. The resource-based view of strategy proposes that competitive distance can be developed by offering products or services that are seen as valuable by the customers, the value is rare in that others are not able to offer them, the value and capabilities creating them are not easily imitated by others, and finally, customers cannot easily substitute this value with alternatives. These four components – value, rarity, inimitable, and non-substitutable – can help ensure sustainable advantage and create competitive distance. Value is created by offering something superior to what competitors are offering that best fulfils customers' expectations. Rareness is created by offering a bundle of utility that competitors do not offer. Inimitability is created through the complex combination of resources and competencies; the tacitness of these resources and competencies or legal protection these resources have prevents competitors from copying them. Non-substitutability is created by offering something that has no equal.

An example of high competitive distance is the Swedish company Tetra Pak. It offers plastic-coated, paper-based packaging material for food and beverages. It was able to have all the necessary elements. It is valuable because it does a better job at ensuring food safety and hygiene than other containers. The material is tough and flexible for use with many types of food. The paper-based material does not rust, and unlike tin cans and bottles, it is not fragile or easily damaged. The cuboid shape of the Tetra Pak's package means it fits neatly into boxes and does not waste space, like cylindrically shaped containers such as bottles and cans. The strength and durability of the packaging material makes it possible to store liquids as well as soft, solid food products such as jelly. The paper-based material also makes it possible to use interesting and eye-catching designs on the packaging material. It is inimitable because Tetra Pak's packaging material was, for a long time, protected by patent. In addition, customers need to lease the machine that makes the packaging material for their use. Again, Tetra Pak has full control over the machine. It remains non-substitutable because no other packaging material provides the same utility as Tetra Pak's packaging material.

Third, a clear understanding of the causal model of the competitive advantage needs to be articulated so that leaders and their followers understand what are the drivers of their strategies. These drivers are rooted in the organisational competencies they developed to create their competitive advantages. Companies like Nike recognise that the drivers of their competitive advantages are their strength in design and marketing. Manufacturing is not a key competency needed for them to succeed. Thus, they outsource the manufacturing of their products.

These issues must be clear in the mind of a strategic leader. They form the key ideas in shaping a viable competitive strategy. At the same time, leaders need to recognise that competitive distance is not permanent. It can suddenly be altered with changes in technology and competitors' actions. A strategic leader also needs to be vigilant of their competitors' capabilities and changes in the market.

Closing

Developing strategic leadership competencies requires a transition from an operationally focused mindset to a strategic one. This involves changing thinking habits. Strategic leaders do not assume current successes will last forever. They are always vigilant of threats and will seek new opportunities. They have to feel comfortable exploring the unfamiliar and sometimes even let go of the familiar. They need to be willing to step out of their comfort zones and lead others to explore new territories.

CHAPTER 4

Change Management Competencies

Introduction

I nability to change can be fatal. Nokia at one time had the biggest market share in the cell phone market. It was so successful that its position looked unassailable. Fast forward to 2014. Nokia's dominance was shattered by players who were not even in the cell phone market ten years ago. Apple and Samsung with their smartphones became the key players. New entrants from China – like Lenovo, Oppo, and Xiaomei – started having a credible presence in the market.

When the Nokia cell phone business was sold to Microsoft, its CEO held a press conference. During the conference he remarked, "We didn't do anything wrong, but somehow we lost." In a fast-moving market where competitors can redefine competitive advantage, not doing anything wrong is not good enough. Companies also have to do the right things. Leaders need to understand and do the right things. And when the right thing to do is being redefined by new competitors, the incumbent cannot do more of the same. It needs to change. Developing the ability to change is an important competency for strategic leadership.

Realizing Strategic Intent

A typical outcome of strategic thinking is the discovery of new opportunities, new ways for developing competitive advantage, moves that

64

should be taken to fend off threats, and improvements that can be made to enhance performance. Acting on these insights requires change. This can be in the form of improvements to the way things are done in the organisation. It can also involve exiting current markets and entering new ones. Some of these changes are on a small scale and incremental. Some changes can be major and transformational. In terms of scope, some changes affect only certain parts of the organisation. However, some changes are more pervasive and involve many or all parts of the organisation.

Regardless of the scale and scope of change, it has to be managed carefully. This chapter will discuss what change management is all about and what strategic leaders need to do to plan for change. Besides relying on the current literature on change, the discussion in this chapter will also draw from the author's experience as a partner at Human Capital Development Sdn Berhad (HumanCap). HumanCap is a consultancy firm that includes change management consultancy as one of its main services.

For many people, stability provides a sense of security. This stability is created by doing the familiar. Prior learning helps create routines that then evolve into habits. As explained in chapter 1, with the passage of time, these habits become entrenched in our behaviours. They create a momentum, something management researchers term as "behavioural momentum" that keep people behaving habitually and in a predictable manner. As a result, this behavioural momentum can frustrate attempts to bring about change. Even when people agree with the change, they find it difficult to let go of their old habits and learn new ones.

There may also be those who disagree with or are unsure of the change. Some of those who disagree will oppose it openly, and some will keep quiet but will withhold their support. For those who are unsure of the change, they will most likely reserve their judgement and remain uncommitted. However, these individuals can later become converts and jump onto the change initiative. One thing that is clear is that all change initiatives will have a mix of all these categories of responses. And all of them have to be managed as a part of the change management process.

Making Change Happen

Battilana and colleagues argue that effective change management requires three key activities: communication, mobilization, and evaluation. All these activities are necessary because change involves a departure from the present. This departure requires getting the members of the organisation on board the change initiative. Not only must members understand the rationale and purpose of a change initiative, they also must be organised to take action and to adopt new routines and behaviours. This shift is not easy and has to be monitored to ensure it realises its goals.

One issue that strategic leaders must address in communicating change is explaining clearly the case for change. This includes explaining the consequences of not changing. Consultants like to use the term "burning platform" to describe the key issue that creates urgency for the change initiative. When you are on a burning platform, you either do something to put out the fire or jump into the sea and face the possibility of drowning. The fire may be small but if left to grow will engulf the whole platform and be more difficult to fight. Members of the organisation need to have a clear idea of the burning platform they are facing. Sometimes it may not be clear to everyone because the fire is small. If members do not see the burning platform, they can be easily lulled into complacency and not support a change initiative. For many people, the basic question is why leave the current comfort zone and venture into the unfamiliar if there is no compelling reason to do so? On the other hand, they are more likely to help put out the fire if they are aware of it and understand the threat it poses.

It is important to recognise that communicating change is not a stage in a sequential process. Instead, it is a continuous process to help steer the change initiative. Communicating change basically involves developing understanding, action planning, and finally executing the change. The aim of developing understanding involves creating a sense of shared destiny and developing a sense of ownership of the change. This then has to be followed by communicating the action plan that will be taken to affect the change. This has to be done to ensure that the ideas related to the change initiative do not remain as abstract ideas. Once the plan is ready, it will involve doing and learning from the mistakes and problems encountered. This requires monitoring feedback, using the feedback for improvement, and keeping people engaged and involved in shaping the change initiative.

Translating the ideas generated from strategic thinking ultimately requires mobilizing employees to create the desired new future and develop the capabilities needed to sustain this new future. In warfare, once all the planning has been done and the troops are in position, the actual fighting happens as they advance to contact. In managing change, this involves mobilizing people to take action. Battilana and colleagues point out that mobilizing involves organizing members to adopt the changes initiated into their daily work and procedures. This involves developing new work routines to implement the change.

Insight Box 4.1

Miscommunicating Change

Some of the mistakes this author has seen in managing change arises because of poor articulation of what the change initiative is all about. In one organisation, the corporate communication department was tasked with communicating a strategic change initiative top management had initiated. The department held town hall meetings in all the divisions of the organisation. Yet, many people complained about not understanding what the change initiative was all about. When the implementation of the town hall meetings was examined, it became evident why people could not understand the change effort. The corporate communication department had used a slide deck that was more than eighty pages long for the one-hour presentation. The audience felt overwhelmed by the amount of information given. Above all, they were still not clear what they as individuals were supposed to do in executing the change.

Nevertheless, change does not always happen even after top management has initiated the process. A number of factors work against members of the organisation getting on board the change initiative.

a. Causal ambiguity about what the change entails and the actions needed to realise its goals often causes members of an organisation to not commit to change. This can happen even when the intent of top management is understood by members lower down the hierarchy. They may accept the ideas associated with the change initiative but are usually hazy about what they have to do as individuals.

b.   Individuals are not always able to visualise the changes to their work necessitated by a change initiative. Laying out a specific action plan that details the specific actions is needed. This includes explaining the adjustments required in work processes. However, this can also be an iterative process whereby individuals can also be involved in identifying the changes that should be done to their jobs.

c.   Perceived increased burden can also make members of an organisation reluctant to embrace the change initiative. Changes to routines and procedures require new learning and can increase workload. According to Shin, Taylor, and Seo, such an experience can be burdensome and stressful. It is important to explain that this increase in workload is typically a transitional stage in change. Once the people are familiar with and have attained the targeted level of competence in the new processes or task, the situation should return to normal.

d.   Political behaviour can get in the way of mobilizing people for change. Some leaders at various levels may resent the change. They may simply not support the change initiative and make it difficult for others trying to support the change.

e.   For many people, the most basic question is "What's in it for me?" There has to be some benefit that they should enjoy from the initiative for them to want to embrace the change initiative. This should be a part of the issues addressed in the articulation and engagement process.

The employees' direct leaders are important bridges in the effort to mobilise people during change. An organisation is simply a chain of command with leaders at every level acting as bridges, connecting the top to the bottom. A conscious effort is needed to map out these bridges to make sure all the identified leaders are involved in engaging and mobilizing their subordinates. Evidence in the research done by this author and his students shows that the quality of relationship that employees enjoy with their direct leaders can affect their level of resistance to change. Direct leaders play important roles in filling in information gaps and planning the specific steps that should be taken to execute change. Thus, in addition to mapping out the bridges, the organisation needs also to assess the quality of relationships the employees have with their direct leaders. In organisations that use 360-degree appraisal, the information gathered can help with this assessment. Where the relationship between employees and their direct leaders in particular workgroups are weak, more attention should be given to improving their relationships or to supplementing and supporting the leaders.

Battilana and colleagues point out that getting people involved in change requires developing their capacity to work together. Leaders need to bring people together into a coalition to support the change. It is not enough that they accept the change as individuals. Each individual needs to work with others to help implement the change. Achieving this requires that leaders understand the need to create structural arrangements, transitional and permanent, that bring people together to solve problems and create the new arrangements, processes, and tasks needed to put the change in practice.

In addition to direct leaders, organisations need to recognise informal leaders who are sometime as influential and, in some cases, more influential than the direct leaders. These informal leaders can be union representatives, a charismatic peer, or a person of high status in a workgroup. These individuals can be roped in to help win over support for the change initiative. However, it is important to note that this should be done in a way that does not undermine the authority of the direct leader. Authority and decisions on matters such as work assignments, changes to tasks, and procedures must remain with the direct leader. Informal leaders should be used to supplement the direct leaders, not substitute for them. The role of informal leaders should be in helping with the communication process and providing feedback on issues encountered in the change process.

One of the key issues in mobilizing people is acquiring the resources and developing the capabilities needed to create the desired future state. Current resources and capabilities mix is the product of the learning and experience on what it takes to develop current competitive advantages and outcomes. The new desired future will require a new resources and capabilities mix to create new outcomes. The resources needed can be in the form of funding, knowledge, people, and time needed to execute the change. Marino points out that capabilities are the products of an organisation's processes and competencies. Developing new capabilities can involve acquiring new technologies, improving understanding of markets, and speed of decision-making within the organisation. It can also include restructuring the organisation, improving and possibly reengineering processes, and redesigning jobs, as well as providing training. All these have to be properly assessed and the necessary steps to develop them planned.

Insight Box 4.2

Left Out Leaders

HumanCap's experience in change management consultancy shows that failures in change initiative can be because a part of the management hierarchy is not on board. In one engagement where HumanCap was involved, it was the level below top management that was reluctant to change. As a result, this level became the impediment to the change initiative. Subordinates below this level were complaining that their direct leaders were not providing much guidance about the change initiative. Another example is the TQM initiative at a manufacturing plant of an MNC that used to operate in the Klang Valley, in the suburb of Kuala Lumpur. The managing director started the initiative as an effort to boost the performance of the plant. He had the full support of the union. However, the initiative stalled. Closer examination showed that many engineers, who were at middle management, did not feel comfortable with the TQM initiative. They were so accustomed to working in a directive manner that they found it awkward that they now had to consult with their subordinates, listen to their suggestions, organise quality circle discussions, and involve them in planning improvements.

At the same time, it is also important to recognise that the bigger the scale and scope of a change initiative, the more important it will be to understand the role of culture and climate in an organisation. Climate is the visible, recurring patterns of behaviour and felt part of culture. Members of an organisation can sense and feel it. Culture, on the other hand, evolves over time and becomes embedded into the assumptions, norms, and values of an organisation. The more visible part of a culture expresses itself in the form of the climate members of an organisation experience. But some aspects of a culture are tacit and may not be fully understood, even by members of an organisation. As such, it is important to audit and make explicit what aspects of an organisation's culture and climate can help and hinder change. This can help the organisation chart the changes needed to its culture and climate.

Quite often, it is more practical to focus on changing the organisational climate. This involves focusing on the aspects that are visible to the experiences of people in the organisation. Culture change, especially at the level of norms and values, are more difficult to do. This author's experience shows that members of an organisation may sometimes not understand their own culture. This becomes problematic when some aspects of the culture are dysfunctional and impede improvement. In one organisation where HumanCap was involved, we were asked to assess the culture of the organisation. One aspect of the organisation's culture that we found to be dysfunctional was the highly politicised climate that prevailed there. Many felt worried by amount of negative behaviours they saw. This included managers backstabbing and undermining one another. When this author presented this finding to the organisation's top management, one member of the team retorted, "So what? Isn't politicking common in all organisations? Why is it a problem?" This author then presented a more detailed analysis which revealed the impact of the intense politicking in the organisation. Many in the organisation felt the highly politicised climate meant that they should keep their ideas to themselves and must be mindful of the various cliques in the organization. Many felt they must always look over their shoulders before saying something. This author then said, "If you do not consider these to be problems, then it is not a problem. But is this the climate you want to have here? Mind you, this organisation is talking about change that involves encouraging more innovation." Everybody went silent. The person who raised the question quickly avoided eye contact with this author.

Managing Change

At HumanCap, the change management consultancy work is based on a model that involves a number of key steps. Strategic leaders can use these steps to plan and prepare their organisations for change. These steps follow.

1. Confirm desired future state.

    An important starting point in any change process is to confirm the desired future state. Quite often the information available in official documents does not provide a complete picture of the intention of the stakeholders behind the change initiative. There are often tacit reasons and goals for the change initiative. It is very important that this is understood. Confirming the desired future state involves three key activities – stakeholder engagement, defining the business case for change, and benefit realisation assessment.

    a. Stakeholder engagement

        This involves seeking more in-depth input from key stakeholders on the purposes and goals of the change initiative. The primary stakeholders who should be engaged at this stage are those in top management, including the board of directors, as well as those who may have an influence on the outcome of the change program. In some situations, this can involve the union. Even when the change is initiated by a member of top management, it is important to touch base with other members of the top management team to ensure that the desire for change is mutual and shared among all members of that team. For managers who are being groomed for strategic leadership positions, the chance to participate in stakeholder engagement is a good opportunity to understand the thinking of key stakeholders, especially members of top management. The key steps in conducting stakeholder engagement are

        i. Identify key stakeholders.

            This involves identifying those who may have a high interest in the change initiative and can influence the outcome of the initiative. Besides key stakeholders, such as members of top management, stakeholders can sometimes include suppliers and customers. In one of HumanCap's past stakeholder engagement sessions, we included customers. We found that our client's assessment of its capabilities and standing and the feedback we received from their customers were different. This enabled us to provide feedback to the client and helped them fine-tune their change initiative.

ii. Develop a list of issues to discuss.

To ensure stakeholder engagement is done effectively, it is important to identify the issues that need to be discussed with them. The main purpose of a stakeholder engagement discussion is to gain depth of insight on the change program. This includes understanding the business imperative of the initiative and the benefits that are desired from the change initiative.

iii. Prepare interviewers.

Once the list of issues has been prepared, it is important to train and develop consensus on them among those who are going to meet the stakeholders. The engagement can be done through interviews or focus group discussions. When direct engagement is not possible, other means of communication can be used.

iv. Analyze data.

Those involved in stakeholder engagement should come together to share the input they've obtained. This is where the feedback obtained is discussed to form a big picture of the change initiative. This includes understanding ultimate goals, motives for the change, expectations, attitudes, and potential conflicts and barriers.

v. Prepare stakeholders' report.

The outcome of stakeholder engagement should help bring into focus the motivations for change and what the organisation wants to achieve. In addition, support from key stakeholders is important during change. One inference that should be made from the stakeholder engagement is identifying DRAF; that is, who are the drivers, resistors, allies, and fence sitters. Drivers are the people wanting and seeking to create the change. Allies are those who are not the drivers but have a positive view of the change initiative and can be depended on for support. The fence sitters are those who are unsure and have a neutral stand of the change. Resistors are those who oppose the change and may impede the change initiative. This assessment will help plan the change intervention later on.

Insight Box 4.3

Resistor Plant Manager

An example of a stakeholder who may not necessarily be an ally is the case of the plant manager of a petro-chemical plant. The plant belonged to a conglomerate and was established as a joint venture effort with a Japanese company. The Japanese partner was to supply the raw material for the plant and market the output. Six months after the plant started operation, it encountered many problems and incurred substantial losses. Corporate head office needed to turn around the plant. We would expect all the parties involved to work together to solve the problems at the plant. The plant manager blamed the Japanese partner for its problems, accusing it of supplying the raw material at a high cost. This author was hired as consultant. Discussions with various stakeholders showed that the problem was much more complex. Closer investigation showed that part of the problems at the plant were due to technical and people issues. The plant experienced frequent disruptions and long shutdowns because of the lack of technical competence among its people. However, for the plant manager to admit to this would have meant admitting his failure. Instead, he deflected the blame by pointing the finger to the Japanese partner. In doing so, he was attempting to avoid taking responsibility for the crisis and resisted the attempt to overcome the problems at the plant. Even though the plant manager was a stakeholder who should be interested in overcoming the problems at his plant, he was, in fact, a resistor. The head office realised this and later decided to remove him from the plant.

---

b. Defining the case for change

One of the key outcomes of stakeholder engagement is defining clearly the case for change. This involves understanding the burning platform that makes the change necessary and agreeing on the desired future state. In some change situations, the case for change may have to do with making operational improvements to support an existing strategy. The strategy itself is not being changed. The operational improvements are done to enhance the execution of the strategy. However, there are situations where the change is done to support a shift in the organisation's strategy. In this situation, operational-level improvements need to be based on the new strategy. Besides understanding the case for change, stakeholder engagement should also assess the 4Cs of the case for change; that is, a) the level of *clarity* on why the change is needed, b) the extent of *congruence* in the understanding of the case for change among stakeholders, c) how much *commitment* there is to the goals envisioned in change process, and d) how much the understanding of the case for change has *cascaded* in the organisation. This assessment will help strategic leaders plan the change initiative more comprehensively.

c. Benefit realisation analysis

Organisations embark on change to create better performance. For businesses, this often involves improvements in the value delivered to customers. For non-profit organisations, this often involves improvements in the services given to end users. The outcomes desired in a change initiative are usually in the form of benefits gained by the organization, as well as the benefits delivered to customers or end users. These benefits must be clearly understood so that one does not undermine the other. For instance, an organisation may change its process to make a task easier for its employees or to reduce cost but end up creating inconvenience for its customers or end users. Likewise, an organisation may provide better goods or services to its customers or end users but does so at a higher cost that ends up wiping its profit and busting its budget. Benefit realisation analysis is done to define clearly who the change initiative is supposed to benefit and in what ways. Creating benefits in change process must address two things.

Insight Box 4.4

Measuring Everything but Managing Nothing

An example of trying to assess everything are the KPIs developed by a university to measure its performance. The corporate planning unit of this university was tasked with monitoring the progress and achievements of the university. However, when this unit started developing the strategic KPIs, it had so many components that it became overwhelming to measure and monitor. Besides indicators such as teaching and research quality, the indicators developed included measures of satisfaction with the landscape and the local bus service that enters the campus. While it is nice to have a beautiful landscape, by itself it does not have a strategic impact on the standing of the university. As for the bus service, it is offered by a private company as a part of the municipal transportation system and is not within the control of the university. Creating so many performance measures simply overwhelms the system and makes it difficult to manage anything.

First, what customers or end users should gain from better value delivery? Second, how will the organisation be able to capture value; that is, maintain or improve profit from the enhanced value delivery? The information gained from the stakeholder engagement should help define the benefits that should be created by the change initiative. This will help define the performance metrics for the change initiative.

2. Analyze current position.

Before change can be executed, it is important that strategic leaders take stock of the current state the organisation is in. Specifically, an understanding of the current position will enable strategic leaders to understand where the change should begin and the magnitude of effort needed to affect the change. In change management, this assessment is focused on understanding those aspects of the organisation that are relevant to the change effort. In order to not lose focus, it has to begin by understanding what has to change. Measurements are then developed to these areas that need to change. There is no need to assess everything in the organisation because some aspects of the organisation are of low importance in terms of contribution to strategic outcomes.

In order to have a focused assessment of the current state of the organisation, it is important to identify first what will be changed in the change initiative. This will help the organisation focus on the important issues instead of trying to measure everything. Once this is done, the readiness of the organisation to undergo change can be assessed. Three key elements in analyzing current position are as follows.

a. Change impact analysis

Change impact analysis is done based on the output of the benefit realisation assessment. It focuses on identifying the changes that need to be made to create the intended benefits and to ensure that the deliverables of the change initiative are completed. This includes assessing changes needed to the organisation's structure, technology, and people. The underlying purpose of change impact analysis is to assess the extent current technology, structure, and people can deliver the intended benefits envisioned by the change initiative. The gaps identified will serve as a basis for planning change intervention. In large-scale change initiatives, all these aspects will be affected. Specifically,

i. Operational capabilities

Assessing operational capabilities involves examining the organisation's structural design, processes, and job design. It involves using the information from the benefit realisation assessment to determine the changes needed to support the change. Key questions that need to be raised include whether current workflow and job design can deliver the desired benefits to the customers or end users, whether the current pattern of interaction between different parts of the organisation enabled by the current structure need to be changed to enhance performance, and whether the existing processes need to be revamped or improved to create the desired benefits.

ii. Technological capabilities

This century has seen tremendous changes in technology that affected our daily lives. Forty years ago, people knew of mobile phones as something used only by the hero in the "Get Smart" television series. Today, mobile phones are ubiquitous and have changed the way most of us communicate and conduct business. For many organisations, technologies can improve performance and improve processes. Strategic leaders need to address how technologies can be a part of the equation in creating and delivering the benefits envisioned in the change initiative. This includes understanding the limits of current technologies in the organisation. Technology can be used as an enabler to enhance

---

Insight Box 4.5

Changing Climate by Bringing in New Blood

When Eddie Tie took over the leadership of VitaLife, a Sydney-based health product company, the company was in the red and had to be turned around. Its very survival and existence was under threat. He believed that everybody needed to go the extra mile and work long hours to turn around the situation. But he found that his employees at the head office in Sydney at that time were more accustomed to working within the regular office hours. He realised that he needed to change the culture and climate of the organisation. However, changing the culture was not going to be easy. Old, entrenched habits are difficult to undo. It requires changing the norms and values people have become used to. And this was going to be difficult and takes time, something that was a luxury in a company that bleeding. Instead of trying to change values and norms, Eddie did something more practical by recruiting new people who were more accustomed to working long hours and exerting extra effort. By bringing in new blood, he changed the climate at the VitaLife head office. This helped the turnaround effort considerably.

---

current process and workforce. It can also substitute current processes and workforce.

iii. Competencies pool

An organisation is a pool of competencies. The capability that an organisation has is the result of a synergistic combination of these competencies. This competency pool, along with operational capabilities and technology, creates organisational capability. The core of any change process is changing the way people behave. Structure can be redrawn and technologies can be acquired, but all these will come to naught if the people involved do not change. In addition to providing training, developing new competencies also involves managing motivation and creating a positive work experience. Affecting behavioural change is the most challenging aspect of every change initiative. It requires changes in attitude and in skills, knowledge, and abilities. As Kahn points out, our behaviours are affected by our psychological states. People who feel positive are more likely to be motivated in their jobs.

iv. Culture and climate change

Culture shapes how people behave. Culture exists at many levels, including norms, values, behaviours, and artefacts. Some aspects of culture are the product of history and experience and may be tacit. These tacit elements of culture may not be visible even to members of the organisation. Climate is simply the more visible aspects of culture. Yet, both culture and climate have strong influences on work behaviours. Some aspects of an organisation's culture and climate can be functional, and some can be dysfunctional. Change involves changing the dysfunctional aspects of an organisation's culture and climate. It is typically easier to change climate because people can feel and describe it. At times, organisations need to do some critical reflection to examine why it is behaving in a certain manner to make the tacit aspects of its culture explicit. Only then can the tacit aspects of culture be changed.

A key output of change impact analysis is to form a picture of what has to change. This will require an understanding of the current state of the structure, technology, and people in the organisation. The gap between the current state of an organisation's structure, technology, and people and what is needed to take the organisation to its future state are areas that will need change intervention.

Smaller-scale changes that involve a limited scope will typically not require changes to the structure. For instance, the implementation of a new email software is a small-scale change that would not require changes to structure and major processes. However, a shift in strategy that involves changes to an organisation's competitive approach may involve changes in many of its aspects. This includes changes to the jobs affected by the change initiative. Depending on the scope of the change initiative, the change effort can involve extensive changes to many jobs or be limited to only a few jobs. The analysis should decide whether the affected jobs have to be redesigned, whether it will require reskilling, whether it will need new technologies, whether it can be performed by the current employees, and whether it should be outsourced.

b. Change readiness assessment

Once the changes that need to be done have been analyzed, the next step is to assess the readiness of organisational members to undergo change. Change readiness assessment is an assessment of the readiness of employees to support and participate in the change initiative. Past writings about change management had been primarily concerned with resistance to change. The term "resistance" implies that those who do not support and participate in the change initiative oppose it. However, current research shows this is not always the case. In some situations, the lack of understanding of the change initiative prevents people from committing and getting involved with the change. This lack of understanding can be in the form of causal ambiguity, where individuals agree on the desired outcomes but are unclear on the actions needed to realise them. Fear and insecurity can also make people hesitant to change. The lack of readiness to change can also be due to the absence of leadership at the middle and lower levels of the

Insight Box 4.6

Improving Loan Processing

An example of the interaction between technology, people, and structure is the introduction of a new information system in a bank that was done to shorten loan application processing time. Under the old system, loan processing had to rely on using multiple databases to assess the credit risk and understand the credit history and various other information about loan applicants. In large branches, the huge volume of loan application required that these tasks be performed by different individuals using different databases. They had to work sequentially to process the loan application, and only the last officer in the sequence was responsible for deciding on the approval. The change impact analysis showed that integrating the three databases into one system would enable one person to obtain all the needed information from one point and complete the processing in a shorter time. The analysis also showed that each officer would now be responsible for approving the loan instead of just performing one activity in the approval process. The loan processing officers had to be trained to use the new system and to make the approval decision. The analysis also showed that loan processing now no longer had to be organised sequentially. It also showed that the bank could reduce the staffing level needed for loan processing and redeploy its personnel to other tasks. Besides introducing a new technology, this change also required changes to work process and developing people's ability to accept bigger responsibilities and make decisions. An initiative involving the introduction of a new technology such as this would only be successful once the related processes have been revamped and the necessary training given to the employees involved.

organisation. This leads to the failure to mobilise people and guide their actions. As a result, people do not know the specific actions they need to take to support the change initiative. It involves the following steps.

i. Develop a model of change readiness.

It is important that change planners develop a model of the readiness of organisational members to undergo change. This model should be based on the information obtained from the change impact analysis and benefit realisation assessment. These two activities will help identify *what* has to be ready and *who* has to be ready to execute the change. For instance, in change initiatives during the implementation of information systems, perception of the readiness of the technology infrastructure can be a variable. If members of the organisation perceive that the system is not ready, they are more likely to have reservations about the initiative. On the other hand, in organisations that are trying to undergo strategic change that involves changing its culture, assessing which aspects of the culture that are dysfunctional and can impede change should be a variable in the model. For organisations introducing the just-in-time inventory management system, assessing readiness can include employees' perceptions of the readiness of their procurement departments and vendor readiness to support the system. Typically, there are variables that should be included in all change readiness assessment models. This is in addition to the ones identified in the change impact analysis and job impact analysis. These are variables related to clarity of understanding of the change initiative, the level of ownership respondents feel towards the change initiative, the extent they feel they have undergone the necessary preparations to implement the change. The model should also assess the presence – or the lack of it – of active leadership of the change process by the respondents' direct leaders.

ii. Develop assessment instrument.

The change readiness assessment is usually done using a questionnaire. The questionnaire instrument is developed based on the model of change readiness developed earlier. The items or questions on the questionnaire are simply the operational measures of the variables in the model. Once a questionnaire instrument is developed, it should be pilot tested to ensure it is easily understood by respondents, that the questions indeed measure the variables of interest, and all the relevant issues have been covered in the questionnaire.

iii. Identify participants in the assessment.

Depending on the model developed, the change readiness assessment can involve everyone in the organisation or only those directly affected by the change. Besides informing people of the change readiness assessment survey and asking them to respond to it, guarantees on the confidentiality of their responses need to be given to the respondents. This helps assure an honest and truthful response.

iv. Conduct assessment.

Once the participants have been identified, the appropriate medium for conducting the survey should be chosen. In most organisations, this can be done using electronic survey applications. However, in some organisations, access to computers can be limited, and hard copy questionnaires will be needed. The deadline for responding to the survey must also be specified. A contact person should be provided in case anyone has questions on the survey.

v. Analyze survey data.

The analysis of the survey data should be done to help the organisation understand the level of readiness of the workforce to implement the change. It can also pinpoint current strengths and weaknesses as well as potential problems and resistance to the change initiative. Besides providing descriptive data, such as mean scores and frequencies, it is important to also examine the relationship between variables. It will provide a basis for understanding the causal relationship between the variables in the change readiness assessment model.

vi. Review the change readiness report.

The final outcomes of the change readiness assessment are the scores of the variables in the change readiness model. Issues that are indicative of problems should be identified and red-flagged.

Besides providing a descriptive overview of the state of readiness to change, decision makers typically wants answers to the, "So what?" or, "What's next?" questions. Thus, the final report needs to also provide recommendations on the remedial steps that should be taken to address them.

3. Develop change intervention plan.

The convergence of information obtained from the confirmation of desired future state and analysis of current position should then be used to identify change interventions needed to create the change. At the most basic level, this will require doing the following.

   i.   Deciding on program mix

   The organisation needs to decide on the program mix it needs to maintain. This includes deciding on which initiatives, products, and processes need to maintained, discontinued, and phased out gradually. Programs that still deliver value to end users and provide the organisation with the opportunity to capture value should be maintained. On the other hand, programs that are no longer serving the end users' interests or cannot provide value to the organisation should not be maintained. Some programs should be phased out gradually to provide the current market to adapt. This ensures that the organisation does not damage its commitment to current customers. At the same, it should not overcommit by continuing to produce products and maintain processes that are delivering diminishing returns. This decision on program mix helps organisations understand what has to change and what has to be maintained.

   ii. Capabilities development planning

   A new strategy often requires new capabilities. The information gained from the stakeholder engagement, benefit realisation assessment, change impact analysis, and change readiness assessment should be brought together to create a capabilities development plan. These capabilities are created through a combination of improvements to an organisation's structure, technology, and people. These are the three dimensions

Insight Box 4.7

Turning around Malaysia Airlines Berhad

The turnaround of Malaysia Airlines is an example of a strategic change that involves extensive adaptation that requires new capabilities. In addition to selling off some its aircrafts, Christoph Mueller, the new CEO who took office on May 1, listed the following steps that Malaysia Airlines Berhad (MAB) was planning to take: i) corporate procurement will be done on better terms and conditions, ii) MAB will be downsized and will outsource some functions, iii) some employees will be terminated, iv) steps will be taken to improve MAB's damaged brand image in important overseas markets, v) employees will be given new contract conditions benchmarked against competitors, vi) staff training to develop future leaders will be initiated, vii) the damaged relationships between the staff and management, unions and management, and even between departments will be fixed, viii) there is a need to overcome the problem of some personnel still working in silos, ix) steps need to be taken to pay more attention to details in service delivery.

These changes in MAB will inevitably involve changes to capabilities that involve structure, technology, and people. For instance, improving procurement will probably involve changing standards and criteria and possibly even the procurement process. It may also involve appointing people who will not succumb to pressure from opportunistic politicians and corrupt vendors. Paying more attention to details in service delivery may involve changing procedures and the use of new technologies. Its employees may have to be retrained for this purpose. Likewise, overcoming the silo mindset among MAB employees may require greater use of cross-functional teams. In addition, these employees will have to undergo attitude changes to enable them to work across functional boundaries.

of capabilities development. As mentioned earlier, they are very closely related and influence one another. New technologies alone may not enhance performances if they continue to be based on old, ineffective processes and procedures. Likewise, technology and structural issues will affect people. As such, it is important to ensure that the change intervention has a synergistic impact by realigning the three dimensions.

iii. Manage lack of readiness and resistance

One aspect that may have been discovered in the change readiness assessment is a lack of readiness to change and resistance. A well-designed change readiness assessment should be able to inform change leaders of the nature of the lack of readiness and resistance, its magnitude, and where it is more pronounced in the organisation. It is important to not equate lack of readiness to change with resistance. People who lack readiness to change are not necessarily resistors. Sometimes they lack information, do not know how the change is supposed to affect their jobs, or do not possess the necessary skills. Some of these issues can be resolved by interventions such as training and process improvements. There are also issues that have to be addressed through better communication planning. Overcoming resistance, however, will require more than just these steps. Dealing with resistance can be by co-opting influential resistors into the change process, creating a critical mass of support among employees, building overwhelming momentum for the change initiative, offering rewards, and sometimes even using power coercive tactics that may involve the use of punishment. However, leaders may not be able to overcome all the resistance. There may still be those who just do not want to be a part of the change. Some of the ways to deal with such individuals include ignoring and even isolating them, minimising their influence and impact, and perhaps even persuading them to leave.

Insight Box 4.8

Letting Resistors Go

When Eddie Tie was recruited from Malaysia to lead as the group CEO of VitaLife at the company's head office in Sydney, Australia, a member of his management team tendered his resignation. Eddie wanted to understand why this manager resigned, so Eddie met up with him. The manager simply said that he no longer felt like working at VitaLife because it had lost its "Australian character." It became evident to Eddie that this manager resented having a Malaysian as the company's CEO. (Never mind the fact that VitaLife was founded in 1947 by a Singaporean who had family roots Kuching, Malaysia, who decided later on to move the company to Australia!) Given the irrational and prejudicial reason given by the manager, Eddie didn't persuade him to stay. Some resistors are best ignored.

iv. Developing communication plan

Lewis points out that articulating a change initiative is more than just sharing information of a new vision. It also involves convincing members why their behaviours and routines have to change. It is also important to recognise that the message articulated is crafted according to the target audience. Lewis and colleagues propose a list of key tactics to be used in planning communication.

I.   Use the communication plan to articulate a message and engage people by seeking their input and getting their involvement.

II. Use informal networks and line supervisors to convey messages and to prevent panic.

III. Disseminate information about roles, tasks, responsibilities, and procedures to get people to understand how the change initiative will affect their daily activities.

IV. Manage the information flow by breaking down the change program into aims of specific units and departments.

V. Be motivating when explaining the change process to encourage action and risk taking.

VI. Formulate a plan that makes use of multiple mediums to share information, build understanding, discuss implications, gain commitment, and alter behaviours.

VII. Create and articulate a vision that is unambiguous, simple, and personally relevant.

The above discussion highlights the fact that communicating change is more than just having a kick-off ceremony or a grand speech by the CEO. More importantly, articulation and engagement are about helping everyone undergo a sense-making process and cultivate a shared understanding of the change initiative. Leaders also need to understand that in order to influence their followers, they must show that they are willing to be influenced. This is why engaging the followers involves having dialogues and listening to their concerns. In addition, a good communication plan should convey the message through multiple mediums and channels. The message conveyed must be in a form that is meaningful and can be understood by the audience. This often involves breaking the message into small bits and communicating over a period of time.

In large-scale change initiatives, change intervention sometimes involves taking it in small steps at a time. This can be by creating pioneer initiatives in the form of pilot projects to implement the change first. The choice of where to begin can be guided by a number of criteria. One option can be by initiating it at a hurting system. This refers to a part of the organisation that is experiencing major problems and is hurting badly. Intervention at a hurting system is badly needed. Since it is already facing problems, an intervention will most likely make things much better. Another option can be by identifying a ready system. This involves starting the initiative at a part of the organisation that is receptive to change. Starting at a ready system has a higher chance of success because of the support readily available there. This approach provides the opportunity for members of the organisation to learn from change done on a small scale first. Success in these interventions can help build confidence and provide a showcase of how to execute the change.

Insight Box 4.9

How Change Management Made a Difference

The adoption of a new financial information system by two organisations, one a university and the other a major corporation employing more than 20,000 employees, highlights the differences in approach and outcome. The former basically introduced an online financial system but had no change management plan, no business continuity plan, and the people responsible made very little effort to communicate the transition. The head of the university's finance division made little effort to lead the change and communicate with other employees, behaving more like a leader in absentia. As a result, many problems appeared once the new financial system was rolled out. Some payments were delayed by months, claims took a long time to be processed, and some people received their salaries late. Members of the finance division behaved as though it was no big deal that people had to endure considerable inconvenience as a result of the absence of a change management plan. It was only when many complaints surfaced that a small attempt at communication was made. Even then, it was very much a monologue.

The corporation, on the other hand, introduced a financial information system that integrated the financial management system across more than a dozen subsidiaries and involved billions of ringgit. It was much more complex and on a much larger scale than the university's change. Yet, when the new system was launched, it went flawlessly. The reason for this was that this corporation saw the implementation of the new system as a change management process and put in place a proper change management plan. Months were spent communicating about the change and developing the readiness of the system, and tests were conducted to ensure flawless implementation and business continuity. When the "go live" date arrived, the transition from the old system to the new one happened without a glitch.

4. Executing Change and Transition Planning

Executing change ultimately requires implementing all the interventions. It involves making operational the new capabilities. Doing this involves a transition from the current processes and capabilities to the new ones. All this has to be done while ensuring that current operation is not disrupted. Key elements of executing change and transition planning include the following.

a. Business continuity planning

Change often involves making changes to an organisation's operation. This can be in the form of introducing a new technology, changing current processes and procedures, and developing new skills and abilities. Simple as it sounds, there are many instances where the transition from the old system to the new system does not happen smoothly. Customers and end users may not be prepared for the new system and are caught by surprise. Equipment may not be ready, and personnel involved may not have been adequately trained. The new technology adopted may not have been properly tested. A number of steps can be taken in planning for business continuity.

i. Decide on service level standard.

The organisation needs to decide what it considers to be the service level standard that is required to ensure business continuity. Essentially, this standard defines the maximum level of disruption that can be accepted. This standard differs across organisations and depends on the nature of the activities and their impact. For instance, for a water supply company, a disruption of a few hours is acceptable. However, for an air traffic control system, even a one-minute disruption is unacceptable and can lead to disastrous consequences. A business continuity plan must ensure the organisation is able to operate and comply with its service level standard.

ii. Identify continuity control points.

Once a service level standard has been set, the next step is to examine what can undermine the attainment of the standards. These are the continuity control points to ensure that the service level can be maintained. These continuity control points must be managed so that there is no breakdown in their activities. In some situations, it can be by having both the old and the new systems operating in parallel or by having the old system as a backup to the new one.

iii. Assess threats and risks.

This simply involves asking the basic question about what can go wrong. This can involve breakdowns at the critical control points or something as simple as the personnel responsible not turning up for work. Mitigation plans need to be developed to deal with these possible threats and risks. Some organisations are so complacent about business continuity that they do not bother to have a business continuity plan. For instance, when a personnel responsible for a particular task is on leave, users are simply told to wait for him to come back!

iv. Prepare a transition plan.

To make a smooth transition, all the necessary preparations must be made in advance. This includes training, updating information, preparing the new processes and procedures, communicating the transition, and planning the switch to the new system. All those affected by the change must know what it will involve, when it will happen, and how it will affect them. Two key actions are needed in planning the transition. The first is to decide on the dates the new system goes live and when the old system will be decommissioned. Second is to prepare a complete checklist to make sure everything that needs to be done is ready.

v. Develop a recovery plan.

There is always the possibility of a breakdown of the new system. A recovery plan needs to make clear the procedures for resolving problems, the people responsible for resolving the problems, the escalation procedure – that is, when it should be raised to higher levels of the organisation and to whom.

vi. Test the system.

This involves testing the new system prior to implementation. For many new technologies, this will involve conducting a user acceptance test. The testing is not just about the technology adopted but also the running of the complete system under different conditions.

vii. Implement the change.

The implementation is marked by the launching date, usually called the "go live" date. If all the above steps have been done properly, there should be minimal problems at the implementation stage.

b. Scheduling and coordination

In many cases, change initiatives go hand in hand with project implementation. Close coordination between the change management team and the project management team is important. Implementing the various projects and initiatives under the change initiative requires close coordination between change leaders and those who are supposed to be affected by the change. This includes coordinating with internal as well as external parties. Internal people need to be informed ahead of time of any intervention that is going to be done. For instance, training must be scheduled at the appropriate time and should be of a reasonable duration. Many managers involved still have to support ongoing operations and need to ensure adequate staffing of their operations. They will need to reschedule job assignments. For some positions, the cyclical nature of their workloads should be taken into consideration when planning activities. For instance, do not expect people from sales and finance to be able to attend long trainings at the end of the financial year. They will be busy closing the company's accounts and finalizing their numbers. For external parties dealing with an organisation, they need to know how a change in the organisation is going to affect them and when it will take effect.

c. Issues management

Whereas risk management is about anticipating possible problems and taking mitigating steps, issues management is about dealing with unanticipated problems. As unanticipated problems arise, leaders need to assess them and decide which ones needs urgent attention. The ones needing immediate attention are those that are likely to a) impede the ability of the change initiative to deliver the desired benefits, b) are unlikely to resolve itself or are not temporary in nature, c) tend to be enduring and have the potential to grow. In taking mitigating steps, the following should be done: a) assign the person responsible for the resolving the problem, b) set deadlines for resolving the problem, c) allocate any resources needed to resolve the problem, d) make sure the necessary authorisation has been given to the person responsible to act to resolve the problem, e) define the line of accountability of the person responsible.

5. Evaluation

Evaluating change is a continuous process. The key concern of evaluation is whether members of the organisation are making the transition towards working and adopting the new processes and routines. Three key elements must be dealt with here. The first is establishing early warning mechanisms to monitor whether the desired changes are happening. In the acquisition of new technologies, this can include monitoring whether the procurement process has been properly implemented. This includes assessing whether the terms of reference in the request of proposal documents truly reflect the requirements of the change initiative and have addressed all the important issues. Likewise, for skills development, it is important to ensure the proper procedures have been established and followed in selecting training providers. The second is the performance level of the components being changed in the organisation's system. This can include monitoring whether the technology acquired is performing at the expected level. For training, it can also include assessing the competency level of the people trained to execute the new processes and routines. Likewise, for process improvement initiatives, the evaluation should also monitor whether processes that were reengineered are operating flawlessly at the desired levels. The third element involves assessing whether the changes adopted have indeed led to improvements in the desired performance parameters.

It is important for strategic leaders to treat the evaluation as a learning process and not use it for punitive purposes. Members of the organisation need to feel comfortable to voice their concerns and point out any problems encountered. It is quite natural that there will be confusion and uncertainties as people try out new ideas. Mistakes will be made. Some decisions will be made with imperfect information. It will take time for people to adjust to new behavioural expectations and new work routines. It is important that a quick feedback loop is created to enable improvements to be done quickly. This will help members of the organisation get out of the "valley of despair" that is sometimes encountered during setbacks in change programs. Managing these disruptions and uncertainties is important to make sure the initiative is not derailed by the problems.

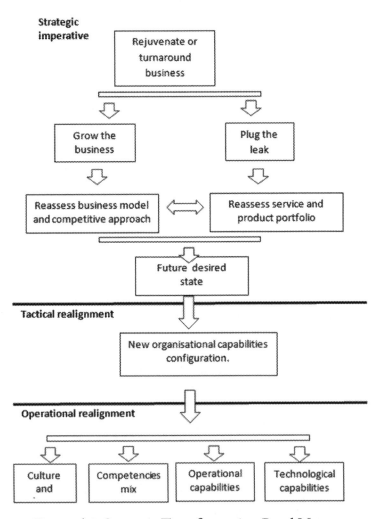

Figure 4.1: Strategic Transformation Road Map

The model of change presented here can be used for more limited change initiatives, such as during the implementation of a new technology or for strategic transformation. The difference between the two types of change is the scale and the locus of the change process. Strategic transformation would typically address the strategic imperative of the change, perform tactical realignment, and undertake process realignment (see figure 4.1). These three steps will involve doing the following.

1. Define strategic imperative.

    The motive for a strategic transformation must be clear. In broad terms, organisations initiate strategic transformations to either improve performance or to turn around poor performance. The former is usually proactive change done in anticipation of challenges or to raise the bar to spur the organisation towards the next level of performance. The latter is usually when the organisation has started to incur losses. Deciding on the strategic imperative for change is top-management responsibility. It precedes the change initiative. Two key assessments are needed once the strategic imperatives are understood.

    a. Plug the leak.

        Organisations running at a loss need to identify what products or activities are draining it financially. This typically involves identifying products or services that are not making money. Stopping these products and services is an important first step in any turnaround situation. Even for companies that are still profitable, they need to identify whether there are products or services that are not meeting its profitability targets.

    b. Grow the business.

        Improving revenue requires reassessing an organisation's business model and competitive advantage. In essence, this involves asking the basic question of whether the company is competing effectively and whether it should change its business model or the way it is competing. Doing this will involve understanding how the market is evolving and what competitors are doing.

    c.   Define future desired state.

Once the strategic imperative is understood, leaders need to define the desired future state. In a turnaround situation, this involves attaining profitability. For organisations seeking to boost performance, this will involve setting new performance targets. More importantly, top management must be clear of the new capabilities the organisation will need to enable it to create the targeted outcomes.

2.   Tactical realignment.

Once the desired future state for a change initiative is understood, it is necessary to assess the new capabilities configuration that is needed to create the new future state. As mentioned earlier, an organisation's capabilities configuration is the synergistic combination of the competencies residing in its people, processes, culture, and technology. As an organisation changes its strategy or relies on new forms of competitive advantage, it needs to relook at its capabilities configuration. This includes assessing which capabilities need to be maintained and which ones need to be eliminated. It may also need to acquire new capabilities.

3.   Operational realignment.

Once an organisation is clear of the changes needed to its capabilities configuration, the next steps is to reconfigure its competencies pool, culture and climate, technological capabilities, and operational capabilities.

The role of change management begins once top management has decided on the strategic imperative and desired future state. Nevertheless, those responsible for managing the change initiative need to begin by confirming the desired future state. This includes conducting stakeholder engagement, defining clearly the case for change, and understanding the benefits the organisation wants to realise from the strategic change. The analysis of current state then has to be performed to understand the new capabilities configuration needed. This includes conducting a change impact assessment to assess what has to change and a change readiness assessment to gauge people's readiness to change. Once this is done, change intervention planning can be done.

Closing

Leading strategically requires that leaders have the ability to translate the ideas born out of their strategic thinking into action. This often requires that leaders change the courses of their companies and initiate change. It is therefore imperative that strategic leaders understand what managing change entails. They need to understand how to rebuild the organisation's capabilities and competitiveness. This includes creating the impetus for people to get out of their comfort zones and embrace change. At the heart of this change process is changing people in a systematic and organised manner. It is not something that can be left to fortune or good luck. Strategic thinkers do not rely on luck. They let fools do that.

CHAPTER 5

Leading with Conscience

Introduction

Individuals who hold leadership positions have the ability to use their power and influence to shape the behaviours of others. They are expected to use this power in a just manner and for achieving greater good. We expect our leaders to be better than us and to be worthy of our trust. But we have also seen many instances where leaders violate this trust. In some cases, leaders simply become greedy and abusive. They use their positions for personal gain. Quite often this is at the expense of the organisation and society.

The various crises that we've seen show the profound impact of leader misconduct. Abusive leaders led to the collapse of Enron, Barings Bank, and Tyco. In Malaysia, the BMF scandal in the early 1980s almost brought down Bank Bumiputera. And there is, of course, the 1MDB scandal which has made Malaysia famous for having a leader who had a humongous amount of dubious fund in his personal account, supposedly money "donated" to him by foreigners. There is the YAPEIM saga, also in Malaysia, which has become an example of the extravagant use of funds by a religion-based organisation that is supposed to serve a charitable purpose. We also hear of many allegations of fraud under a previous leader of a local airline. Whereas in Enron, Barings Bank, and Tyco those responsible were finally brought to court and convicted, Malaysia is special in that those responsible for these scandals remain free.

Strategic leaders are supposed to create value and bring benefit to society. What we see instead are leaders who seek benefits for themselves and destroy value in the process. They also harm society. Bank Bumiputera had to be saved through injection of funds from Petronas. This is money that could have been used to improve education and health services. Perhaps Malaysians could have enjoyed toll-free highways if our money was not wasted bailing out such companies. *Businessweek* wrote an article about the 2008 financial crisis in the United States, criticizing business schools for producing managers who are hasty and more concerned about value extraction instead of value creation. These managers just want to make fast money, even if it harms the organisations they represent. Instead of behaving like strategic leaders, they are toxic leaders who harm everyone and everything around them. They have no consciences and have lost their moral bearings. In the short term, they extract value for themselves, but in the long term, they destroy value.

In an age where performance is measured using KPIs and stakeholders are quite willing to turn a blind eye to how the KPIs were achieved, moral boundaries become fluid. In business, we see companies adulterating their products to cut costs and maximise profits. This was the case in the scandal involving the sales of contaminated milk in China. Corruption has become endemic, and abuse of power is common. In government, politicians meddle with decision-making in the public sector to steer business to those close to them. In countries with corrupt governments, it is common to see last minute revelations from the political masters, instructing civil servants assessing bids for government contracts to "consider" companies that were not even considered qualified for shortlisting. Civil servants who don't seem to understand what "consider" means are bound to find themselves transferred elsewhere or their careers derailed.

Holding a leadership position is a trust. This is especially the case for strategic leadership positions. A study by Dr Ho Joann from Universiti Putra Malaysia shows that managers' commitment to behaving ethically is shaped by their leaders' commitment to ethical standards. There is a vicarious effect taking place when managers observe the behaviours of their strategic leaders. When strategic leaders behave ethically and are mindful of the moral and ethical boundaries, it has a signalling effect to the rest of the organisation. Followers understand that their leaders treat these issues seriously. Their own behaviours will be shaped by what they see in their strategic leaders. All of us are born with good qualities in us. The Quran describes the creation of humankind as being in "the best of stature" and that our surrounding and socialisation can help preserve and nurture this stature or corrupt and undermine this stature. In organisations, the actions of strategic leaders can help nurture or undermine this stature.

After the 1997 Asian financial crisis, a lot of attention was given to improving corporate governance. Ethics became a hot subject. Steps were taken to improve managerial capabilities to ensure problems from the past do not recur. This includes changing regulations, structure, and training. While all these are helpful, they are not sufficient. When a society has to rely on an elaborate set of rules and regulations to ensure ethical behaviour and create benefit for society, it shows that we have failed to build the moral character of our people, especially those who ascend to leadership positions. It shows that our educational system has failed.

Society needs leaders who are guided by their consciences in every organisation and at all levels. This is especially important for leaders at the strategic level. As Axiata's Dato Jamaluddin Ibrahim points out, strategic leaders have to consider the impact of their decisions and actions on society. They have to be mindful of how they affect the environment and livelihood of members of society. A failure to do this will leave organisations with a moral vacuum. The organisation becomes like a ship sailing without a compass.

Understanding Conscience

Conscience can be broadly defined as human knowledge of right and wrong, and it includes our moral consciousness and use of moral reasoning in decision-making. It is a mental awareness that prompts us to distinguish between right and wrong. In Buddhism, conscience is said to be a "self-luminous spark of thought" that is revealed at the inner core of ourselves. In Catholic tradition, Saint Augustine defines conscience as the voice of God, whispering to us. In secular tradition, Piaget considers conscience as the cognitive ability to engage in moral reasoning. The notion of conscience in Islam is tied to two key concepts, *taqwa* and *ehsan*. Loosely translated, "taqwa" means the fear of God. However, a more precise definition of "taqwa" defines it as the state of mindfulness in observing the boundaries of behaviour. Ehsan is a state where a person feels God's presence in his or her life as though one can see Him. Islam sees the convergence of these two concepts as creating a sense of awareness of God's presence that motivates people to live within the proper boundaries of behaviour. One's behaviour is defined not by self-interest but by the desire to seek His pleasure.

Having conscience is more than just knowing what is right and wrong. People with consciences are able to integrate moral reasoning into their thinking and decision-making. They are able to assess ambiguous situations and new moral dilemmas and reason out their stances and actions. Among the manifestations of this conscience is the considerate way they treat others. Leaders with a high level of conscience exhibit the following behaviours.

Insight Box 5.1

Courage at a Crossroad

Bishop Desmond Tutu, a Nobel prize winner, is a leader who stood against apartheid rule in South Africa. He opposed the US policy of constructive engagement with the apartheid regime in South Africa. He advocated for foreign countries to stop investing in South Africa. In 1985, both the United States and the UK finally stopped investing in apartheid South Africa. A defining moment in Tutu's role as a non-violence activist was during the assassination of the black leader Chris Hani. Tension escalated, and the anger of the black community was at its peak. It was easy to use the incident to foment violence against the white community. Yet, Bishop Tutu managed to appeal to the crowd of 120,000 people who attended Chris Hani's funeral to not resort to violence but to instead chant with him, "We will be free. All of us, black and white together." Instead of letting the emotion of the moment influence his actions, Bishop Tutu used his moral judgement to make the right decision and steer people away from further bloodshed. His stance during this incident had major strategic significance. South Africa could have spiralled into violence and become a totally different country had Bishop Tutu simply kept silent or followed the angry mood prevailing at that moment.

---

a. Driven by a higher sense of purpose

Being driven by a higher sense of purpose is one of qualities of leaders with consciences. To these leaders, leadership is not just about power and personal interests. It is more about making a difference in bringing some benefits to others. For those leading businesses, profit is the reward for doing something good and beneficial. It is not an end by itself.

b. Concern for others

Leaders with consciences are mindful of how their behaviours affect others. They think of the interests of others and are considerate towards those they deal with. This behaviour is an extension of their concern for doing what is right and behaving fairly.

c. Possess conscience-based sensitivity

Volling and colleagues point out that leaders with consciences have a sense of moral and emphatic emotion. They are sensitive to anything that comes near the boundary between right and wrong and are able to sense the ethical dilemma that it may present. Moral emotion means that they develop emotional reactions to wrongdoings. Emphatic emotion means that they are able to be aware of and understand the emotions of others. This makes these leaders mindful of the consequences of their actions on others.

d. Able to use moral judgement

Related to the previous point is the ability to use logical reasoning to determine right and wrong. This means that leaders with consciences do not let their emotions and prejudices cloud their judgements. Having a sense of moral judgement is also about understanding that diversity and differences of opinion are part of the realities of life. Thus, leaders with consciences accept that respecting those who differ from them is part of the moral standard that to be adhered to.

e. Altruistic motives

Leaders with consciences are driven by the desire to do good. Griffin and Hesketh point out that this involves having proactive and inhibitive motivations. Proactive motivation is the desire and motivation to do good on one's own initiative. Inhibitive motivation is the desire to avoid causing harm to others and accepting responsibility for one's actions.

f.   Moral courage

Leaders with consciences do not just have a sense of what is right and wrong. They also have the courage and persistence to behave based on their moral standards. They do not bow easily to pressure or compromise their commitments to doing the right thing and shunning the wrong. They do not succumb to temptations that require them to abandon their principles.

When Conscience Guides Leaders

Professor Muhammad Yunus, a Nobel Prize winner and founder of Grameen Bank, initiated micro-financing projects in Bangladesh. He is a good example of a leader who is driven by his conscience. His motivation was to help the poor help themselves by doing something strategic; that is, by providing small loans to enable poor people to become self-reliant and get them out of poverty. Muhammad Yunus, who earned a reputation as "Banker to the Poor", helped the poor by lending to them, something banks would typically not do. Leaders who lead with consciences fight for something bigger than themselves. Professor Yunus could have just walked away from the poor women he saw in rural Bangladesh. He was then a professor at a university and already had a comfortable life.

Tawakkul Karman is another Nobel Prize winner. From Yemen, she persisted in fighting for human rights in spite of hostile treatment from the ruling regime in her country. She could have just retreated into silence after being thrown into jail. South Africa's Bishop Tutu could have called for revenge and violence against the white community after Chris Hani's assassination. It was not easy to tell Hani's followers to remain calm given the circumstances. Each of these leaders reached a crossroad but chose a path that the ordinary person may prefer to avoid given the difficult circumstances before them. All three were thinking about the greater good and not just their personal interests. They were determined and willing to persist in their causes. And they were rational in their decisions and the steps that they took. They did not let prejudices and emotions determine their actions. Because of this, all three created strategic impacts that made them outstanding leaders.

Insight Box 5.2

Helping the Poor to Help Themselves

Professor Muhammad Yunus was inspired by his mother, who always made it a point to help any poor person who sought her help. He came with the idea of lending to the poor after seeing a poor woman who made bamboo stools on one of his field trips. The woman had to buy raw material and relied on a loan for it. He found that after all her effort, she had to pay back the loan at an exorbitant rate of 10 percent per week. As a result, the woman was left with very little balance for herself. Muhammad Yunus felt that there had to be a better system and lent his own money to help the woman. Since then, he formed the Grameen Bank and introduced the micro-credit program to lend to the poor. Today, Grameen Bank employs 19,800 people, has 2,564 branches, and lends money to 8.29 million poor people. The non-performing loan rate of Grameen Bank is only 3 percent, way lower than other banks. Professor Muhammad Yunus is an example of a leader with conscience who was concerned about others and understood the suffering of the poor. He channelled this energy into searching for a more strategic way to help the poor. This reduced their dependency on loan sharks and welfare handouts and made them self-reliant.

Leading with conscience is by no means limited to social and political leaders. Business leaders are also known to define their business in terms of creating value and benefit for society. John Mackey, the founder of Whole Foods Markets, describes going into business as being about serving others. He said, "Most people want more transcendent values. They want to believe and understand how their work is contributing to helping other people making the world a better place."

The late Anita Roddick, who founded The Body Shop, described her thinking about business succinctly when she said, "If I can't do something for the public good, what the hell am I doing?" Soichiro Honda, the founder of Honda, alluded to the importance of having conscience when he said, "The value of life can be measured by how many times your soul has been deeply stirred." Konosuke Matsushita, the founder of Panasonic, highlighted the same point when he said, "All I did through my career was to work unstintingly, devoting my best to the job at hand from day to day, and following faithfully the dictates of common sense and my own conscience." It is because of his conscience that he firmly believes in producing quality products. To Matsushita, producing quality products is not just about being profitable. This commitment grows from a conscience that considers it a moral imperative to serve customers well. He said, "I believe a manufacturer's most important responsibility to the customer is to make defect-free products."

For Datuk Pua Khein-Seng, the CEO and co-founder of the Taiwanese firm Phison, entrepreneurship isn't just about chasing money. It is more about creating value out of nothing and developing people, whether employees, suppliers, or clients. Wealth and ego can make people forget who they are when they are successful. Datuk Pua points out, "Entrepreneurship is about chasing ideals, about feeling successful from being able to create something

---

Insight Box 5.3

Driven by a Bigger Sense of Purpose

Tawakkul Karman is another example of a leader with conscience. In many ways, Tawakkul Karman defied the stereotype image of Muslim-Arab women as a marginalised and suppressed group in her role as a civil right leader who stood in defiance of the Salleh regime in Yemen. She almost lost her life during an assassination attempt. Her opposition to the corrupt and abusive regime in Yemen landed her in jail a number of times. She inspired women in Yemen to come out and stand against repression. She founded Women Journalists Without Chains to unite women journalists in Yemen in their campaign for justice. Karman fought for something bigger than herself. In spite of all the hardship she had to endure, Karman showed moral courage and persistence in standing for her beliefs.

---

from nothing, from having trained employees and seeing them live well, buying houses or cars, and starting a family."

It should be noted here that all these entrepreneurs created successful businesses. Their concern for doing something for the good of others enabled them to focus on really understanding their markets well and giving their best in serving them. Let there be no mistake. These leaders were not turning their businesses into charity organisations. They had to ensure their businesses were profitable. However, their attitudes and outlooks about how they should impact others and contribute to society went beyond thinking about profit maximisation. They were guided by conscience. They did not simply follow what others were doing purely for the sake of maximizing profit. That could have been the shortest route to profitability. Instead, their consciences made them choose the route not taken by others.

For example, in the 1970s, Honda decided to redesign its engine in order to exceed the California air emission standard that came into effect then. At that time, other manufacturers simply installed catalytic converters to their existing engines to reduce emission. This more ecofriendly engine made Honda's first Civic model a runaway success. Soichiro Honda, the company's founder, was so please with the success that he declared that he was happy Honda was able to beat the American car manufacturers in exceeding their country's standard. However, his engineers commented to him that to them it was not about beating the Americans. It was about leaving a better future for their children. Soichiro realised his mistake and was so embarrassed by his comment that he said, "I felt that I should have stepped down on that day."

The Body Shop's business is based on offering products that are natural, do not use ingredients from animals, and do not involve testing on animals. The company relies on a network of poor rural suppliers to supply ingredients for its products. This enabled the company to them improve their livelihoods. And as mentioned earlier, Panasonic's commitment to quality comes from its conscience and belief that the right thing to do is to give its customers the best.

Jim Womack made an interesting remark when observing Volkswagen's intention to become the world's biggest car company by 2017. When he heard of the announcement, his immediate reaction was that he believed the plan would come to a bad end. Indeed, by 2015, Volkswagen had grown in terms of sales but became embroiled in scandal. The company was caught cheating by using software to give a false output during emission tests for its diesel models. Its single-minded pursuit of the goal to become the biggest car company in the world made it forget its customers. Womack commented that when a business has a vision that just takes care of itself, not the customers, it is going to flop. Instead of setting delivering value to customers as its goal, it became more concerned with its ego and pride.

Foss points out that organisations can frame their goals based on three key categories. These are hedonic goals, gain goals, and normative goals. Hedonic goals are concerned mainly with achieving pleasure and pride. Volkswagen's desire to be the biggest car company in the world is a form of hedonic goal. Gain goals are about enhancing financial outcomes. Normative goals are about acting in the proper manner to provide collective benefits. Most organisations have elements of hedonic, gain, and normative goals. The choice of which goals become the dominant and overarching ones shapes the forms of collaborative behaviour that emerge in organisations. Normative goals emphasize serving greater good and makes this the focus of the collaborative behaviour in organisations. Hedonic goals make people focus on managing images and impressions. Quite often the focus becomes about pleasing the ego of the leader. Gain goals tend to make people focus on maximizing profits. Other concerns become secondary or unimportant. Gain goals tend to make people focus on financial goals. This often leads them to work towards attaining short-term performance indicators. When normative goals are the dominant goals, people see profit as a reward for serving a greater purpose. Fame is only a side benefit of having done a good job in serving a greater purpose. Leading with conscience is about leading by framing normative goals for the organisation.

As mentioned earlier, having conscience defines not only a person's commitment to ethical and moral standards. It is also about how they deal with others. Leaders with consciences are more considerate, willing to listen, and have respect towards others. Leaders who treat others in this manner create positive work experiences. This positive experience raises the level of motivation and commitment to work. It is also more likely to nurture creativity in the workplace. Creating this positive experience is important in the exercise of strategic leadership because the search for new opportunities or deciding on responses to threats requires creative thinking. Leaders with consciences are able to provide the climate that supports creative thinking.

Leading with conscience is even more important at the strategic level. The change that often comes with strategy change often involves doing the unfamiliar. Leaders sometimes have to venture into new areas where the moral and ethical standards may not be clear and are still debated. They need to listen to their consciences when deciding on issues. Strategic leaders need to understand that they may not have all the answers on what needs to be done. They have to be willing to accept the imperfections in their own knowledge and understanding and to listen to those around them. Strategic leaders need to create an open climate that enables discourse and debates on ambiguous issues in their organisations.

Leading with conscience is also important for teamwork. Because leaders with consciences are driven by a higher sense of purpose, they tend to be more inspirational and unify the team with a sense of common fate. Again, the exercise of strategic leadership requires that followers remain focused on their goals and purposes as they respond to changes in the environment. It is easy for the team to succumb to the pressure to cut corners and compromise on quality and even safety. This is more likely to happen when the leader is not guided by his or her conscience. Strategic leaders also have to set high moral standards to ensure that political behaviours in their organisations take place within acceptable boundaries. Political behaviour in the organisation must be motivated by the desire to do good and not for undermining or hurting others. It must be for the purpose of spurring learning and generating better insights and not for obstructing change and improvement. Strategic leaders set the tone for how people should behave in their organisations through their own behaviours and actions. They can lead with their consciences or lead driven by greed and relying on coercion.

When Leaders Lack Consciences

There is no shortage of stories in the business press of toxic leaders who destroy businesses. Many are written based on scandals in the United States and Europe. Malaysia, unfortunately, is not spared from such an experience. Some veteran managers at a local conglomerate are familiar with the history of difficulties the founder of the company experienced when he started the business in the 1970s. He needed a loan to fund the business and approached a bank. The manager who processed the loan agreed to approve it on the condition that the founder pay him a certain amount of kickback. The founder was guided by his conscience and refused to make the payment. He managed to get a loan from another bank, and the rest is history. His company grew into a major conglomerate.

As for the manager who demanded the kickback for the loan approval, he was subsequently implicated in the BMF scandal and was jailed in Hong Kong. This manager was primarily driven by his selfish self-interest. He probably believed that he could use his position in a corrupt manner forever. Besides losing his moral compass, he also became more like a ship without a rudder that, in the end, ran aground in a Hong Kong jail. The fact that he rose up the ranks at this bank to then become a part of the top-management team at its Hong Kong subsidiary shows how organisations can fail to screen out bad leaders. Small indiscretions at the lower level may not cause major damages. But when such leaders rise to the strategic level and continue to not have conscience, the consequences of their actions are dire.

For leaders with no consciences, their utmost concerns are staying in power and using it for personal gain and benefit. They become toxic and cause harm and damage to others and even themselves. When such leaders are at the strategic level, the harm they cause can have far-reaching impact. Management researchers have identified a number of ways these leaders dominate and manipulate. Padilla identified three foundations that enable a toxic leader to use their positions in an abusive manner. The first is the personal character of the leader. These leaders can be persuasive and charismatic, but they use these abilities to serve their personal power. Whereas leaders with consciences are motivated by higher senses of purpose, leaders without consciences make their personal interests, gains, and grips on power their main obsessions.

The second condition that enables a toxic leader to stay in power is a conducive environment. These leaders are good at using their charisma to conjure perceptions of imminent threat to their organisations and followers. Even when the threat is real, such leaders are more likely to exaggerate it and present themselves as the saviours. Lipman-Blumen points out that toxic leaders do this by creating a grand illusion. Whereas leaders with consciences create noble visions to motivate followers to reach a better future, the grand illusions created by toxic leaders are used to conceal problems, counter critics, and distract attention from real problems. A typical message in the grand illusion presented by toxic leaders is presenting themselves as the saviours and that in spite of all the problems around them, things will get better or are still good. They tend to also rely on a negative framing of problems by blaming others for the predicament faced. Lipman-Blumen mentions the example of Jeff Skilling, one of the figures behind the downfall of Enron. Skilling kept on insisting that the company's stock price would rise at a time when the company was, in fact, imploding. In politics, this grand illusion can be in the form of creating a narrative of threats from foreigners, Muslims, Jews, and other minorities. As usual, the toxic leaders concerned will present themselves as the saviour of their people.

The third foundation mentioned by Padilla and colleagues is willing followers. Toxic leaders are able to stay in power because they continue to have the support of some followers. It seems ironic that people will support toxic leaders. Part of the problem is that not everyone considers toxic leader behaviour as toxic. Some followers have a high tolerance of abuse and low equity sensitivity. They may have low consciences and moral standards. Another reason has to do with the personality of some followers. Management researchers recognise that individuals have different levels of the desire to be led. De Vries and colleagues introduced the concept of need for leader (NFL) as a person's desire to have a leader facilitate task performance. High NFL individuals tend to prefer being led and are not comfortable working on their own. This need is learned and can be the product of conditioning. Individuals can develop this outlook as a result of being told that they are not good enough or that their leaders know better, and they should depend on their leaders. The grand illusion mentioned earlier can also cultivate this outlook. As a result, high NFL individuals tend to be more accepting of their leaders even when they are toxic. There are also followers who accept toxic leaders because it serves their interests. Such followers tend to be incompetent yes men or yes women and sycophantic followers. They see aligning themselves with the toxic leader as beneficial for their interests and advancement. They are the colluders in the abuse.

These three foundations form what Padilla and colleagues call the triangle of toxic leadership. It amplifies the negative consequences of leaders who have no consciences. It is like a ship led by an incompetent captain who is steering the ship onto a rock. The captain considers anyone who disagrees with him or her as insubordinate and will have the person thrown overboard. The captain justifies his or her actions by insisting there are sea monsters lurking in the water along alternative routes. The captain appoints a timid, incompetent navigator who spends his or her time defending the captain's erroneous actions. Instead of reading the navigation charts and helping steer the ship through a safer route, the navigator makes the problem worse. This situation began with a leader who has no conscience, impervious to what is right and wrong, indifferent to the feedback from others, and who lets his or her personal interests, ego, and emotions shape actions.

Leaders in high positions sometimes find it easy let their egos take over. The conscience takes a back seat. They begin to feel invincible and start believing they are too smart to listen to others. Management researchers use the term "managerial hubris" to refer to this phenomenon. Picone and colleagues explain that this happens when leaders fail to understand their personal limitations as well as their organisations' limitations. They develop a sense of invincibility and start taking actions that expose the organisation to unusually high risks. They tend to exaggerate their achievements and fail to recognise the contributions of others. Those who dare to disagree with them will find themselves marginalised and often put in cold storage.

Bringing Conscience to the Fore

We develop conscience throughout our lives. Boddy points out that only a psychopathic personality has no conscience. We learn our values and morality from those around us. We develop a sense of what is right and what is wrong. We are taught to respect others, to be helpful, and not to harm others. The environment we grow up in influences the extent we become more or less committed to these standards of behaviour. Even as adults, we continue to be socialised by the values of society and our workplaces.

Culture, religion, and education also play important roles in developing conscience. All of us have to make decisions about right and wrong; what we should and should not do every day. We also interact with others and have to be considerate when dealing with them. When a society sets a high standard of behaviour, we tend to have a more caring and benevolent environment. Societies thrive and remain cohesive when its members are guided by conscience. It enables us to coexist without an elaborate set of rules and laws to control our behaviours. Conscience is a basic and needed resource for our human and social coexistence. Being led by leaders with consciences helps bring us together as an entity to strive for a higher purpose.

Insight Box 5.4

Distance and Conscience

Distance from those who are responsible can sometime diminish our sense of empathy towards their problems. It makes it easier for decision makers to act without thinking about the An example of such a situation was described by Dato Ahmad Bakri Shabdin, the Chief Secretary of the Ministry of Youth and Sports during the 1998 Commonwealth Games hosted by Malaysia. The ministry had hired many volunteers to help run the games. Unfortunately, the allowances for these volunteers were often paid late. The officers responsible for managing the matter were slow in dealing with the problem. Unhappy with the situation, Dato Ahmad Bakri instructed his aide to ask the Accountant General to delay the next salary payment to his own officers by seven days. When payday came, everyone realised that they had not been paid and started complaining. Dato Ahmad Bakri quickly responded, "Now you understand what it feels like to receive your salary late. Like you, the volunteers also have families, bills to pay and children to feed." It did not take long for his officers to get their act together and resolve the problem. We sometimes let our consciences recede into the background when we are able to dehumanise a problem. People are just treated like claim forms or employee numbers. Bringing the human dimension of a problem closer to home helps bring conscience to the fore.

Most of us dislike dealing with inconsiderate and insensitive individuals. This includes leaders at the highest levels. Leaders in strategic positions often have their consciences tested. This is because they can choose whether to make a decision that benefits their organisations or just their personal interests. Because of their high positions, they can choose to listen to dissenting opinions or just dismiss such opinions. The power that they have makes it possible to be demanding and coercive when dealing with their subordinates or be empathetic and understanding. Strategic leaders can get away with being opportunistic, abrasive, and dictatorial. The impact of these behaviours can even be positive in the short term. Quite often, they destroy the organisation in the long term.

Abusive behaviour among leaders can be due to the leader becoming more insulated as he or she rises up the hierarchy. As leaders gain more power, privilege, and status, they can become more detached and intoxicated with their power. They start feeling more distanced from those who they lead and those who are affected by their actions. As such, it is easy to ignore conscience when making decisions. It is easier for someone at the corporate head office to make decisions about laying off workers than the direct supervisors who deal with the affected workers face-to-face. This physical and psychological distance makes it easier for leaders in senior positions to make unpleasant decisions. To them, people are just numbers and cost reduction targets. However, for the direct supervisors, such a decision affects people who they have come to know and who have families to care for.

An incident that highlights this point is the reaction of an American B-52 bomber pilot who decided to join a helicopter gunship during a sortie in Vietnam. The helicopter flew low level as they searched for the enemy. Once they spotted enemy soldiers, they'd go in for an attack. The bomber pilot found it shocking to see real people being shot at and killed as the helicopter started shooting at enemy soldiers. The bomber pilot seems to have forgotten that every time he goes for a bombing run and bomb whole areas and villages, he'd usually kill dozens and maybe even hundreds of people. But since bombers attack from a high altitude, and the pilots never get to see the people they are killing, they are able to maintain physical and psychological distance from their victims. Distance makes it easier for one to insulate one's mind from the consequences of a decision.

Sometimes the role one is given can change a person. A person starts behaving according to the role expected from the position. During the Second World War, it was observed that one way the Nazis controlled the Jews held in concentration camps was by appointing guards from amongst the detainees themselves. It was observed that these Jewish guards were often more ruthless on their fellow inmates than the Nazi prison guards. The same can be said regarding the behaviour of Israel. While often invoking the Holocaust and injustices arising from anti-Semitism to gain sympathy for Israel, Israelis are ruthless when it comes to their treatment of Palestinians. They have this uncanny ability to discard their consciences when it involves the Palestinians.

An interesting study that highlights how conscience can take a back seat in our actions is the Stanford University prison experiment done by Professor

Philip Zimbardo in 1971. Students were randomly divided into two groups. Members from one group were to become prisoners and held in cells. The members from the second group were assigned the role of prison guards. All participants were psychologically stable, healthy, and had no criminal background. Yet, as the experiment progressed, the students who assumed the role as prison guards started behaving in a nasty manner towards the prisoners. They started harassing and torturing the prisoners. The situation deteriorated quickly, and what was supposed to be a two-week experiment had to be stopped after six days. The students took their roles seriously and started internalizing the behaviours associated with their roles. One of the conclusions of this study is that an individual's behaviour can be easily shaped by the role the person assumes. The influence of the role can be so strong that it exerts a stronger influence than the individual's personality.

In the situations described previously, it is not that the individuals involved have no conscience. They simply chose to ignore it and let it recede into the background. Instead, the role they assumed defined how they behaved. We also see this in our driving behaviours. All drivers have to take driving lessons and driving tests to get licenses. We know the safe way to drive and the behaviours that endanger us and others around us. We drive carefully and courteously during the driving lessons and driving tests. Yet, our driving habits can change easily once we have our licenses. Some drivers start speeding, drive aggressively, go through red lights, and jump the queue. The difference in the way we behave before and after getting our driving licenses is simply because by the time we are more confident, we let conscience recede and take a back seat in determining how we drive.

This raises the question of how we maintain our consciences. How do we make sure it continues to be at the fore in guiding our behaviours and actions? Ordinary people get derailed when they ignore their consciences, not unlike a jungle trekker who decides to not use a compass when walking through a thick jungle. In organisations, leaders set the tone through the goals that they consider priorities. In addition, their own behaviour signals that preferred among their followers. Likewise, the reward system developed in the organisation indicates to followers what the organisation considers important. When the organisation signals that being guided by a moral compass is not important, it is more likely to be ignored.

Sometimes leaders who set aside their consciences start developing illusions of their own importance. They develop oversized egos and start being dismissive of those who disagree with them. In business, this develops into managerial hubris. Picone and colleagues point out that leaders can develop excessive self-confidence, pursue ambitious and highly risky ventures, and develop a high desire for power and control. In politics, these leaders become dictatorial and start using the instruments of state to suppress dissent and clamp down on opponents. These leaders do not hear the voice of God in them simply because they are not even listening for it. What can leaders do to avoid such a derailment?

A key starting point in ensuring that we are always guided by our consciences is to constantly assess our thoughts, perceptions, ideas, and emotions. Necsoi and colleagues argue that this can be done through developing a self-reflective conscience. The purpose of self-reflective conscience is to enable us to understand and adapt to our internal condition – for example, emotion and elation – as well as to external conditions. This involves making reflection a part of the process of maintaining and nurturing our consciences. Three elements need to be present during this self-reflection process. The first is intense curiosity. The second is acceptance of confusion. The third is acceptance of doubt.

Improvements happen when we are not content with the status quo. We believe that things can be better. Nelson Mandela, Mohammad Yunus, and Tawakkul Karman all believed that things could be better in their respective societies. That's what drove them to persist in their efforts. Likewise, Thomas Edison is reported to have conducted 1,200 experiments to figure out the best material to be used as filament for the light bulb. Curiosity made them all believe that the status quo – whether it was in the realm of scientific advancement, social justice, or poverty eradication – was not good enough. This motivated them to keep on looking for ways to improve. The determination to keep on trying is driven by intense curiosity and the belief that there is a better solution than the one already known. This is what makes conscience that is guided by curiosity an important foundation for strategic leaders. In addition to keeping them guided by their moral compasses, it also keeps them searching for better solutions. Doing things the way they had always been done is not good enough for these leaders.

The exercise of leadership, especially at the strategic level, involves dealing with problems with considerable novelty and uncertainty. Leaders make informed decisions based on the information available to them. However, these decisions can still be wrong and have shortcomings. Good strategic leaders understand that business problems and their solutions are not like mathematical equations. They are not precise, and solving them is sometimes an evolving process. Leaders never have perfect information, and the reality they face is not stagnant. Even when there is a lot of information available, the ability to accept and process this information is limited. This is a phenomenon cognitive theorists term "bounded rationality." This highlights the fact that most decisions are not made based on complete information and that rationality can be relative to one's ability to process information. Accepting that there is a certain amount of ambiguity and uncertainty about the reality faced by the leader is important. This makes the leader realise the need to keep an open mind and to continue to learn and incrementally improve decisions. Leaders need to have a healthy level of doubt about their decisions.

Acceptance of doubt is necessary to avoid complacency and to make people reflect on their decisions and actions. A healthy level of doubt prompts us to think and question ourselves. Accounts of various prophets in the Bible and Quran show that even prophets display doubts from time to time. The Bible mentions how Moses was told to throw Aaron's staff during his confrontation with Pharaoh. The staff turned into a serpent and attacked the snake thrown by Pharaoh's sorcerers. In spite of knowing it was God's power that turned into a serpent, Moses was mentioned in the book of Exodus as having retreated backward because he was shaken by what he saw. The Quran mentions in the chapter Al Baqarah verse 260 an incident where the prophet Abraham asked God how He creates life and death. God then asks Abraham whether he does not have faith. Abraham answered that he asked the question in order to make his faith stronger. Leslie Hazelton made an interesting observation about how prophet Muhammad reacted after receiving revelation. Instead of feeling jubilant and excited, he was overcome with fear and doubt. Her account is consistent with what Muslim historians write about prophet Muhammad's state after revelation. Prophet Muhammad had to be assured by his wife, Khadijah. It shows that it is normal to have a certain amount of doubt because addressing doubt helps build certainty and conviction.

One's sense of what is right and wrong is sometimes influenced by the context and circumstance we are in. It takes considerable rethinking and reflection to question the appropriateness of our actions and attitudes. Doubt makes us question our actions and decisions. It makes us assess whether we could have been wrong or whether we did our best. It is human nature to misjudge and make mistakes. It is also human nature to sometimes succumb to our instincts even when they are not appropriate. The process of exploring and discovering often involves confusion and uncertainty. The ability to deal with this confusion and accepting it as a part of a learning process helps us deal with doubt and improve our judgement.

The trinity of doubt, curiosity, and confusion is what makes us learn continuously. The quality of our decisions will only improve when we have a healthy level of doubt and curiosity. It is when we have doubt that we are willing to question and be questioned by others. Curiosity drives us to try new ideas. This creative exercise will inevitable involve some confusion as we explore options and possibilities. On the other hand, managerial hubris happens when leaders become overconfident with their decisions and close their minds to the possibility that they may be wrong or have not gotten everything figured out. This applies to decisions about business opportunities, about a person's abilities, and on the appropriate thing to do during challenging situations.

It is important to recognise that leading with conscience requires an active mind that continuously reflects on actions and behaviours. This includes accepting that things can be better and that leaders can be wrong or not know enough. Sometimes even the notion of right and wrong changes with society's experience and values. Continuous reflection ensures that a leader's conscience does not recede from awareness. It ensures that he or she does not easily succumb to the temptations of greed, power, and position.

To sum it up, leading with conscience involves observing the following.

i.   Lead by framing your goals in terms of a higher purpose.

In business, it is easy to think that the ultimate goal is generating profit. If we consider profit as a reward, it has to be something earned for achieving a higher outcome. For instance, an insurance company earns profits as a reward for helping its clients manage their risks and protecting them from losses. Likewise, an airline is rewarded with profits for transporting passengers safely to their destinations. Profit is not an end by itself. It is a reward for achieving a higher purpose. Framing their businesses as driven by a higher sense of purpose helps strategic leaders keep their followers focused on higher ideals. There are two levels of higher purpose. The first is about understanding the essence of the value the business is trying to create to earn the reward from it effort, as mentioned earlier. The second sense of purpose is related to the business's role as citizens in society. Businesses need to see that, ultimately, they have the duty to improve the well-being of society. Businesses should not neglect the less privileged and the marginalised. As Bakri Musa argued, wealth creation should be like the rising tide that raises all the vessels in the harbour. It is important for leaders to cultivate this outlook among their followers to ensure that they are always connected to improving the general well-being of society. A society where there is less poverty, better education and health care, and is inclusive will be more prosperous, peaceful, and have more harmony.

ii. Be mindful of your moral boundary.

It is easy to fall off the cliff if one does not know where the edges are. Likewise, it is easy to deviate from moral standards if one does not have a sense of moral boundary. A person's moral boundary is defined by one's morality and ethics. As mentioned earlier, the notion of conscience in Islam is tied to the concept of taqwa. Even though taqwa is often erroneously translated as "fear", the explanation of the concept of taqwa by Umar Al Khattab shows that it is more than just that. Umar describes taqwa as akin to walking along a path that has many thorns. It makes us alert and mindful of the boundary of where we should go and what we should avoid. Fear alone is not enough if one has no sense of the boundaries of behaviour that should be observed. It can create a false sense of piety that is based more on emotions than knowledge. Leaders need to draw the line between what is right and wrong, the appropriate and inappropriate to ensure that they and their followers do not trod into the grey area and cross over to the other side.

iii. Be curious, and have a healthy amount of doubt.

A healthy amount of curiosity and doubt makes us think and question. It makes us question ourselves and be open to input from others. Doubt and curiosity are powerful forces that make us seek continuous improvement. They nudge us to go the extra mile. Be open to being questioned. Recognise the fact that there are no straightforward answers to some of the problems that leaders have to deal with at the strategic level.

iv. Develop genuine relationships, and cultivate commitment when leading others.

Leadership, especially at the strategic level, can be intoxicating. It confers power and influence on leaders to coerce and compel others. However, such a leader-follower relationship will be shaped by fear and desire to conform. Followers will suspend their own creativity and sense of initiative. They comply mainly because they have to earn a living under the leader. However, when followers view their relationships with their leaders as being based on mutual respect and influence, and that the leader takes the time to communicate and engage them in decision-making, they are more likely to feel committed and develop a sense of ownership of the decision. They are also more likely to exercise creative effort as they perceive their leaders as being receptive to their input.

v. Be a good listener, especially to those who disagree with you.

Related to having doubt is the willingness to listen. This is especially the case in dealing with those who disagree with us. People who agree with us usually do not offer additional insights. Those who disagree with us are more likely to provide new perspectives and insights.

vi. Create positive experiences for others to create enduring positive results.

Leading with conscience involves setting a high moral and ethical standard. It is an important aspect of creating a positive climate in an organisation. Most people are not comfortable engaging in unethical behaviours. Researchers recognise such a situation leads to a troubled conscience that can undermine motivation. In addition, leaders with consciences provide followers with a work experience that is uplifting. Such a positive experience has a strong impact on followers' motivations. Leaders achieve this by giving personalised attention to their followers, create opportunities for them to grow, provide meaningful tasks, constantly give feedback to them, and seek their input.

vii. Make it a point to stop and listen to that "voice" in your heart.

Most of us were raised by parents who want us to grow into good people. We develop a sense of right and wrong. We also learn from friends and from our educational experiences. These values are always there in us. Our hearts keep on whispering to us these values throughout our lives. To ensure that leaders lead with consciences, they have to pause and listen to the voices in their hearts.

viii. Be the example of the values and norms you want others to follow.

Leading is not merely preaching. Instilling noble values is not just about putting up posters of corporate values. Leaders must walk the talk and make it a part of their leadership responsibilities. Do not abdicate the responsibility to incorporate communication or consultants. The corporate value of an organisation must be an extension of the leader's conscience and not a copy and paste job of someone else's values.

Closing

There is no shortage of examples where the pursuit of profit maximisation causes leaders to develop a narrow outlook of their roles and the purposes of their organisations. Maximizing gain and fame is sought at the expense of the greater good. Instead of leading with consciences, they cultivate greed. As a result, the leader and the organisation are derailed. In some of these cases, it was due to unethical actions. Others failed simply because their leaders felt too certain and confident of themselves. They stopped being curious and ceased having healthy levels of doubt. The powers that they have as leaders at the top of the organisation make it easy for them to dominate others and ignore feedback. In the end, the failure to lead with conscience destroys our moral characters and economic value.

CHAPTER 6

Persuasion and Influence Competencies

Introduction

It is not always easy to get people to accept change. This problem is amplified when it involves strategic change in organisations. Aryee, Chen, and Budhawar argue that an organisation is a social marketplace where individuals engage in transactions to obtain favourable returns. Horton points out that organisations are not merely a rational model of economic activities but are also places where competition of ideas, political activities, and conflict takes place. Even though organisations are supposed to operate based on rational and objective rules and procedures, it is not always possible to develop a complete set of rules and procedures to govern every single decision and problem that emerge. This is especially the case at higher levels of the organization, where problems are less structured and are sometimes novel.

As organisations grow and have many products and initiatives, it is normal to see that leaders have to compete for resources. All leaders want funding for their projects and activities. They also want the best people and equipment. Once a leader secures these resources, it is not easy for them to give them up. The amount of resources a leader has signals the importance of his or her role and status in the organisation. On the other hand, being allocated a small amount of resources signals the low status and unimportance of a project or initiative.

Yet, strategizing requires the willingness of an organisation to reallocate its resources to deal with current and emerging challenges. Changing focus and priorities must be supported with changes in the way an organisation allocates its resources. Companies sometimes have to deal with changes in technology by abandoning their current technologies and investing in new ones. Kodak was doomed when it failed to make this change. Companies like NCR continue to be successful because they are able to make changes to their technology bases. For NCR, this required changes to its resource allocation. It was able to do this as it responded to changes in the competitive environment.

A strategic leader recognises that getting people to change is not a simple, straightforward process. This is especially the case when the strategist is trying to persuade other leaders to change proactively. This means making changes before the organisation suffers and experiences losses. However, people tend to feel the need to change only when an organisation has started incurring losses. People are more willing to make sacrifices when they perceive that their survival is at stake. They are less likely to be willing to make sacrifices when they think the organisation is doing well. Leaders can be lulled into complacency during good times. Yet, waiting for an organisation's profit to be hit before doing something is going to be harmful. Jobs may be lost, customer goodwill will be damaged, and morale may erode. Even in business, prevention is better than cure. This is why persuasion and influencing skills are important for a strategist. Other leaders need to be persuaded to change before the ship starts sinking. For companies like NCR, changing was inevitable because technology was making its traditional products, manual cash registers, obsolete. There are occasions when strategic leaders need to persuade their organisations to make drastic changes like these. This is not an easy undertaking and requires careful use of influence and persuasion.

Developing Influence

Influence can be categorised in two broad categories. Influence can be compliance-based or credibility-based. The use of compliance-based influence can be through power-coercive tactics or through the promise of rewards. Power-coercive tactics involve the use of threats and impositions. The promise of rewards appeals to the "What's in it for me?" mindset. Compliance-based influence is largely achieved by relying on people's fears, obedience, and self-interests. Compliance-based influence tends to breed a short-term outlook and does not always lead to commitment.

Credibility-based influence relies on the use of conviction, trust, and respect towards the influencer. Reward can also play a role in credibility-based influence. However, the mechanism of its use is different from compliance-based influence. Instead of appealing to self-interest, rewards are usually framed as the consequences of committing to higher-level goals and performing according to those goals. Credibility-based influence focuses on cultivating belief in a common destiny and commitment. This book mentioned in an earlier chapter that leading with conscience is built around a commitment to a higher sense of purpose.

Effective leaders recognise that they have to be skilful in using both types of influences. During pressing moments, leaders may have to exert their authority and decide without consulting and explaining their decisions. There may be moments when they may have to deal with difficult and problematic subordinates which may require using the threat of punishment. However, reliance on compliance-based influence creates a short-term impact. The commitment people show is usually superficial. People behave to avoid punishment or gain reward without really being committed to what they are doing. During strategic change, this is not sufficient. Strategic change can only be sustained when people are committed to the desired outcomes and behaviours needed to support them. The desired outcomes require commitments to the future state envisioned. It is not possible to promise reward at every point and to everyone during a change initiative. Neither would it be possible to use coercion and threaten people with punishment to make them enthusiastic about making the journey from the present state to the desired future state.

The essence of credibility-based influence is about getting others to willingly accept a strategic leader's influence attempt. Our willingness to be influenced by a leader is shaped by a number of considerations. The first is the leader's character. People trust leaders they perceive to be sincere, reasonable, fair, and motivated by the desire to do greater good. These qualities are a part of the leader's character. This notion is similar to John Maxwell's notion of personhood where a leader's influence is due to who he or she is. Maxwell argues that the weakest form of influence is when a leader's ability to influence is entirely based on the position held and the use of the authority that goes with it. Most people would prefer to avoid leaders who are abusive, unfair, unreasonable, and concerned mainly about their self-interests. People are usually more guarded with leaders and peers who are seen as untrustworthy.

The second consideration is competence. We accept being influenced by those who we perceive to be competent. Researchers call this competence-based trust. However, we accept the influence of people who we consider to be competent as long as the subject matter in within their area of expertise. We comply when a physician tells us to take off our clothes. But we wouldn't comply if a professor told us to do so. We accept the former's influence because we assume the physician is competent and has a valid reason to ask us to take off our clothes. In the short term, we usually have no means of knowing the person's character. When a person is trusted because of both character and competence, people's willingness to accept someone's influence is going to be much higher.

For a strategic leader, the ability to inspire people and make them self-driven is a powerful form of influence. People are more willing to listen to leaders who are seen as credible. Strategic leaders have to develop this credibility through their competence and character. Leaders who have credibility-based influence are more likely to be respected, trusted, and believed. People need to believe in the ideas presented by a leader before they will commit to a goal. This commitment helps make them become self-managing when undergoing a change process. This is important during strategic change because it often requires individuals at the lower levels to exercise their discretion and make decisions on the needed changes. It easier for them to exercise their judgement when they are clear of outcomes expected at their levels.

Principles in the Use of Influence

Robert Cialdini introduced the notion of principles of influence. Below are six of the principles developed by Caldini. This book adds one more principle to the list.

1. Reciprocity
   It is human nature to feel indebted to those who have done us some good. We tend to reciprocate by paying back the favour from another person. We are more likely to buy lunch for a friend who has taken us out for lunch before. We develop reciprocal relationships with others because no individual can be completely self-sufficient. Expectations of reciprocity help glue the transactions between individuals and develop it into a relationship. Gouldings explain that in the early stages of a

relationship, we tend to evaluate the other person's character by her or his reciprocal behaviour. We do this by developing expectations that the other person would be willing to reciprocate in the short or medium term. We expect the other person to reciprocate with something of a similar value. Reciprocity is more than just more exchange of favours. Reciprocity signals to us the other person's sense of fairness. Reciprocity also indicates to us how much the other person values the relationship with us. It also indicates to us the extent the other person is dependable. Someone who only seeks favours from others but is not willing to reciprocate is more likely to be seen as an opportunist or a parasite. Over the long term, our expectations of reciprocity are less immediate. When we know and trust someone, we do not expect him or her to always pay back immediately. However, we tend to expect the person to be available when needed. Family members and close friends help one another without expectations of immediate return. But we know we can turn to them when we need help. Individuals who help others are more likely to develop this goodwill that makes people more willing to help them. For strategic leaders, being helpful towards and supportive of them in their times of need can be capital that enhances their influence with others.

2. Consistency

Most people feel obliged to honour their promises. We seek consistency with what we say and declare. Violating a promise or declaration signals hypocrisy and shows that we cannot be trusted. Behaving in ways that are consistent with our word is a part of maintaining our self-images. It is a part of our notions of being honourable. Leaders whose behaviours are consistent with what they say are more likely to be seen as credible. Others are more likely to accept their influence attempts. Similarly, when the help of people who have made a pledge to a cause are sought, they are more likely to oblige. One study compared the turnout at a neighbourhood cleanup. One group of residents was asked to sign a petition about public hygiene before the cleanup campaign. Another group was not approached to sign the petition. When the neighbourhood cleanup was held, a higher percentage of those who had signed the petition turned up compared to those who were not approached for the petition. People are more likely to take action when it is consistent with a commitment they've made earlier. Leaders can use consistency as a form of influence in shaping the behaviours of others.

3. Authority

People are more likely to obey and follow the instructions of a person who is perceived to have authority. Drivers are more likely to follow the instructions of someone in uniform controlling traffic flow than someone dressed in sports attire. We are more likely to believe that someone dressed in a white coat carrying a stethoscope knows more about our health than someone dressed like a clown. The authority a person is perceived to have can come from many sources. It can come from ability, reward, or punishment. It can also come from the perceived expertise that someone has. For strategic leaders, establishing expertise depends on their abilities to provide sound logical arguments and back them up with evidence. Leaders who are able to back their ideas and recommendations with facts and data are more likely to be able to influence others.

4. Social proof

Marketers rely on endorsements from famous individuals and celebrities for their products as a form of social proof. Seeing others use or adopt a product is perceived as proof of the efficacy of the product. Cosmetics firms will use pretty models and actresses in their advertisements to give the impression that using their products will make the rest of us as pretty as they are. Managers often cite other leading companies as having adopted a particular practice to justify their proposals that their companies adopt the same practice. People feel more comfortable trying an idea that is supposedly tested and proven elsewhere compared to an untested idea. Fads are sometime created based on social proof. Leaders can use social proof to support their ideas and arguments. However, they need to be cautious to make sure that there really is merit to their ideas. Social proof can be deceiving. For the individual customer, the mistake of buying a cosmetic product that does not work can be easily stopped. The cost is not that much, and the damage done is usually in the form of a deflated ego and unmet expectations. For an organisation, adopting a new idea and making disruptive changes based on social proof only can be damaging. It can undermine the organisation's current capabilities and make things worse. Strategic leaders have a moral responsibility to make sure there is sound justification for a new strategic idea. Social proof can be used to complement the evidence justifying the idea. Social proof should never be used as a substitute for sound analysis.

5. Scarcity

Perceived scarcity can be a form of influence when it motivates the perceiver to act. Businesses often advertise "while stocks last" or "limited offer" or "limited edition" to create the perception of scarcity to influence customers to quickly make a purchase. The notion of scarcity in strategizing, however, is not and cannot be about misleading others. Good strategists recognise that competitive advantage is never permanent; ideas and technologies become obsolete, resources can deplete and become ineffective, and motivation can go up and down. Likewise, opportunities are not there out there forever. Customer loyalty is just temporary, and threats can emerge from anywhere and anytime. All these are various forms of scarcity that the strategist has to deal with. Making others in the organisation recognise these scarcities can help galvanise support and win commitment to new ideas. Many people are inclined to feel complacent and content during success and abundance. Doing more of the same becomes the norm. They do not want to venture out from their comfort zones. A strategist needs to be able to get people to realise the limitations of success, or what Bill Gates described as "the junction around the corner." Members of the organisation need to understand the consequences of not being proactive and the impending scarcities. As Andy Grove, former CEO of Intel, points out, "Success breeds complacency. And complacency breeds failure. Only the paranoid will succeed." When others understand the scarcities the organisation is facing or is about to face, they are more likely to be paranoid and open to new ideas and influence.

6. Personal liking

Authority, reciprocity, and consistency can lead us to form a judgement on whether we like or dislike a person. In addition, the person's underlying personality makes people consider him or her as nice or nasty. Most people accept the influence attempts of people they like. Nasty people are followed only because they have the power to punish or reward. Leaders who lead with consciences are more likely to be liked and followed by others. A leader who is universally liked by those around him or her do not gain personal liking through pretension. This leader is liked because people genuinely believe he or she is a nice individual. Some politicians develop personal liking through pretensions. They appear during natural disasters for their photo opportunities with the media. They make claims of "striving for the people" even as they enrich themselves. Such leaders can fool some people some of the time. But it is just a matter of time before their true characters are exposed. In the end, they lose influence. In organisations, leaders work in close interaction with their peers and subordinates. These people see and know the leaders' true characters. Only those who are genuine will be liked and have influence.

7. Common destiny

A sense of common destiny is a powerful force that brings people together. John Drury conducted many studies on how people behave during disasters. He points out that natural disaster victims are usually quite organised when dealing with their predicaments. Even complete strangers can join hands and work together to get out of the situation. This is largely because of the sense that they all share a common destiny and need to work together to overcome the odds. The same dynamic operates in organisations. Vision and mission statements are supposed to create a common destiny that galvanises people towards course. Appealing to this sense of common destiny can help win over the support of others in two ways. First, people are more likely to accept the influence attempts of strategic leaders who can frame their ideas as a part of the common destiny shared among members of the organisation. A new idea that is seen as presenting some continuity from the present is more easily accepted. Second, people are also more likely to accept a new idea that has mutual relevance for everyone. The strategic leader needs to present the new idea as something that serves the interests of everyone. Both situations are concerned with tapping into the sense of common destiny as a form of influence. It should be highlighted that cultivating this sense of common destiny requires meticulous effort and serious communication. It is not just about pasting posters of vision and mission statements on the walls. Many organisations fail to create the sense of common destiny in spite of having vision and mission statements. This is mainly because these statements were not properly thought out. Some are just modified versions of the statements from more successful organisations. And some are socially desirable statements that are not rooted in the reality the organisation is facing or the capabilities it possesses.

The above discussion can be summarised into a number of important lessons in developing influence. First, if someone wants others to support her or him, the person needs to be willing to support them. This is part of the reciprocity people expect in a relationship. Of course, a leader needs to be able to distinguish between good ideas and bad ideas. Support good ideas and those who created those good ideas, and people are more likely to support the leader when she or he presents a good idea.

Second, in a work situation, the judgement that others form on how much they will accept another person's influence attempt depends on how much credibility, consistency, and competence the person has displayed. This means that the level of influence a strategic leader has is not something that can created in a spontaneous manner. Credibility goes hand in hand with consistency. A leader who appears to be concerned about others only when something is needed from them may be perceived as an opportunist.

Third, a leader who wants others to embrace a new strategic idea needs to do his or her homework first. The authoritativeness of a strategic idea comes from the facts and data to support it. The idea must be backed by strong and logical arguments.

Fourth, the idea presented must also create a sense of urgency and explain the consequences of not acting. The strategic leader needs to convey this urgency through energy, passion, and behaviour. If the leader wants followers to act quickly, he or she must be decisive and quick in taking action. If the leader wants followers to attached priorities to certain issues, he or she must be willing to provide the necessary resources and support to enable them to do so.

Finally, the idea must be framed as part of a sense of common destiny. Other leaders need to understand how this new destiny affects them and their priorities, roles, and functions. People lower in the organisation need to understand how this new destiny will affect their jobs and responsibilities. This will help develop a sense of ownership to the idea.

The above understanding also highlights the fact that influence requires long-term investment. Most of the principles are outcomes of long-term actions. People form judgements of a leader's character, consistency, sense of shared destiny, and willingness to reciprocate through their long-term interactions with the leader. All these cumulatively shape the amount of long-term influence a leader has.

The Art of Persuasion

It is very important to recognise that not all influential persons are persuasive. Persuasion has a lot to do with how a person communicates and presents ideas. It is partly a verbal skill, and it is partly about emotional intelligence. The latter relates to understanding others as well as understanding one's own emotions during the communication process. Persuasion involves achieving some key milestones in the communication process. These are changing attitude, developing commitment and ownership, and taking action. Others must be persuaded of the merit and benefit of a new strategic idea. They need to have a positive attitude towards the idea. It is only when this is achieved that people are willing to commit and develop ownership of the new strategic idea. Finally, once there is commitment and ownership, it will be easy to plan for actions to be taken. Some basic tips in persuading others follow.

1. Be certain when communicating ideas.

   A sure way to not be persuasive is by portraying doubt and uncertainty. Senior leaders assessing strategic ideas do not want to just listen to hunches and impressions. They want ideas that are sound and have been given considerable thought. Expressions such as "Maybe we should …", "We are still thinking about it …", "We are not so sure yet …" and, "Why not just try first …" do not convey certainty. These expressions may be acceptable when discussing ideas in QCC sessions. Strategic ideas are supposed to be impactful and have major ramifications for the organisation. Senior leaders do not want to waste their time discussing half-cooked suggestions. If they want such ideas, they'll look for them in the suggestion box.

2. Understand how much time you have.

    Whether it is a meeting or personal encounter, time is always a constraint. Do not prepare a forty-slide file for a ten-minute presentation. Even in personal communication, find out how much time the other person has.

3. Be clear of your objectives.

    Always be clear of what you want to achieve given the time available to present an idea. Is it to get an approval, to request more resources, to request the establishment of a cross-functional task force to develop the idea being proposed further?

4. Organise your ideas clearly and logically.

    Organise your ideas in a way that is logical and understandable to the audience. Sometimes the same issue has to be presented in a different manner to different people and groups. Make sure the ideas are logical, consistent, and can be backed by evidence. Highlight how the idea presented is new, better, and beneficial. Be prepared to explain more if you are given more time to explain your ideas. And be prepared to compare your ideas with other options being considered.

5. Communicate with others, not to them.

    Persuade others by communicating with them and not to them. Use "we" instead of "I" and "you". Make people feel like they are a part of the effort to develop the new idea. This helps develop a sense of common destiny and togetherness.

6. Read how others are reacting.

    Observe the reaction you are getting from the audience. Know when to stop and open up to questions. Engage the person listening to you by asking questions. Anticipate questions and objections, and prepare answers for them. Do not be self-absorbed, and do not let your presentation become a monologue.

7. Manage your own reaction to others.

    Be aware of your own behaviour and impact on others. This includes reading and sensing the audience's verbal and non-verbal reactions. Be energetic and confident if you want others to have confidence in your ideas. At times, the listener may object and become confrontational. Be aware of your reaction to the listener's reaction. Do not be dismissive of objections and disagreements. Reason out your ideas calmly, and avoid being confrontational.

8. Have a firm landing.

    End the persuasion effort by having a clear conclusion. This is, of course, tied to your objectives. If it is a personal discussion, it can be agreeing when to meet again to work out any issues raised. It can also be agreeing on the next steps to be taken or who else to present the idea to.

Tips in Persuading Others

While the principles of influence discussed help us understand the levers that can enhance a leader's influence, leaders also need to have persuasion skills. This depends a lot on how they approach others and present their ideas. Some basic tips leaders can observe in improving their persuasion power include the following.

1. Do not wait for meetings to present ideas.

    Meetings are a bad place to sell new ideas. There are often many issues on the agenda, and there are also time constraints. Given these limitations, it is sometimes difficult to get undivided attention. Leaders need to touch base with others before the meeting. Test the new idea, and see how people react. Try to win support before the meeting. The reaction a leader receives from others can help him or her prepare better for the meeting that is going to decide on an idea. Try to understand any resistance to the new idea and how it can be managed.

2. Identify influential individuals.

    There are always individuals who have a high level of influence. Identify them, and engage them before the meeting. Win them over, and make them your allies. If they disagree with the idea presented, understand why. Ideally, the leader should try to win them over. This may not always be possible. At a minimum, get them to at least understand the new idea so that they keep an open mind. And continue to communicate and engage with them.

3. Challenge your own thoughts.

New strategic ideas are basically hypotheses. No one knows for sure whether they will work. It is therefore necessary to have your ideas challenged. Create a climate where subordinates and peers feel comfortable to question and challenge a new idea. New ideas that are rigorously debated and scrutinised will only get better and become more convincing.

4. Listen to and understand objections.

In modern organisations, expertise is dispersed. Knowledge does not reside in one person. As such, it may not be possible for one person to know everything. Fostering organisational learning involves bringing together various personal insights and knowledge to enhance collective learning at the organisational level. New strategic ideas should be the outcome of such a process. The process of learning is continuous. When others disagree and object to a new idea, treat it as a learning opportunity. However, this learning will only take place when all involved are willing to listen and understand one another. Listening to others also creates the opportunity for others to become participants in creating and developing the new idea. It helps develop ownership of the new idea. Influence grows when it is shared. As such, leaders need to be open to the influences of others in order to have more influence.

5. Respect the authority and interests of others.

An organisation consists of many interests and people with authority. All these individuals tend to prefer the status quo that preserves their authority and protects their interests. Even when a new strategic idea is good, others may still oppose it. This is because it is seen as undermining established authority and interests. Work with these individuals to get them on board. Respect their authority and understand their concerns. A sure way to lose the battle of strategic ideas in an organisation is by stepping on everyone's toes. This will offend and alienate others. Instead of listening to the new idea, they become more concerned about protecting their authority and interests. Choice of words and how an idea is presented are important. Generally, smart people do not like a new idea being presented to them as an ultimatum. Find common ground when presenting a new idea. Create as many allies as possible.

6. Be prepared to be unconventional.

   Winning support for an idea sometime requires the willingness to be unconventional. It is not always easy to persuade others of a new idea, especially ones that others are not familiar with. The story in the Insight Box 6.1 on how the Post-It Notes was promoted internally illustrates how an unconventional approach can help push a little-known initiative into the market. Showing a working example of an idea can also be a way to make it more convincing. It is more convincing than concepts and abstract ideas.

7. Be the scribe.

   One tactic smart leaders use to shape the outcome of discussions, especially brainstorming sessions, is to be the one writing down the ideas generated on the whiteboard. The person doing this has control over which ideas get more attention and which ideas are marginalised. Use this opportunity to keep the discussion focused on key issues. It is quite normal that discussions on new ideas are easily distracted by peripheral issues. However, this must done in good faith to make sure a there is meaningful debate of ideas and options.

There may be occasions when managers find themselves having to propose ideas that are not necessarily in line with the preferences of one or more of their superiors. It is always difficult when the new idea involves disagreeing with a view held by superiors. Claman proposes that managers observe the following guidelines when dealing with such a situation.

Insight Box 6.1

Persuasion in Creating a Market for a Product

The Post-It Notes is today a common part of the tools that many of us use at work. The birth of the Post-It Notes at 3M has an interesting history. It was not a part of any formal project decided by top management of the company. Nor was it funded by a budget. The company's marketing function did not know the product was being developed.

Post-it notes require the use of adhesive of a certain strength. It must be sufficiently strong to stick to where it is placed. But the adhesive should not be too strong such that, when it is removed, it shears and tears the paper or surface. A scientist at 3M had developed a glue with such a property but couldn't figure what it should be used for. A colleague of this scientist needed a bookmarker that did not fall off for his hymnbook. So he suggested using the glue for such a bookmarker. The idea worked, and Post-it notes were born. But the product didn't have a market, and these 3M scientists were not sure how to get it adopted and marketed as one of 3M's products. So they sent samples of the Post-it notes to the secretaries in the company. Soon, the secretaries were calling them, asking for more. The scientists told the secretaries to direct their calls to marketing and, in effect, created a demand for Post-it notes. The rest is history. This is an example of subtle persuasion used to get a company to adopt and market a product that most people have never heard off, and management did not even know was being developed in their company.

1. Be strategic when presenting your view. Think through what you are going to say, your motives and objectives. Be careful to not be seen as having a political agenda.

2. Make sure you are right. Do your homework, and make sure you can back your ideas with facts and data. You may have only one chance, so don't blow it by being unprepared.

3. Test your ideas with others, including those near the superiors. This will give you an idea of how the superiors may react.

4. Prepare a presentation that is concise and straight to the point. Keep your presentation focused and easy to digest.

5. Find a respected and credible person to take a look at the presentation. Get his feedback and reactions.

6. Consider getting a peer of your superior to present the idea. People tend to trust people who they know and comfortable with.

A good and convincing presentation to superiors is not only about selling ideas. It can also enhance a manager's standing and credibility and help his or her career.

Networking and Influence

The expression "knowledge is power" has been said by so many people that it is not very clear where it came from. The power conferred from having more knowledge translates into more influence. While many will agree there is a lot of truth in the statement, bringing knowledge together is not always easy. A lot of the insights and knowledge needed to make strategic decisions is dispersed within and outside the organisation.

Hargadon points out that individuals who are at the crossroad in the flow of knowledge will be in positions to benefit from the flow. They will able to access more knowledge than those located from the crossroad. Leaders can extend their access to knowledge by networking with others. A strategic leader needs to develop internal as well as external networks to access and bring knowledge together. Internal networking can be developed by cultivating relationships with others outside one's work unit. In addition, access to networks is also about accessing the space where people interact. The pantry, water cooler, and corridor are important areas where people interact and exchange ideas. In some companies, the pantry is located in the middle of the office. At the Steelcase Global Shared Service office in Kuala Lumpur, the pantry is the first thing one sees when entering the office. This physical arrangement enables people to interact in informal settings. Leaders can tap into these informal interactions to seek new ideas. Leaders who keep to themselves in their corner offices will become disconnected from these networks.

Insight Box 6.2

Learning from Outside

Microsoft built its initial success by developing a disk operating system. When the browser was invented, Bill Gates did not see the Internet as providing a potential market for Microsoft. The company very much ignored the development of Internet-related technologies. It was more focused on its Windows product.

It was when Microsoft managers went to university campuses that they noticed how much the Internet was becoming a central part of students' lives. They realised that the Internet had enormous potential, and Microsoft did not have its feet in place. These managers went back the head office and persuaded Bill Gates to start getting involved in Internet-related technologies. It took considerable deliberation for Bill Gates to agree to the idea. Finally, in May 1995, he sent out the now famous "Internet tidal wave memo" that announced the company's decision to go big in the Internet. Had the company been inward looking and only sought to learn from one another, Microsoft might have been crushed by the inevitable Internet tidal wave.

Toyota had a similar experience when it started the Prius project in the 1990s. The team tasked with the project was given the basic assignment of developing a car for the next century. The team made significant improvements in the design, including improvements in fuel consumption by around 50 percent. However, Toyota's management was still not satisfied with the outcome and demanded more improvements. As the team looked for ideas, they finally discovered a promising technology that would redefine their thinking about cars. It was a battery developed by Panasonic that had a long life and was rechargeable. This finally led to the birth of the hybrid car that combines battery and petrol engine. In the end, Toyota's ability to develop a radically new product was made possible by a technology developed outside the company.

In both cases, new strategic ideas came as a result of contact with outsiders. Being networked with external parties can open the way to new opportunities and possibilities.

In modern organisations, change and innovation are more about bringing knowledge together to create something new. Instances where an innovator creates something totally new is rare nowadays. More often than not, leaders create new value by acting as knowledge brokers. This involves bringing together knowledge to create new combinations and applications. Meyer explains that knowledge brokering requires that the broker knows what needs exists and where the needed knowledge is located. Leaders who are effective knowledge brokers can become very influential because they are seen as the ones who can "connect the dots". When they come up with new ideas, they are more likely to already how to develop and implement them.

To be effective knowledge brokers, leaders need to have a good social network. Internal social networks help leaders understand where the organisation's knowledge and resources are located. This enables them to assess new possible combinations of knowledge and resources. Knowledge brokering involves getting as well as giving and sharing knowledge and resources. Leaders who are good at doing this are not only able to find new ways to create value, they also develop many allies who can be strong supporters when they propose new ideas.

Besides internal social networks, strategic leaders need to also develop external social networks. Information about threats and opportunities, new technologies, and impending changes in the environment are not always publicly available. Researchers on innovation found that people are more likely to discover new ideas from those who are not in constant contact with them. People who are in constant contact tend to share their ideas together and become fairly similar in their knowledge. Their thinking tends to become alike. Such people are more likely to discover something new, ideas that are not already a part of their common thinking, from outsiders. Outsiders who should become a part of a strategic leader's network include customers, regulators, technology vendors, and even competitors. Corporate leaders like John Chambers, who was Cisco's CEO, made it a point to spend half their time outside the company, talking to customers. They understand that the reality is out there and not within the insular walls of corporate head office.

Both internal and external social networks can enhance the knowledge a leader can access. Having this advantage can boost the leader's influence and stature in the organisation. The leader will be better able to understand changes in the environment and how the organisation's internal capabilities can be leveraged to respond to these changes. It can help provide the authoritativeness in the new strategic ideas the leader presents.

Closing

Strategic leaders have to deal with problems that are sometimes ambiguous and novel. Others may not necessarily see what they see. As such, it is not always easy to get others to accept new strategic ideas. Strategic leaders also have to be able to translate their cognitions into actions. They also have to get others to change to support the new ideas. Persuasion and influence skills are important competencies in enabling them to manage changes effectively. This is necessary to ensure commitment and sustainability of the change initiative.

CHAPTER 7

Developing Talent Competencies

Introduction

Modern organisations are complex and need more than just a person to lead. While there will always be one CEO in a company, the CEO needs the assistance of managers at all levels to be effective. This is especially the case when the organisation has to respond to changes in the environment. Such a response often requires adapting the way the organisation creates and delivers value. This, in turn, requires changes to the way people work at all levels. This requires having leaders across the vertical hierarchy who can help realign the organisation.

The modern corporation can be considered akin to a soccer team. It takes more than just a capable striker for the team to win a match. The striker often requires the midfielder and wing players to bring the ball up to near the rival's goal. All these players have to coordinate their movements. Likewise, when defending against an attack, the players of a team have to coordinate their retreat and need to be able to defend against enemy attack and quickly launch a counter-attack. It is not sufficient just to have a star striker on the team. All the other players must also be effective in their positions. Some, like the wing and midfielder, have to be versatile enough to go on the offensive and also retreat to a defensive position when under attack. The same is true with modern organisations.

Indicators of Failure to Develop Leadership Talent

The lack of talent in organisations often expresses itself in many ways. The first is a phenomenon called leadership deficit. This is a situation where the organisation experiences a shortage of suitable leaders for advancement to senior positions. There may be many managers who are suited for their current jobs. But these managers are ill-suited for advancement to senior positions. One contributing factor causing leadership deficit is the lack of investment in long-term leadership development. Some organisations are mainly concerned about preparing people for their current work but underinvest in preparing people for strategic leadership roles. As a result, these organisations have people who are good in their current positions. These organisations tend to make the mistake of thinking that when these managers are promoted into a strategic position, they will be just as good and effective.

To illustrate this point, consider the case of an outstanding surgeon. Training makes the surgeon an expert in the field. In the operating theatre, the surgeon is the boss and gets to dictate what happens. No one else knows as much as the surgeon. Nurses and junior doctors cannot and should not question the surgeon's decisions during the operation. The situation in the operating theatre involves the life of a patient. The surgeon is admired for expertise and decisiveness. The surgeon's leadership style is justifiably autocratic. However, when this same surgeon moves to the position of a hospital director, he or she will need to deal with many issues he or she was not trained for. Since the new problems are not as urgent as the ones faced in operating theatres, the people around the new director are not as obedient as the nurses and junior surgeons. Whereas surgical procedures are often governed by well-defined protocols, the situation is very different in administrative situations. Sometimes other administrators and even subordinates can make life difficult for those in administrative positions. The former surgeon finds herself in the administrative position like a fish out of water. The director's performance declines, leading to frustration. An outstanding surgeon does not necessarily make a good hospital director.

The second manifestation of a lack of talented leaders is an organisation's inability to respond to strategic challenges. The case of Malaysia Airlines reflects this situation. When Christoph Mueller assumed the position as CEO of Malaysia Airlines Berhad on 1 September 2015, he basically found that people there worked in silos. The airline's employees could not see the big picture, and their horizons were limited to their immediate jobs and functions. Mueller found that a key issue he had to address was how to break this silo mentality. When leaders have silo mentality, they lack a strategic outlook and become myopic. Mueller realised that he had to overcome this problem in order to turn around the airline. This is the reason he made talent management a key element in his turnaround plan.

The third problem often encountered with the lack of leadership talent is the ability of lower-level managers to translate the intents of top management into action. This is especially the case during change. In our consultancy work in change management at HumanCap, we often see a familiar problem among many of our clients. Change initiatives often stall because middle management is not on board. Lower-level managers are aware of the change that is initiated. However, they are not able to translate the ideas articulated by top management into actions that should be taken to create the change. Middle managers are so focused on leading operational issues that they lack the understanding and ability to visualise the adjustments needed at lower levels to support the change initiative. As a result, middle managers are not able to lead lower employees to support and execute the change. Instead of serving as a link between top management and lower levels of the organisation, they become the gap that impedes the change.

One of the most glaring signs that an organisation has failed to develop its talent is when the retirement or departure of a member of top management creates a sudden leadership vacuum. The organisation cannot find internal people to fill the vacuum, or the one chosen to fill a vacancy turns out to be ill-prepared for the job. At times, the race for promotion becomes a competition between incompetents. As a result, performance suffers.

Another sign of the failure to develop talents is the rise of bureaucrats. As mentioned earlier, operational-level work tends to be governed by rules and procedures. This tends to nurture a more bureaucratic work habit. When these managers ascend to higher positions, they can't shed off this habit. As a result, instead of using judgement and imagination when dealing with strategic challenges, they tend to fall back on their procedures and rule books. Instead of taking the organisation forward to the future, they tend to keep it anchored to the past. One example is the member of a top-management team of an organisation. Those who had seen the person make decisions are amused by how dependent the leader is on rules. Meetings are often about referring back to the rule book when making decisions. When presented with novel problems that have no rules applicable to the situation, the person simply avoids making decisions and prefers to procrastinate.

The failure to develop leadership talent can also create a pool of insecure managers. Jack Welch argues that organisations need people who have self-confidence and intellectual self-assurance. Nurturing this sense of self-confidence and intellectual self-assurance requires that top management creates a climate where people do not fear discussing contentious issues. Welch points out that insecure managers create complexity and make things difficult for others. Look at any organisation that has elaborate rules and time-consuming procedures, and you will see that behind these rules and procedures are insecure leaders. Their insecurities make them become obsessed with control, domination, and protecting their power.

Besides creating leadership deficit, the failure to develop leadership talent can also create apathy in the organisation. If talent development involves challenging managers by raising the bar and stimulating search for ideas and learning, the unintended consequence of the absence of these activities is a sterile climate in the organisation. It creates a climate that nurtures complacency and a "play safe" attitude. Doing more of the same is the way up in these organisations. Thinking creatively and critically is not welcomed. As one former vice president of a Malaysian telecommunications company remarked, "Great minds think alike; fools do not differ." This climate produces managers who are unwilling to deal with difficult issues. It is unlikely they will be able to challenge others to push the needle. As a result, mediocrity becomes the norm.

The above problems create what Sanchez terms "competency bottleneck". The aspirations of top management cannot be realised because people lower down the hierarchy simply do not have the ability to support and implement them. Instead of propelling the organisation forward, the lack of talented leaders holds the organisation back and causes strategic initiatives to stall.

Strategic leaders need to recognise that developing leadership talent is a key activity. It is not a side issue or nice-to-do matter that can be treated lightly. Organisations like Petronas recognise this as a major challenge. Many of the earlier generations of Petronas managers have retired, and its current managerial force is much younger. There is a gap between the accumulated experiences of the earlier generations of managers and the younger ones in the company. This is the reason Petronas is spending RM500 million (about USD120 million) per year on developing its talents. Axiata, a much smaller company, spends RM20–30 million (about USD7.2 million) each year for its talent management program.

Leaders sometimes make the mistake of thinking that developing leadership talent can be relegated to a lower-level manager. They fail to recognise that developing strategic leaders is not an easy and mundane task. Developing leadership talent is not a recipe-based learning that involves teaching procedures such as the five steps for delegation or the six steps in planning. Instead, developing strategic leaders involves the ability to think and develop judgement skills. These managers need to have the ability to deal with ambiguity and make difficult choices under conditions of imperfect information. It also involves the ability to use influence in an ethical manner. In most organisations, the people who have the experience in these skills are members of top management. As such, they are the best trainers for their company's talent management program. And since the outcome of a talent management program are candidates for succession to senior leadership positions, it is important that members of the top-management team know these candidates and constantly engage them. Developing leadership talent must be a responsibility of top management. Dato Jamaluddin Ibrahim, group CEO of Axiata, explains that he personally chairs meetings that decide on the talent development plan of Axiata's managers.

Leadership Competency Model

Many organisations today rely on leadership competency models to plan their talent development programs. Ulrich defines a leadership competency model (LCM) as a framework comprised of a set of skills, behaviours, qualities, and attitudes that precedes quality leadership and performance. LCMs provide a basis for formulating a talent development program. It serves as a basis for determining the competencies that should be developed among managers. In addition, LCMs are also used when selecting candidates for talent management programs. A risk companies that do not use LCMs may face is that their talent development activities may lack focus and consistency. Instead, the content of their programs may end up being determined by their training providers. Some organisations rely on generic LCMs that were developed by consultants.

These are standard models that are used across many organisations. Among the popular LCMs used by several Malaysian organisations is the one developed by Development Dimension International.

Some organisations develop their own LCM based on the unique requirements of their organisations. This approach requires customisation of the LCM. The argument for using customised LCMs is that they reflect the business challenges faced by the organisations. However, not many organisations have the know-how to develop their own LCMs. They often have to employ consultants to develop them. Evidence from the research done by this author and his student shows that Malaysian companies that use LCMs are more effective in their talent management efforts than companies that do not use LCMs. Effectiveness was measured by the extent those who underwent the talent development program fulfil expectations once they are promoted to higher-level positions. And those who use customised LCMs were found to be more successful than those who used generic ones.

Colgate Palmolive's LCM consists of five key competencies. These are i) inspiring leadership in others, ii) acting courageously, iii) providing a strategic perspective, iv) building a collaborative environment, and v) delivering outstanding results. The talent management program is designed to develop these competencies. Each of these competencies have three subcompetencies. Managers at Colgate Palmolive are assessed on the extent they demonstrate these competencies. Each subcompetency has descriptors of behaviours that are indicative of each subcompetency and behaviours that indicate a person needs improvement.

The LCM at 3M is grouped into three categories: fundamental competencies, essential competencies, and visionary competencies. Fundamental competencies include i) ethics and integrity, which is about exhibiting uncompromising integrity and commitment to 3M's core values; ii) intellectual capacity is related to the ability to assimilate and synthesise information rapidly, recognise complex issues, challenge assumptions, and face up to reality; and iii) maturity and judgement, which is about possessing resilience and sound judgement when facing challenges.

Essential competencies include i) being customer-oriented by consistently working to provide superior value to customers; ii) developing people, creating a workforce that values diversity and respects individuality as well as promotes learning and development; iii) inspiring others, which is about having a positive effect on the behaviours of others and motivating them; and iv) maintaining business health and results, which involves identifying and generating success and delivering results as well continuously searching for ways to add value.

Visionary competencies encompass i) having a global perspective; ii) providing vision and strategy, which involves creating a customer-focused vision and aligning everyone towards a common goal; iii) nurturing innovation by supporting experimentation and rewarding risk taking; iv) building alliances through beneficial networking and creating opportunities; and iv) creating organisational agility by benefiting from 3M's culture, leading change, and teamwork.

The LCMs used by these companies were developed to address the unique requirements of their businesses. It is important to recognise that LCMs are not meant to be static. They should evolve and reflect the challenges faced by the business.

Talent Pool versus Talent Sea

Most companies assess their managers for selection into the talent development program. Some companies create a dedicated group of high-performance, high-potential managers to undergo talent development activities. This group is usually called the talent pool of the organisation. The use of talent pools makes the talent management program more cost effective and focused. However, some companies prefer to not use a talent pool. The reason is that the creation of a talent pool can create an entitlement mindset among its members. These companies also do not want those not included in the talent pool to feel alienated. Instead, these companies consider their whole managerial force as akin to a talent sea. There are merits to both arguments. Evidence from our research involving Malaysian companies shows that companies that use talent pools perform better in developing managers who fulfil expectations when they are promoted.

In Malaysia, companies that use a talent pool include Telekom Malaysia (TM) and the country's national electricity company, Tenaga Nasional Berhad (TNB). Among the companies that treat the whole managerial force as a talent sea include Steelcase Manufacturing Malaysia and Malaysia Airlines when it was led by Idris Jala.

Talent Review

For organisations that rely on talent pools, candidates are assessed through a talent review process. Performance appraisal result alone is not enough to predict a person's ability to lead at the strategic level. Yarnall reports that only around 19 percent of high performers are ready for strategic leadership. Conducting a talent review helps to ensure that besides current performance, candidates are assessed for their potential to grow further. In addition, talent review is also used for assessing the progress of those who underwent the talent development activities and their readiness for promotions. Even for companies that do not use talent pools, managers are assessed for their leadership potential to help chart their development plans and assess their readiness for promotions.

At Steelcase Manufacturing Malaysia, candidates are assessed on two dimensions – leadership potential and performance. The assessment of leadership potential involves assessing the likelihood that an individual can and will grow into a successful leader at one or more levels above his or her current position or into a role with significantly expanded leadership responsibilities. In assessing each candidate's leadership potential, the company uses a set of criteria which includes a) leadership promise, b) personal development orientation, c) mastery of complexity, and d) balance of values and result. Leadership promise is related to a candidate's motivation to lead, the ability to bring out the best in people, and authenticity. Personal development orientation is concerned with the candidate's receptivity to feedback and learning agility. Mastery of complexity assesses the candidate's adaptability to different work situations, conceptual thinking ability, and ability to navigate ambiguity. Balance of values and result is related to the candidate's ability to balance adherence to the company's core values and his or her passion for delivering results. In addition, the talent review process also identifies the individual's towering strength, career interest, career limiters, and developmental actions.

At TNB, managers need to have worked at least eight years before they can be considered for inclusion in the talent pool. They also have to achieve a score of at least 75 percent in their performance appraisal for three consecutive years. Managers can become candidates for the talent management program through nomination by their direct leaders or by nominating themselves.

The assessment of candidates for TNB's talent pool uses the Leadership Potential Inventory (LPI) instrument. The LPI is used to assess each candidate's leadership potential. The LPI examines ten attributes that are categorised into four dimensions – leadership promise, balance between values and results, personal development orientation, and mastery of complexity. These dimensions are the same ones used by Steelcase because they are both based on the model developed by the consulting firm DDI. The LPI assessment uses a set of assessment questions that is filled in by the candidate's immediate superior and the department head. The superiors making the assessment are also asked to rank the candidates they are assessing. This ranking is a forced ranking, where each candidate is placed into various percentile categories. The raters also have to provide a description of the candidate's behaviour that warrants the ranking given. The outcomes of the line managers' and department heads' assessments are then brought to a meeting with the head of divisions and the vice president of HR for moderation. The purpose of this moderation is to ensure consistency.

Another tool used by TNB is CRIM. This tool assesses each candidate on six dimensions: i) eagle vision, ii) creativity, iii) result, iv) change, v) interpersonal skills, and vi) integrity. Each candidate is asked to conduct a self-assessment using a questionnaire that measures these six dimensions. They are also assessed on these dimensions by their line managers as well as by consultants. The consultants use a combination of tools that includes case study, role play, and interview to profile each candidate.

Depending on the size and the resources available in an organisation, the talent review process can be quite simple or fairly sophisticated. One IT company uses a panel to review its managers. This panel examines the performance appraisal results and makes an assessment of the potential of each candidate. The approach taken by this company is largely because its employees are deployed to project teams and are often rotated into new teams once a project is completed. They often work with different people and report to different team leaders. Thus, to get more comprehensive pictures of their performances and potentials require the input from multiple team leaders. Some companies established dedicated assessment centres to perform the talent review. Candidates undergo a battery of tests at these assessment centres. The output of this assessment includes information such as their personality types, growth potentials, skill deficits, and career preferences. The use of a talent review provides additional information that can help reduce any bias and favouritism during performance appraisal.

Talent Development

As mentioned earlier, the focus of talent development programs is developing strategic leadership competencies. Unlike basic management skills that are often procedural in nature, strategic leadership competencies involve developing the ability to deal with ambiguity and uncertainty. Strategic issues that have to be addressed at the top management level often involve new problems and challenges.

Insight Box 7.1

GADP at Axiata

Axiata's talent management program is called the Group Accelerated Development Program (GADP). The program has 144 managers in this talent pool. Candidates are assessed based on three basic criteria: competence, cultural fit, and job fit. In assessing a candidate's competence, Axiata looks at functional skills, professional skills, and leadership skills. Functional skills are about the technical competence possessed by the candidate. Professional skills are about one's ability to work in cross-functional teams, the ability to connect the ideas and issues, and motivation. Leadership is related to a candidate's strategic thinking skills and business acumen. Cultural fit is about the fit with the work culture. Some of Axiata's businesses are very fast paced, and some of its businesses move at a much slower pace.

Candidates are selected based on their abilities to fit with these aspects of work culture. Job fit is about ensuring the candidate is posted or promoted to a position that suits his or her ability. Dato Jamaluddin Ibrahim explains that Axiata seeks managers who have what he terms "needle moving" abilities for its talent management program. These are people who are able to go the extra mile and boost the performance and velocity of the company. They are like the race car driver who pushes the speed of the car to maximum. Their focus must go beyond productivity – that is, cutting costs and increasing efficiency – and towards seeking new market segments, technologies, and opportunities. These are the qualities Axiata considers important to becoming strategic leaders.

Problems are less structured and require inductive reasoning to define the pertinent issues and make decisions. Solutions developed are often new and untested, and the efficacy of these solutions will only be known as they are tried. These solutions are the business hypotheses that leaders develop of the problems and how to solve them. Strategic leaders need to be open-minded and quick to recognise effective solutions and less-effective ones and adjust their decisions.

An example is how Microsoft reacted to the Internet. The Internet has been around since the 1960s. It was then known as ARPANET, and development on the project started in 1963. However, its use was limited to researchers, and it was not user friendly. Two developments made the Internet spread quickly in the 1990s. One was the invention of the personal computer that made it possible for individuals to own computers. The other important development was the invention of the web browser that made using the Internet easier. The development of various protocols expanded the types of information that could be shared on the Internet. By the 1990s, the Internet was accessible to anyone with basic computer skills. Yet it took time for companies to realise the potential of Internet. Bill Gates initially did not show much interest in the Internet because he felt it did not have the potential to be profitable for Microsoft. It was only after his subordinates saw how university students were using the Internet and persuaded him to take it seriously that Gates decided Microsoft should venture into the Internet. This shows how the process of strategic sense making can be slow, requires the willingness to engage in critical discussion, and the ability to act quickly once a potential is recognised.

As Mintzberg points out, strategizing involves imagination and creativity. It often involves scanning for threats and opportunities. Decisions made at the strategic level require the ability to see the forest and not just become fixated with the trees. As such, developing strategic leadership competencies is about developing wisdom, decision-making skills, and the flexibility to deal with new and novel situations. It also requires the ability to lead across functional boundaries. Managers need to get out of their tendencies to think from a functional perspective and focus more on an organisational perspective. For those from a technical background, they need to have the ability to frame the problems faced by their organisations from a business perspective. As such, developing strategic leadership competencies is much more difficult. It goes beyond training managers on how to supervise and delegate or the steps to follow when managing projects or on how to chair a meeting. In addition, talent development programs must rely on activities that have high learning transfer; that is, the ability to transfer what is learned to the workplace. Ensuring this requires that a talent development program incorporate a good learning mix, deliberate practice, experience density, and reflective learning.

Designing Learning Mix

One important decision in designing a talent development program is deciding on the learning mix that will be used. Talent development programs require more experiential and work-based learning. Formal classroom-based learning has its place. It provides knowledge but tends to take place in a sanitised environment that is sometimes a simplification of the realities managers have to face. Work-based learning involves learning by doing and can include job rotation, special assignments, and junior board programs. Its emphasis is more on the ability to use the skills learned and ensures better learning transfer. Work-based learning is also used to broaden the skills, experiences, and outlooks of managers. It forces them out of their comfort zones, which are based on their current functional disciplines, and requires them to work in other functional areas. In addition, work-based learning exposes managers to the messy world of organisational problem-solving. It forces them to exercise judgement by dealing with the complexities of real-world problems. When properly planned, work-based learning amplifies the learning delivered in classroom settings.

For Axiata's Dato Jamaluddin Ibrahim, exposing people to different experiences is an important part of developing managers for strategic leadership positions in Axiata. His belief in this approach is influenced by his own experiences at IBM at an earlier part of his career. He started his career at IBM mainly doing programming work. The work itself was very structured and had a high degree of uncertainty. He was using technical skills that he was good at. IBM then moved him to sales. It challenged him and required him to venture out of his comfort zone and learn new skills. It was a major shift for him because sales involved a lot more ambiguity and required skills that he did not have. It also involved a lot more uncertainty because the outcome can be unpredictable. Later on, IBM moved him into sales support, which involves a lot of planning, and then to marketing management. This cultivated in him cross-functional thinking abilities and made him appreciate the broad range of issues a business has to address.

The same approach is now used in Axiata. A chief financial officer who was being groomed to become the CEO of one its subsidiary was rotated into the marketing function to broaden his exposure and experience. Another manager was moved from his functional area into corporate planning as a part of the job rotation to enable work-based learning. Dato Jamaluddin personally chairs the meetings that decide on the rotation of Axiata's managers.

In some organisations, particularly government-linked corporations (GLCs) in Malaysia, work-based learning can include being cross-posted to other GLCs. This is done to broaden the experiences of managers and enable better understanding and possibly the transfer of best practices. Work-based learning can also involve being assigned more complex and difficult assignments. In some organisations, the ultimate work-based learning is being assigned to build and commission a new plant. Such an assignment involves many skills. Managers have to deal with local authorities, government departments and agencies, technology providers, vendors, contractors, and the various functions within their own organisations. Managers need to have an understanding of budgeting and finance, project management, government regulations, technical issues, logistics, marketing, and above all, possess people skills. Managers have to deal with some of the most difficult people as well as some of the nicest people. Some managers may even find themselves being tempted with bribes from corrupt vendors and contractors. And managers may have to deal with dirty politicians and officials who want to be bribed. All these will stretch a manager's skills, patience, imagination, and challenge one's conscience.

In Shell, undergoing work-based learning is a part of the experience managers have to gain to be promoted to senior positions. The company published a document called *The Experience Navigator* that lists the experiences one must have to qualify for promotion to a senior position. For some positions, this can include having been involved on teams responsible for cost reduction, having worked on cross-functional teams, having had a work experience outside a manager's country of origin, and so on.

Work-based learning can be difficult to implement. Managers find the extra work required to be burdensome and can find it stressful. Their direct leader may not be supportive of the idea of having them rotated to other areas. Some managers also find job rotation risky. Their performances in the new jobs may not be impressive given that they are doing new things. This can undermine their performance appraisals. This is why it is very important to plan work-based learning carefully. Implementing it haphazardly is a sure way to fail. A clear policy regarding work-based learning and staff career development needs to be formulated. Direct leaders need to be informed ahead of time of any rotation or cross-posting that will involve their managers. This will enable them to plan and redistribute work accordingly.

Relationship-based learning involves methods such as mentoring and coaching to complement formal learning and work-based learning. Relationship-based learning enables the sharing of insights, experiences, and tacit knowledge. Besides mentoring and coaching, some companies like Shell introduced a shadowing program. In such a program, a junior manager is required to shadow a senior manager. The junior manager attends meetings with the senior manager. He or she observes the senior manager's actions and behaviour. Besides learning from the senior manager, the junior manager is also expected to give feedback to the senior manager. Relationship-based learning can also be difficult to implement because it requires the commitment from the junior manager and the more senior mentor or coach. In some situations, the relationship-based programs fail because of the sense of hierarchy that prevails in an organisation. Senior managers do not like being shadowed by a junior and find it unnerving to have to listen to feedback from their juniors. Some mentors may just be too busy and not give necessary time and attention to the mentoring relationship. Some companies have to resort to setting minimum targets on how often mentors have to meet their mentees to ensure the mentoring program works.

The basic rule of thumb in deciding on learning mix is to use a 70:20:10 combination of experiential-based, relationship-based, and classroom-based learning. Evidence suggests that achieving this mix is not easy. This is largely because experiential-based and relationship-based learning programs are more difficult to manage and implement. Those who are able to successfully incorporate work-based learning and relationship-based learning are more likely to be more successful in their leadership development efforts.

Some basic guidelines in designing the learning mix of a talent development program follow.

a. Plan the work-based learning closely with training providers to ensure that it is linked to the training given.

b. Work closely with the direct leaders of the managers involved to make sure they support having their managers involved in new work assignments.

c. Provide advanced information about the plan so that any new assignments given will not disrupt current work being done and enable the direct leaders to plan work distribution in their work unit.

d. When the work-based learning involves job rotation or cross-posting, make sure the receiving work unit is ready to accept the manager being deployed there and help him or her adjust into the new job.

e. Provide training to mentors and coaches involved in the relationship-based learning activities. Do not simply assume they know how to mentor or coach those under their guidance.

f. Prepare a sound communication plan to inform all those who are going to be involved in the work-based and relationship-based learning activities that will be implemented and get their buy-in.

Besides the use of a learning mix that includes formal learning, work-based, and relationship-based learning, research in other disciplines provides important insights on how to develop strategic leaders. Developing the capabilities related to strategic leadership competencies also requires a learning experience that incorporates deliberate practice, experience density, and reflective learning.

Incorporate Deliberate Practice

Various researchers in sports education point out that skills enhancement require practice and repetitions. To gain mastery, learners need to be given the opportunity to try the skills being taught, make mistakes, learn from the mistakes, and make repeated attempts. This approach is termed "deliberate practice". Malcolm Gladwell argues that it takes 10,000 hours of practice for someone to become an expert. This applies to the performing arts, sports, and other areas of skill development. The underlying belief behind this idea is that talented performers are made and not born. They learn continuously and repeatedly to improve and perfect their skills.

Likewise, becoming a strategic leader is a journey of continuous learning. Getting to the top position typically involves a lot of practice and failures along the way. Making mistakes is a part of the experience in the journey to the top. As mentioned earlier, when a manager is rotated to a new job, it is possible that performance may decline slightly. He or she may make mistakes and not be as competent in the new job. Providing the opportunity to try again and learn from his or her mistakes is important for development. This gives the opportunity to improve and develop competence. Incorporating deliberating practice also requires a supportive climate when managers make mistakes. Each mistake should be turned into a learning opportunity.

Some basic guidelines in incorporating deliberate practice in a talent development program include

i.   Define clearly the outcomes of each learning experience and the competency level expected.
ii. Deliberate practice goes hand in hand with work-based learning. So design the work-based learning activities to provide multiple opportunities for the managers involved to try new skills.
iii. Create a supportive climate so that people feel comfortable making mistakes and see it as learning experiences.
iv. Make sure feedback on mistakes as well as successes is given to enable effective learning.
v.   At the same time, manage the learning experience so that mistakes made are within acceptable limits and do not cause major damages and losses.

Create Experience Density

In addition, judgement and strategic thinking skills can also be improved by incorporating experience density in the talent development program. Experience density is developed by exposing the learner to stresses and challenges. This is achieved by exposing them to challenging assignments, tight deadlines, and unfamiliar problems. This creates the stress that will draw out the creativity of the learner. It will also help develop the individual's psychological resilience in dealing with challenges often encountered at the top management level. On the other hand, if the learning experience is easy and mundane, managers will not feel the need to use their judgement and creativity. Instead, they are more likely to use familiar solutions to deal with problems.

Noel Tichy describes how US Special Forces creates stress and pressure during their exercises and training programs. A training program may involve conducting a hostage rescue operation. This will usually involve planning for the operation. For a special forces team, planning will involve analyzing intelligence on the target. The rescue plan developed is based on the intelligence gathered. However, the training is designed such as that once the team executes the rescue plan, it will find that the intelligence given to them is not accurate. The team will find that instead of six enemy soldiers defending the location, as described by intelligence, there are in fact ten soldiers. Likewise, instead of the enemy soldiers being armed with light weapons, some of them have rocket-propelled grenades. This deviation from the information given is deliberately incorporated into the training program to force the special force soldiers to make decisions on the spot, improvise as they go on, and be flexible with their plan. Change and facing the unanticipated create stress and forces these soldiers to use their creativity and judgement. Tichy argue that people will learn more when they are taken out of their comfort zones and pushed into the learning zone. On the other hand, those who continue doing their work by relying on existing rules, procedures, and known solutions are less likely to seek new learning opportunities.

Talent development can also incorporate experience density by introducing increasingly difficult and challenging assignments. Training programs can also use teaching methods that force participants to think and rethink their decisions. Business games and multi-scenario case analyses can be used for this purpose. Participants can be given a case that contains certain information about the competitive situation faced by a company. They will be asked to develop a solution on how the company should deal with the competitive situation. Once they've presented their proposals, they will be given a different set of information on the situation faced by the company. This can come in the form of an increase in raw material cost by 25 percent, a new regulation introduced by the government that requires changes to how the company does business, or a move by an unknown competitor who introduced a product that is 30 percent cheaper than the one offered by the company. This will force the participants to stretch their imaginations in dealing with the problems depicted in the case.

Eddie Tie, the group CEO of VitaLife, creates experience density by insisting that his managers always propose to him three options when dealing with a problem. It doesn't necessarily mean that he will select one of the three options given. However, insisting on three options forces his managers to think thoroughly about the problem, explore options, use their creativity, and not just rely on known solutions. And he insists that they get straight to the point and keep their ideas short and simple. As Eddie said, "Tell the truth in three minutes; don't bullshit in thirty." Experience density can also be created by assigning managers to crisis management teams. Managers need to think rationally and maintain their cool when dealing with crises. They need to work as a team and coordinate their actions with others. Jeff Immelt, who succeeded Jack Welch at General Electric, is said to have developed his leadership skills by dealing with crises early in his career.

Some basic guideline that should be observed in creating experience density in a talent development program are

i. Experience density can be created in a manager's current job or when the person is rotated or cross-posted to other jobs.
ii. Create experience density by incorporating as many cross-functional assignments as possible.
iii. Complement this effort with workshops or courses on stress management and creative thinking.
iv. Plan the level of difficulty and complexity so that they are raised incrementally.
v. Monitor the reactions of the managers involved to the stress and difficulties they are experiencing.
vi. Encourage these managers to use their creativity and to think outside the box in dealing with difficulties.

Encourage and Structure Reflective Learning

Insight box 7.2

Training and Reflection

In one MNC operating in Malaysia, reflective learning is incorporated early in the learning experience. Discussions are held at the end of training programs. The trainer will sit down with each participant and link up with his or her direct leader through teleconferencing facilities. The trainer will then share feedback on how the participant performed during the training program with the participant and the direct leader. This feedback discussion enables the participant and the direct leader to plan the next steps that can be taken to ensure transfer of the learning experienced during the training program. Feedback discussions like these provide the opportunity for the participant to also reflect on his or her attitude and achievements during the training program. Cultivating this mindset right after training programs helps make reflective learning a natural part of a manager's development throughout his or her career.

Dealing with stress and challenges can be taxing. Sometimes it can lead to disappointments and emotional reactions. This can cloud a manager's ability to think clearly and derail him or her from learning from the difficulties encountered. For learning to take place, managers need to reflect on the problems and situations faced. Reflection helps nurture the ability to think rationally and logically. This process, termed by Dewey as "reflective learning", needs to be incorporated into the learning process. It involves rationally examining and exploring an issue encountered during a learning experience to gain insight about how the learner dealt with the issue.

Hoyrup proposes that reflective learning involves hypothesis-driven thinking where the learner assesses and reassesses his or her understanding of the cause-effect model of the problem that needs to be solved. Chapter 2 describes strategic thinking as requiring causal thinking. This involves developing a causal model of the problem or a business strategy. This model is basically a hypothesis because in some ways, it is the product of an educated guest. One will not know the soundness of the model until after it is implemented. A strategic leader needs to closely monitor performance to ascertain the validity of the causal model. One of the aims of reflective thinking is to assess the hypothesis and decide whether a leader can continue to depend on it to solve business problems. The hypothesis can be invalid because it was based on an erroneous causal model. The cause hypothesised to be the root of the problem may not, in fact, be the real cause. It can also be invalid because of changing circumstances that make the model inaccurate, irrelevant, or unnecessary. Strategic leaders need to be able to reflect critically on their ideas and the solutions they develop. This reflection should help learning and adaptation.

In addition, reflective thinking also involves intellectualizing difficulties. This is important to enable managers to not react emotionally to difficulties. Instead, reflection can be used to enable them to deal with difficulties in a logical and rational manner. Intellectualizing difficulties goes hand in hand with reassessing the causal model used to deal with a problem. Talent development programs should incorporate moments for reflection so that learners can assess their weaknesses, question their assumptions, seek opportunities for improvement, and maintain their objectivity when dealing with difficult and stressful situations. This can be aided by mentors and coaches.

At the core of reflective learning is the willingness to question assumptions. This relates to assumptions managers make in their decisions. The discussion on reflective learning implies that it is done at the individual level. It can also be aided by trainers and facilitators. Some companies incorporate reflective learning on a large scale by organizing structured programs to do this. Besides reflecting about their personal weaknesses and experiences, these companies encourage their managers to even question top management's decision. General Electric has a strong tradition of leadership development programs for its managers. This includes organizing its Work-Out sessions to find opportunities for improvement. These sessions are held over a few days. As Jack Welch, then CEO of General Electric, describes it, the objective of these Work-Out sessions is to "get rid of thousands of bad habits accumulated since the creation of General Electric."

During these sessions, leaders are put in front of around a hundred of their people to discuss how to improve performances. This includes talking about what these hundred people like and dislike about their jobs, why they are not realizing their potentials, what should be improved in the organization, and things that the company should change. People are expected to challenge their leaders and raise critical questions about the status quo. These Work-Out sessions are how General Electric enables reflective learning on a large scale – reflective learning on steroids. It is by raising critical questions and questioning assumptions that managers are able to develop candour. Jack Welch defines candour as the ability to see reality as it is. On the other hand, in organisations where there is no critical debate and questioning of assumptions, leaders start becoming insular and see what they want to see. Instead of reaching out to their managers, top management creates as much distance and hierarchy as possible between them and their subordinates. As a result, their perceptions of reality are distorted.

Incorporating reflective learning on a large scale is not always easy. Some leaders find being questioned and criticised as unnerving. They feel insecure and vulnerable when questioned. Being questioned pushes them out of their comfort zones. Some will react by putting those who are vocal in cold storage. Look at any organisation that failed to understand and adapt to the changes in its environment, and you will find many such insecure leaders. These leaders are more likely to develop followers who are docile, unimaginative conformists. Instead of developing their subordinates into strategic leaders, these leaders prefer to encircle themselves with mediocre followers and live in their worlds of make believe. For Jack Welch, leaders have to overcome these insecurities or get out of the way. The Work-Out sessions are used to get leaders to understand this. Welch points out, "Ultimately, we're talking about redefining the relationship between boss and subordinates. I want to get to a point where people challenge their bosses every day, "Why do you require me to do these wasteful things? Why don't you let me do the things you shouldn't be doing so you can move and create? That's the job of a leader – to create, not to control. Trust me to do my job, and don't make me waste all my time trying to deal with you on the control issue." For Jack Welch, good leaders are those who are willing to listen, use influence and be influenced by their subordinates. Welch explains, "Above all else though, good leaders are open. They go up and down and around their organisation to reach people. They don't stick to establish channels. They're informal. They're straight with people. They make a religion of being accessible. They never get bored telling their story."

Activities like General Electric's Work-Out sessions create a culture where leaders are comfortable to raise questions and being questioned. When ideas are debated and subjected to scrutiny, they become better. This is especially the case when dealing with complex problems. No one person can possibly know everything about the problem. Reflective learning helps cultivate a habit of being open to critical feedback. It helps refine the hypothesis about the problem and the solution needed to resolve it. In terms of strategic thinking, it helps improve the causal model that leaders develop in dealing with strategic challenges and ensures that it more closely reflects the reality the organisation is facing. It also ensures that future strategic leaders appreciate the value of continuous learning and feedback from others. Admittedly, the sense of hierarchy that is common in some organisations can impede such an open flow of communication.

The vice president of a Malaysian bank commented that his CEO had a number of town hall meetings with employees, but these meetings are mainly monologues. The CEO spends a lot of time talking. This is then followed by a short question-and-answer session. Most people who raise questions ask "polite and safe" questions. As a result, things remain very much the same as before the town hall meeting. Departmental and project meetings can also be used to enable reflective learning if they allow for exchange of ideas. Some leaders treat meetings as briefing sessions, where they behave like *mahagurus*, and those attending the meetings are passive students. Again, these meeting are usually 80 percent monologue followed by brief question-and-answer sessions that leave very little room for critical debates.

Dialogue is about sense making that involves exchange of insights and ignorance to develop a common understanding of issues. This common understanding helps the search for new ideas and improvement. Unfortunately, some town hall meetings and even department and project meetings are just boring, two-way monologues that leave little room for reflection. This happens either because leaders do not understand how to enable reflective learning or because they are not comfortable being questioned and having to question their assumptions. Some leaders like to have so-called engagement sessions, not because they want to listen, but because they like being the centres of attention and brag about their successes. Again, there is no meaningful dialogue in these sessions. There are also leaders who show high interest in having dialogues and discussions with their subordinates upon assuming office. However, these dialogues and discussions are held during the first one or two months only, and as time passes, the leader basically isolates himself or herself, and the enthusiasm for engaging the leader's people dissipates.

Some basic guideline in incorporating reflective learning in a talent development program include

i. Design reflective learning at the individual, work-unit, and organisational levels. Some of the insights learned from reflective learning may require improvements at the work-unit and organisational levels. They have to be able to propose changes to the work unit and organisation. It makes little sense to ask people to reflect on their learning experiences but prevent them from making changes at the work unit and organisation levels.

ii. Link reflective learning with relationship-based learning by involving mentors and coaches. Connecting participating managers with more experienced seniors will help them share insights and wisdom.

iii. In the early stages of the talent development program, make reflective learning a structured and scheduled activity. It takes time for new practices to become habits. Mentors, coaches, trainers, and direct leaders should all play their roles in facilitating reflective learning.

iv. Mentors, coaches, trainers, and direct leaders should be trained in how to facilitate reflective learning. A key skill is the ability to use questioning techniques to facilitate reflection.

v. Get the top management team involved and lead organisational level reflections. Whether these reflection sessions are called Work-Out sessions, workshops, or retreats does not matter. The more central concern is creating a climate where people feel comfortable to express their doubts and fears, give critical feedback, and question assumptions. Whereas reflection at the personal level should be about the individual's performance and learning, reflection at the organisational level should be about the organisation.

A talent development program needs to include a good learning mix and incorporates deliberate practice, enhances experience density, and reflective learning to be effective in developing strategic leadership competencies. It helps build the competencies, consciences, psychological resilience, and intellectual headroom to lead at the strategic level. Evidence gathered from Malaysian companies support this contention. Doing all these requires the support and involvement of the top management team. As mentioned earlier, the best leadership trainers are those who have leadership experience.

Leaders cannot say that they are busy with their jobs and have no time to develop leadership talent. For heaven's sake, developing leadership talent is a part of their jobs! Just look at how countries select people for the top echelon of their leadership. Some countries have an enviable track record of putting the best people into the top echelon of leadership. On the other hand, some countries seem to have an unenviable track record of putting imbeciles and bigots into the top echelon of leadership. It is not difficult to see that the former fare better. This is the difference in performance, resulting from paying close attention to leadership development and ensuring really capable leaders rise to the top.

Closing

Organisations need to be responsive to remain competitive. The speed of its response is dependent on the speed of learning and sense making among its leaders. The more people there are who possess strategic leadership competencies, the more the organisation will be able to respond and adapt quickly to changes and challenges. Even though developing strategic leaders for the future is meant to fulfil a long-term requirement, the benefit can be seen even in the short term. The process of developing leadership talent creates many learning opportunities and contributes towards organisational revitalisation. This is why organisations need to invest in developing strategic leadership competencies continuously.

CHAPTER 8

Leadership Talent Suppressors

Introduction

C laude Le Roy is a soccer coach and manager who has an interesting past. He coached the Cameroon soccer team to various successes, including qualifying for the World Cup in 1998. In 2008, he was appointed the coach for the Omani national team. He led the team to win the Arabian Gulf Cup the next year. Earlier, in 1992, he had led Senegal to the quarter finals of the African Cup of Nations. In spite of his successes, his performance as Malaysia's coach in 1994–1995 could not be considered a success. Why does a coach who was successful before coming to Malaysia and after he left Malaysia a fail in Malaysia? Some would like to blame Claude Le Roy for the failure of Malaysia's soccer team. Fast-forward to 2015, and we can see that in spite of being trained by different coaches since Claude Le Roy left, the Malaysian soccer team's performance continue to be, oh, well, so and so. Many Malaysians have their views on what ails the Malaysian soccer team. Perhaps things will get better after this. How much worse can things get after being defeated 10–0 by United Arab Emirates and 6–0 by Palestine (twice!)?

Management researchers recognise that certain conditions can act as suppressors to organisational capabilities. For instance, IT is supposed to make processes more efficient and faster. However, the potential for IT to enhance speed and efficiency can be hindered by bureaucracy. Likewise, the less than successful performance of Claude Le Roy in Malaysia is most probably due to the suppressing effect of various conditions around him there.

Personal Attributes as Talent Suppressors

Chapter 2 describes the personal attributes that are required to become an effective strategic leader. At the same time, there are certain attributes that can undermine, even impede, a person's ability to become an effective strategic leader. Some of these attributes are rooted in a person's personality. These attributes make a person less suited for strategic leadership. One influential work on this issue is by Michael Maccoby, who discussed about the role of personality and leader behaviour. Basing his work on Freud's discussion of the three main personality categories, he argues that these three categories can enhance or undermine a leader's effectiveness. These three categories are erotic, obsessive, and narcissistic personalities. It is not clear why Freud used the term "erotic" in this categorisation. He did not intend to give it a sexual connotation but instead referred to personalities who have the desire to love and be loved. To avoid misunderstanding, this book will use the term "benevolen t" to refer to this quality. All individuals have varying amounts of each of these three qualities. Maccoby argues that too much and too little of each of these personality categories can be bad for leaders. This can suppress a person's ability to become an effective strategic leader.

a. Narcissistic personalities are individuals who are very driven, independent, and ambitious. They have the desire to be admired. They are usually visionary, critically minded, and are not easily impressed by others. They are driven by the desire to take their organisations to next level. And they are willing to provide the leadership to do so. Narcissistic leaders tend to exude a certain charisma, and followers find them appealing. Observe any successful leader, and you are more likely to see individuals who are proud of their achievements, who enjoy talking about their successes, and like being at the centre of attention. However, too much narcissism can also be damaging. Maccoby points out that highly narcissistic leaders tend to be sensitive to criticism. They tend to feel threatened when criticised and may become paranoid about it. They also tend to be less willing to listen, lack empathy, and have a dislike of forms of learning that involve learning from others. When competing, highly narcissistic leaders tend to be ruthless. While a healthy amount of narcissism is normal among leaders, too much narcissism can easily turn them into toxic leaders and make them ineffective strategic leaders.

b. Obsessive personalities are people who are inner-directed, self-reliant, and conscientious. They prefer orderliness and predictability. They are guided by conscience, set high standards, and are concerned about continuous improvement. Leaders with a healthy level of obsession are good team players, supportive of others, and comply with decisions and rules. Leaders who have a healthy amount of obsession are focused in their efforts, meticulous in the work they do, and will strive to move beyond the status quo. They are usually good operational leaders. Leaders usually consider followers who have a healthy level of obsession to be an asset. Having a healthy level of obsession is also necessary to become a strategic leader. It helps them become effective in execution. However, too much obsession can be damaging. Highly obsessive leaders tend to be very controlling, risk averse, and rigid in following rules. They are less open to new ideas and tend to dismiss anything that requires them to consider the unfamiliar. As followers, they are reliable and dependable, but when they rise to positions of leadership, they tend to be inflexible. They are more likely to become stiff bureaucrats rather than leaders. At the same time, too little obsession can also be damaging. Such leaders tend to not pay attention to details in whatever they do, are careless, and are easily contented with the status quo. They do not keep details in perspective when making decisions. They are nonchalant in their attitude towards work and are not concerned with achieving something. Thus, leaders who are too high and too low obsession are less likely to become effective strategic leaders.

c. Benevolent personalities tend to be empathetic, caring, and supportive towards others. At the same time, they are concerned about how others perceive and accept them. Whereas obsessive personalities are inner-directed, benevolent personalities are outer- and others-directed. Their caring attitudes make them good trainers and mentors. Strategic leaders need to have a certain level of benevolence to be effective mentors. It also creates a considerate attitude towards others. However, too much benevolence is less suited for strategic leadership. These individuals tend to be so concerned about being accepted by others that they tend to have difficulty making tough decisions. They are usually not assertive and will change their minds to gain the acceptance of those around them. Individuals with high benevolence can very likeable personalities but are less suited for strategic leadership. On the other hand, individuals who are low on benevolence can be cold and aloof. They are indifferent to the feeling of others and may have problems developing productive relationship with others.

The implication from the foregoing discussion is that organisations need to recognise how people differ in their abilities to lead at the strategic level. Some individuals can be very successful operational leaders but will require a lot more adjustment and learning to become effective strategic leaders. In many cases, it is not easy to change a person's personality. These are enduring qualities that were shaped during the long process of socialisation that we undergo as we grow older. For organisations that rely on the use of talent pools, incorporating personality tests that assess candidates' personality types can be useful in choosing suitable candidates and enhancing the effectiveness of talent management programs.

Leaders as Talent Suppressors

Suppressing effects also operate to suppress the development of leadership potential in organisations. These suppressors prevent managers from blooming into leaders. Sometimes evidence of this can be seen when a manager leave his or her organisation and manages to grow and become a successful leader in a new organisation. Jeff Immelt, who succeeded Jack Welch as CEO of General Electric, and Steve Balmer, who succeeded Bill Gates as CEO of Microsoft, both worked in the same company at the start of their careers. Both were rated as having low future leadership potential by their then employers. Yet, both Balmer and Immelt grew to become influential leaders. Managers, including those considered not promising, can grow to become outstanding leaders under the right conditions. But their talents will not grow if they continue to work in organisations that suppress their leadership talents.

Various elements create a suppressing effect in leadership talent development. They include the following.

a.   Abusive leaders

Abusive leaders come in many forms. Some are dictatorial but may still be honest. These leaders tend to be self-centred and incapable of learning from others. Harvey and colleagues point out that at the extreme end are abusive leaders who are also bullies. These leaders tend to also be opportunists who are willing to exploit others for their self-interests. A common thread in their behaviours is their inabilities to appreciate those around them. They lead with fear and expect people to be obedient conformists. Their subordinates learn to not disagree with them. As a result, smart followers find themselves unable to exercise their judgement and provide their creative inputs. The climate of fear created by these leaders creates a "play safe" mindset. Abusive leaders ensure that there is no check and balance to their power and leadership. An example of such a leader behaviour is in a recent Reuters report about the leadership style at Volkswagen. The company was caught cheating in its emission test and saw the resignation of its CEO. Former managers and industry observers interviewed by Reuters describe a management style under the CEO as one that fostered a climate of fear and authoritarianism. Problems that existed in the company were not resolved because no one dared to bring them to the CEO's attention. One manager explained that it was typical for the CEO to treat other senior managers "quite disrespectfully." Another manager describes the climate in the organisation succinctly when he said, "There was always a distance, a fear and a respect … If he would come and visit or you had to go to him, your pulse would go up. If you presented bad news, those were the moments that it could become quite unpleasant and loud and quite demeaning." In the short run, the company managed to boost performance by doubling its sales. But the emission scandal is going to be costly. The company has to set aside 6.5 billion euros to recall its cars and fix the problem. In addition, it may be slapped with a fine of as much as US18 billion by US authorities. Not only do abusive leaders destroy the leadership talent in their companies, their actions can also destroy the company.

b. Laissez-faire leaders

Another extreme in leadership behaviour are laissez-faire leaders. These are leaders who have a hands-off leadership style and provide very little guidance and leadership. These leaders confuse delegation with abdication of leadership responsibilities. Followers are expected to figure things out on their own. On the positive side, laissez-faire leaders do not create the pressures of abusive leaders. Neither do they obstruct people like suffocating bureaucracies. However, the lack of direction and common sense of purpose make task performance difficult. There is no sense of strategic priority and focus. Skogstad and colleagues found that laissez-faire leaders tend to create a work climate that is characterised by ambiguities and confusion, conflict between employees, and between employees and the leaders. There are basically two types of laissez-faire leaders. The first are pure laissez-faire leaders who are genuinely not interested in providing leadership. This disinterest can be due to incompetence, lack of commitment, or simply laziness. Capable followers under this leader may be able to make some sense of the ambiguities facing them and may still be able to create a common purpose and still work together. However, they will still be working without a clear strategic focus. The second are the opportunistic laissez-faire leaders who portray disinterest in providing leadership but will interfere and overturn decisions when it involves their personal interests. They appear to be delegating authority but will not hesitate to seize it back when it serves their purposes. This type of laissez-faire leadership tends to have a negative effect on morale and willingness of followers to take responsibility. Followers find the work environment to be unpredictable because of the interferences of the leader. In both cases, leaders show little interest in the development of their followers. In addition, their indifference and lack of strategic thinking means that they have no sense of how to develop strategic leadership capabilities among their followers.

c. Dysfunctional relationship

The work relationship is supposed to be a productive one that is based on respect, trust, and merit. It is an economic as well as a social and psychological exchange. Employees expect to be fairly compensated for their efforts. In addition, employees also form relationships and develop a sense of identity at their workplace. These relationships are with their peers, superiors and subordinates. Ideally, employers would like their employees to feel a sense of identification with the organisation. A functional relationship is one that is characterised by mutual support, fair treatment of one another, openness to ideas, and high trust. However, these expectations are not always fulfilled. Instead, dysfunctional relationships may develop and create imbalance and unfairness. These dysfunctional relationships can be due to favouritism, others relying on impression management to advance themselves, and cliquishness. Instead of creating a climate where everyone has a fair chance of being recognised for their contributions and potential, dysfunctional relationships alter the natural state of things. Instead of competence, people are rewarded and promoted because of their personal relationships or for having similarities with key decision makers. This creates a vicious cycle where high potential individuals are left out and feel alienated. Instead, those enjoying a special relationship with key decision makers are promoted and enjoy direct access to them. As a consequence, the high-potential individuals remain hidden and unknown. Their leadership talent is suppressed, and their motivation declines. In the end, they are then judged as non-performers and sidelined from the line of succession. At the same time, the non-performers recognise that they can advance themselves by currying favour and impression management instead of delivering results. They play this game and get promoted. As a result, higher-level positions in the organisation are occupied by mediocre leaders.

d. Mediocre leaders

Managers with high need for achievement and high need for cognition thrive in an environment where people are expected to push the needle and question assumptions and convention in order to improve and progress. However, these managers will find themselves at odds with their leaders and even peers in organisations where mediocrity is the norm. No one will ever admit to being mediocre. In fact, mediocre leaders often rely on impression management to give the impression that they, too, are committed to high standards and goals.

The reality, however, is very different. These leaders tend to be content with small accomplishments. They do not have high expectations of their subordinates. The only time they may seem enthusiastic is when there are direct personal benefits for them. They are uncomfortable with peers who set high expectations, often seeing these peers as burdensome and making life difficult for them. They value having hardworking subordinates who are willing to do their work for them. But they do not appreciate subordinates who present new ideas that may require that they get out of their zones of mediocrity. Managers who work under mediocre leaders will find their potential stunted and their creative contribution not appreciated. Mediocre leaders do not openly reject creative ideas from their subordinates. But they kill these ideas and the creativity of their subordinates slowly by ignoring them or sweeping them under the carpet. They also tend to prefer peers who are like them. When these leaders can influence promotion and appointment decisions, they'll try to make sure equally mediocre leaders get the positions. As a result, mediocrity becomes the collective character of leaders in the organisation. The long-term impact is that these leaders make mediocrity the culture and turn high–potential followers into highly disappointed workers.

Organisational Context as Talent Suppressors

Organisations serve as contexts for the exercise of leadership. Organisations can provide an environment that nurtures strategic leadership talent. At the same time, organisations can also create constraints and impediments that suppress leadership talent. These constraints and impediments include the following.

i.   Suffocating bureaucracy

Modern society has a love-hate relationship with bureaucracy. To be fair, bureaucracy creates value by making processes and decision-making more objective, rational, and consistent. The notion of bureaucracy emerged as a response to the administrative system's inability to provide fair and consistent service in post-feudal society. However, in some organisations, bureaucracy outgrows its value and usefulness and starts becoming irrational. It becomes overwhelming and suffocating. People within these organisations become enslaved to rules and procedures. Instead of having rules and procedures as means to aid processes and decision-making, preserving these rules and procedures become the ends themselves. Quite often these rules and procedures substitute thinking and judgement. Suffocating bureaucracy acts as leadership talent suppressors in three ways. First, the pressure to comply forces people to rely less on judgement and wisdom and more on enforcing rules. It leaves little room for discretion and creativity. Work is mostly about rule-following and does not provide experience density. And since changing these rules and procedures is usually very difficult, it renders reflective learning useless. Thus, leadership talent does not bloom in suffocating bureaucracies. Instead, it wilts and dies. Second, because of the emphasis on rule compliance, performance is less about creative contribution. It negates the need for capable leaders who can think strategically. The climate that prevails in suffocating bureaucracies values followers who are not critically minded. As a result, those who tend to be favoured for promotion are those who are docile followers. Those who are critically minded and willing to question assumptions are seen as inconveniences. Third, when less-capable leaders rise up the organisation, they tend to be incapable and insecure. They encircle themselves with even more incapable leaders. The more decent of these incapable leaders tend to just concern themselves with maintaining the status quo. The more indecent of these incapable leaders will focus their attention on dominating and controlling others. As a consequence, the whole organisation becomes infertile for nurturing leadership talent.

ii. Lack of justice

Normal individuals consider being treated fairly important. Being treated unjustly undermines our dignity and trust. It makes us feel that we have no value and are not respected. This, in turn, makes us resentful and distrustful. Researchers classify justice into three main categories – interactional justice, procedural justice, and distributive justice. Interactional justice is about the interpersonal treatment someone is subjected to. Interactional injustice happens when a person is treated in a rude, humiliating, and indifferent manner. Procedural justice is about the use of fair and consistent procedures in decision-making. Procedural injustice is more likely to happen when a person is subjected to an inconsistent set of rules or the formal procedures are ignored to favour certain individuals and discriminate against others. Distributive justice is about fairness in the distribution of rewards and resources. When people perceive that rewards and resources are not distributed in a fair manner, they are more likely to experience distributive injustice. Admittedly, there will always be complaints of unfairness in most organisations. Direct leaders may misjudge a person's contribution. This can be due to leaders lacking the opportunity to observe and understand the appraised's work. Sometime personal biases can also play a role. However, such unfairness is more likely to be the exception in organisations that treat justice as a serious matter. On the other hand, organisations that ignore justice as a concern are more likely to see frequent and pervasive use of performance appraisal, decisions on rewards, and interpersonal treatment of employees as political tools to consolidate influence, marginalise others, and practice favouritism. The resentment and distrust created by injustice undermines motivation and commitment to the organisation. Injustice signals to potential leaders that their efforts may not be fairly appraised and rewarded. This means that their futures in these organisations are not promising. As a consequence, there is no incentive for them to make the extra effort to develop their leadership competencies. Capable people who feel unjustly treated would prefer to move elsewhere and make their contributions there. Lack of organisational justice suppresses leadership talent by damaging morale, undermining trust, and hurting commitment.

iii. Short-termism

Developing leadership talent takes time. It involves practical experience that is gained over time. Organisations need to be willing to make a long-term commitment to talent management. For instance, in spite of the being adversely affected by low oil prices, Petronas continues to make talent management one of the six thrusts to remain profitable. Short-term orientation can suppress leadership in a number of ways. First, and the most obvious one, is that the lack of investment in talent management means that managers will not be given the opportunity to hone their strategic leadership skills. Second, the lack of long-term commitment signals to the employees that the company is not committed to developing leadership talent. As a result, line managers will be reluctant to allow their direct reports to participate in such a program. The lack of a long-term commitment also signals to the high-potential managers that the organisation is not concerned about giving them a better future. These managers will more likely reciprocate by not showing long-term commitment to the organisation. They will leave the moment there are better opportunities elsewhere.

iv. Hierarchical orientation

One inevitable consequence in the growth of any organisations is the creation of hierarchies. Layers of management are introduced to improve control and coordination. However, over time, this growth in layer becomes a liability. It leads to a hierarchy that impedes communication and coordination. Individual leaders may have more control over activities under their jurisdictions, but they begin to operate like silos. Compounding the hierarchy created by growth is the hierarchical orientation that is rooted in culture and mindset. Countries differ in their hierarchical orientations. Hofstede's study of culture across many countries found that Malaysia scored the highest in "power distance", the term he used to refer to hierarchical orientation. At the macro level, a strong hierarchical orientation impedes organisational learning. Information and knowledge flow is obstructed. Quite often the information is filtered and sometimes reshaped to fit the concerns of the various gatekeepers in the information flow. As a result, decision-making becomes slow and does not reflect the actual situation. At the micro level, work groups are conditioned to defer to hierarchy. Those at lower levels are expected to not question the decisions and opinions of their superiors. Those at higher levels do not feel comfortable with subordinates who are critically minded and speak their minds. Besides norms and values, the sense of hierarchy is often enforced through various artefacts, such as seating arrangements during meetings and different amenities given to the different levels of employees. The message all these send is unmistakable: "You are inferior mortals, and you should remember your place in this organisation." It breeds conformity and rigid rule-following behaviour. As a result, smart and creative followers feel constrained and limited in their abilities to grow. Instead of contributing ideas, they are expected to be passive followers.

v. Obsession with narrow goals

A key idea put forward in this book is that strategic leaders need to lead with conscience. This includes observing moral boundaries and being guided by our moral compasses. However, there are many situations where members of an organisation slip and tumble even when no one in the organisation told them to ignore ethics. Lynn Paine, writing in the *Harvard Business Review*, points out that when someone behaves unethically in an organisation, it is rarely the result of a lone actor. Instead, it happens because of the explicit and tacit approval of others and is usually a reflection of the organisation's values and culture. In some cases, companies deliberately cut corners and cheat. But it some cases, it was not the intention of management to behave unethically by cheating or misleading customers. Yet, ethical misconduct happens. Quite often the decisions and priorities set by top management have a signalling effect on employees. It conveys to employees what is important and paramount. At the same time, it also conveys what is not important and can be ignored or compromised. This happens when top management sets narrow targets and key performance indicators. Leaders in the organisation lose sight of long-term goals and inadvertently make decisions that push them across their moral and ethical boundaries. Instead of leading with conscience, they become opportunistic and myopic in their focus. Instead of developing leaders who can think strategically, the obsession with narrow goals creates leaders who are short-term oriented and concerned only with operational goals. Paine gives accounts of such behaviours and how it ended up hurting companies (see Insight Box 8.1).

Insight Box 8.1

Sell, Sell, Sell at Sears Roebuck

Paine describes how Sears Roebuck became the subject of complaints and investigations by US authorities. These complaints were related to its automotive service business, where customers were sold unnecessary part and services. In the end, the company had to reach a settlement that involved refunds that cost it an estimated $60 million. The crisis was not the result of a deliberate attempt to cheat customers. The company denied any intention to deceive customers, but its CEO admitted that the company's goal-setting system, "created an environment in which mistakes did occur." Sears Roebuck had sought to boost performance by setting high targets and incentives for its employees. Employees were given specific sales targets for a number of products and were paid commissions based on sales. Those who failed to meet these targets were transferred or given fewer work hours. Under pressure to protect their jobs and livelihood, employees began to push unnecessary services and products. This became pervasive and led to the company being investigated by the attorneys general in forty states. Seen from a strategic angle, the targets set ended up hurting the company. It forced leaders in the company to abandon their consciences in order to pursue their targets. Middle-level leaders caught in such situations found themselves under pressure to just push for higher sales per customer. They ceased thinking strategically and became completely focused on operational targets.

vi. Silo mindset

One consequence of specialisation is that it creates people who are focused on their areas of functional responsibility. While this is necessary for efficient use of resources, it can also lead to a mindset that is limiting. People fail to see beyond their functional horizons. As a consequence, they are content when their functional goals are achieved without assessing whether that has helped achieve organisational objectives. For instance, the emphasis on cutting costs may lead to a preference for a stable product line in the production function. While this will help the production function achieve its objectives, it may come at the expense of responsiveness to changes in the market. People tend to be concerned with only their immediate responsibilities and tend to develop a "not invented here" attitude. Problems that started elsewhere or initiatives started by other functions are seen as not being a part of the concerns of other functions. This mindset suppresses the development of strategic leadership talent because it prevents people from developing a bird's-eye view of the organisation. Leaders who emerge from this climate tend to continue to think in silos even after they are promoted to senior management positions.

Talent Enhancers

Developing strategic leadership talent involves creating conditions that can nurture employees' abilities to grow. These conditions include nurturing a climate that is conducive for creativity and critical thinking and encourages collaboration while at the same time sets high expectations and commitment to standards. A number of practices can help foster these conditions.

a. Undo hierarchy

It is tempting to simply view that the antidote to the suppressing effects of hierarchical orientation is less hierarchy. However, hierarchy is both a structural as well as cultural phenomenon. The sense of distance can also be created by how higher-level leaders treat their subordinates. Over time, this behaviour becomes a part of the culture of the organisation. It is difficult to say with certainty why some organisations develop a stronger sense of hierarchical orientation than others. Some may argue that hierarchy is created as a result of insecurities of leaders who do not like to be questioned by their subordinates. Dismantling the layers an organisation without changing how people think and behave will not overcome the hierarchical orientation. Some of the steps that can be taken to undo hierarchy are the following.

i. Creating a norm of authority of knowledge

An important starting point in undoing hierarchical orientation is recognizing that good ideas can come from anywhere in the organisation. This may seem intuitive, but some organisations create a climate where lower-level employees are supposed to know their places and should not differ with higher-level leaders. This climate is often created in subtle ways through artefacts such as seating arrangements during meetings, separate facilities and amenities for higher level positions, and behaviours such as who gets to speak and who are expected to remain silent. Creating a norm of authority of knowledge involves developing an open attitude towards input and critical feedback from everywhere in the organisation. The success of QCC initiatives in Japan is largely because management recognises that improvement ideas can come from even the lowest level of the organisation. For instance, a comparison between Mazda and an American car manufacturer shows that 70 percent of the ideas given by employees through the suggestion scheme in Mazda are adopted. On the other hand, only about 20 percent of ideas given by employees in the American firm are adopted. Besides openness to input, a norm of authority of knowledge also involves cultivating a culture of respecting individuals regardless of their positions and levels in the organisation. This norm helps nurture critical thinking and encourages people to think outside the box. These are among the basic ingredients in developing strategic thinking competencies. In addition, the involvement in dealing with organisational issues helps develop a sense of ownership towards the organisation.

ii. Encourage dialogue

Many of us have probably experienced being asked to give our opinions on issues. Yet, we have no idea what happened to the opinions after we've given them. It is basically a two-way flow of information without anyone becoming wiser. Dialogue is a process of sense making to develop shared meaning. This happens through the exchange of opinions and discussions about the merit of ideas. By sharing ideas, we are subjecting them to scrutiny that helps us improve them or understand their limitations. Crossan explains that individual learning often happens through intuition.

To ascertain the merit of these intuitive ideas, they should be discussed and interpreted at the group level. This process enables individual learning to progress to become a part of organisational learning. A climate that encourages dialogue makes it natural for people to discuss and debate ideas. Dialogue can also help to support the reflective learning that is necessary to support strategic leadership competencies development.

iii. Increase consultative communication

Developing a norm of authority of knowledge and nurturing dialogue will not happen in organisations where communication is top-down and mainly in the form of directives and instructions. Instead, it requires more use of consultative communication, where people are given the opportunity to become a part of the learning and decision-making process. This is especially important when dealing with novel and complex problems. No one leader has the complete picture about the problem. Nor are they likely to find solutions to problems alone. Consultative communication helps management tap into the knowledge of members of the organisation and develop a deeper and more accurate understanding of problems.

b. Leadership by top management

Developing strategic leadership talent requires the active involvement of senior leaders. CEOs like Jack Welch recognise this. He led leadership development programs when he was heading General Electric. Organisations like TNB hold dialogue sessions with members of their talent pool on a periodic basis to help develop their leadership abilities as well as keep them informed of strategic issues facing the organisation. In some of these organisations, members of the top-management team also serve as mentors to talent pool members. The involvement of top management has a vicarious effect on junior leaders because it presents to them a visible role model that they can emulate. It also signals to the rest of the organisation the importance of leadership development for the organisation and ensures that the initiative receives support from other line managers.

c. Opportunity to lead

Leadership competencies cannot be developed in a vacuum. Developing strategic leadership competencies is not an event. It does not begin with a leadership training course and stop at the end of the course. As mentioned earlier, skill development requires deliberate practice. This is also the case in developing strategic leadership competencies. One important aspect of leadership development is providing managers with the opportunity to lead. This can begin with leading small-scale activities and ventures. It can also be in the form of leading task forces and cross-functional teams. Bigger leadership responsibilities can be in the form of leading major project teams.

d. Creative climate

A point highlighted in this book is that strategic thinking involves creativity. Strategic thinkers need to be willing to question the status quo and think beyond existing ideas to push the needle. Such thinking will only grow in a climate that is supportive of creativity. Ekvall proposes ten conditions that constitute a creative climate.

i. Presence of challenge to spur people to search for ideas to take the organisation to the next level.
ii. There must freedom for managers to use their ideas and creativity to search for solutions.
iii. Top management shows support for new ideas by being open, receptive, and attentive to suggestions.
iv. There must be openness and trust for people to feel safe to try new ideas.
v. A climate that is playful and humorous where people feel looking for new ideas is fun.
vi. The sense of urgency to search for ideas is stronger when people perceive dynamism in the way people think and look for new ideas in the organisation.
vii. Debates are encouraged so that ideas are discussed and opposing opinions are assessed.
viii. There needs to be a willingness to take risks as creative ideas tend to be uncertain.
ix. People must be given idea time to search for and test their ideas.

x. A healthy level of conflict needs to be present to encourage people to compete to make improvements.

It is important to note that a creative climate is very much shaped by the behaviours of leaders, especially higher-level leaders. If there is a lack of creative ideas in an organisation, leaders need to assess whether they are sending the right signals on the need for creativity. Leaders convey their aversion to creativity by being unreceptive to change, insisting on a top-down approach to problem solving, unsupportive of any form of risk taking, by being inattentive to input from subordinates, and by being hasty in exploring ideas.

e. Develop a systems perspective

Strategic leaders need to see the organisation as a whole, and this will only happen when they are constantly encouraged to think holistically. When silo mentality persists in an organization, it is usually because no one is doing something to overcome it. "No one" here specifically refers to the top-management team not taking enough steps to deal with the problem. Developing a systems perspective must begin at the top for it to influence the organisation as a whole. People lower down in the organisation will not be able to nurture a system perspective if top management itself continues to operate and think in silos. Some of the mechanisms that can nurture a systems perspective include the use of cross-functional teams, rotating people across functions, and incorporating systems-level goals into the result they are accountable for. Developing system thinking involves the following.

i. Develop the habit of framing issues and problems by thinking at the organisational instead of functional level.
ii. Get everyone to think of the interdependence that exists between people and functions and the downstream consequences of their actions and decisions.
iii. Focus on superordinate goals and not just short-term goals or merely focus on performing activities.

iv. Continuously explain the relationship between the organisation and its external environment in the organisation's internal communication.

v. Frame the organisation's vision and mission as ultimately being about giving benefits to humankind and society.

Closing

Organisations need to be mindful that developing leaders is more than just organizing training programs. Internal conditions in the organisation can suppress or enhance managers' leadership potential. All these have to be managed to create conditions that are conducive for people to grow and become strategic leaders. At the same time, organisations need to dismantle the impediments that suppress the leadership potential of their managers. No amount of training can undo the effects of the talent suppressors. In fact, the more talented members of the organisation will probably prefer to move elsewhere to realise their potential.

CHAPTER 9

Organisational Failure and Strategic Leadership

Introduction

Even though a lot has been written about business success, there is no shortage of business failures. Some successes are not sustainable and ended up as failures. Montuori points outs that one third of the companies in the Fortune 500 list are no longer on the list merely fifteen years later. In fact, some of the companies that were considered highly successful in the past are no longer around. These include Yashica and Kodak in photography; Nokia and Dancall in mobile phones; Trans-World Airline and PanAm in aviation; Sylvania and RCA in consumer electrical products. and Wang, Amstrad, and Commodore in computing. In Malaysia, companies like MEC in consumer electronics, the Chef brand of instant noodles, Sate Ria in F&B, MegaTV and Metro TV in broadcasting, and Accent in personal computing have all suffered the same fate.

Some products are not even around anymore. Personal digital assistants have been made obsolete by advancements in cell phones. Typewriters are facing near extinction. Overhead projectors and slide projectors are also on the way out if not already gone. Only a few years ago, newcomers to any city would need to buy a map to know how to get around the city. This has been replaced by Waze, Google Map, Papago, and Garmin.

Learning about the success of others can be inspiring. But failure has a lot more to teach us. Success is not easy to copy. Just look at people who have attended talks by millionaires-motivational speakers on how to become a millionaire. How many of them do end up as millionaires? Even success stories may not be long-lasting. A company owned by one such speaker – Robert Kiyosaki, Rich Global LLC – filed for bankruptcy in 2014. When those extolled as success stories end up as failures or encounter major problems what lessons can we infer?

Studying success can help us understand what it takes overcome the odds and develop competitive advantage. However, there is the need to be cautious when listening to success stories. First, people who talk about their successes have the tendency to emphasize their own roles in creating the success. In reality, this is not always the case. In some cases, having a strong political connection is all it takes to make money. It is quite common in countries ruled by corrupt regimes to see businesspeople use their connections to win over a contract and then cash out by subcontracting the job to others. In some cases, having a privileged position gives enormous advantage. Only fools will fail in businesses where the profit is assured, where the government guarantees the loan, and the business operates as a monopoly. This enables the business to borrow at a favourable rate and force its products on consumers. This is a common scenario in countries ruled by corrupt elites.

In addition, success is not easy to be examined. It is a combination of entrepreneurial farsightedness, favourable conditions, and possibly to tacit elements that may not even be understood by the people involved. For instance, what makes a company innovative? A macro-level analysis may attribute the innovativeness to the amount spent on R&D. Closer examination, however, may attribute it to the presence of certain creative talent. Others may see it as the product of effective leadership. An organisation's culture is also often said to affect creativity and innovation. For instance, many accounts of Thomas Edison credit him with being an inventive genius. However, recent studies point out that the structural arrangement of his Menlo Park lab – for example, the bullpen layout of his lab – also played an important role in generating a highly creative work environment that made innovation possible.

It is also important to recognise that the successes of others are not always imitable. It is always expedient for others to simply attempt to replicate the success of other organisations. Take the case of Toyota. It is well documented that one of the strengths that Toyota has is its production system, known as the LPS. Many companies have tried to adopt the LPS, but the success rate has been slow. Jadhav estimates that 70 percent of attempts to adopt the LPS failed. What was thought to be a straightforward success formula turned out to not be so straightforward after all. There are many aspects of the management practice at Toyota that are a part of the ecosystem that supports the

Healthy organisations	Sick organisations
• Goals are widely shared among employees. • Employees feel safe and comfortable to communicate difficulties and problems. • Problem solving is pragmatic and not constrained by sacred rules or the desire by top management to dominate. Judgements of people lower down are respected. • There is a noticeable team spirit. • Personal needs are addressed. • There is a collaborative culture.	• Employees feel little personal investment in goals. • Problems are hidden and unsolved; members do not bother to act. • Those at top try to control many decisions. • Lower-level judgement is respected only in limited job scope. • Managers feel alone and isolated in performing their jobs. • Personal needs of employees are ignored. • Members compete when they need to collaborate. • The CEO behaves like an autocrat.

Table 9.1: Randell's Comparison of Healthy and Sick Organisations

implementation of the LPS. Researchers are only beginning to understand this ecosystem. Szulanski uses the term "barren context" to refer to internal conditions that are not conducive for implementing new knowledge. Applying a technique like the LPS in a rigid culture that does not allow employee involvement and is unreceptive to change will make improvement difficult.

Understanding failure can help us avoid the mistakes made by others. Quite often, it can also inform us of the limitations of success stories. Learning from failures can also help us focus on improvement. Pretorius points out that failure is something all business leaders will face in their lives. Yet, failure is something business leaders are least prepared for.

Toyota is known today as a global leader in the automotive industry. However, its journey to the top was not easy and smooth. It first attempted to enter the US market in the 1950s but did not succeed. It was only after two more attempts that Toyota finally made significant headway and achieved success in the United States in the late 1970s. It owed much of its success to the company's improvement orientation. Understanding failure is also necessary because many firms experience failure just after they reach the peak of their success. For some, like Nokia in cell phones, the downward journey was quick. For others, like Kodak, it was slow and not unlike the proverbial frog in a frying pan.

Causes of Organisational Failure

A successful organisation is akin to a healthy individual. A healthy individual is able to care for himself or herself, respond to threats, and strive for survival. On the other hand, failed organisations are like sick individuals. Failed organisations are in a perpetual state of decline. Like the sick individual, the organisation experiences degeneration and is incapable of fending off threats. Randell presents a comparison of sick and healthy organisations (see table 9.1). In healthy organisations, people feel a sense of shared destiny. They understand the goals of the organisation and are committed to it. In healthy organisations, problems are discussed openly. People feel safe to raise issues and voice criticisms. Problem solving is focused on finding solutions instead of rigid compliance to rules and procedures. Leaders feel comfortable involving their subordinates in decision-making. Input and views from members of the organisation are genuinely valued. Leaders recognise that employees have personal concerns and needs and seek to create a supportive climate. Members of the organisation work as a team, and people collaborate to pursue their shared goals.

On the other hand, in sick organisations, people do not feel a sense of ownership of the organisation's goals. Coming to work is about earning a living and performing their jobs regardless of whether it actually contributes towards goal attainment. The CEO behaves like an autocrat and is feared by his or her followers. As a result, problems are not openly discussed. Sycophantic followers play the game of giving the CEO only the good news. On the surface, the CEO starts believing everything is good even though in reality, the organisation is rotting from inside. Those who dare to convey bad news are more likely to find themselves on the receiving end of the CEO's wrath and will be considered non-performers. The CEO is very concerned with control and domination. Opinions of lower-level employees are not valued, and neither are they sought. If they are ever involved in any decision-making it is usually in superficial issues such as deciding on the activities for the organisation's family day or the menu for the annual dinner. The climate is one of distrust. People compete to please the CEO. Quite often, the sycophantic non-performers are the ones who circle around the CEO. And to ensure their influence over the CEO, they will destroy those they consider a threat to their status and influence. As a result, there is no team spirit, and managers feel isolated in their work. They become more inward looking and operate in silos.

Sick organisations are more likely to experience deterioration in performance and decline simply because of their inabilities to learn and adapt. Insights are usually ignored and are not shared. Instead of tapping into the collective learning of members of the organisation, these organisations tend to rely on the views of the CEO or a small group of managers that circle him or her. As a result, both the CEO and these managers tend to be insulated from reality. They have a jaundiced view of the external environment.

Lorange and Nelson explain that organisations that experience decline tend to exhibit certain characteristics. The first is the tendency to engage in self-deception. Top management tends to see only what it wants to believe. They tend to filter and skew information to fit their existing views. Instead of engaging in learning, their view starts gaining the status of superstitious belief. They believe in something in spite of evidence to the contrary. This belief is often the product of emotions and stubborn insistence on an idea.

The second characteristic of an organisation experiencing decline is that it starts becoming more hierarchically oriented. Top leaders seek comfort by creating distance from their followers and the unpleasant realities in the market. Accounts of the downfall of Eckhard Pfeiffer as the CEO of Compaq show that he became more insular. He kept a distance from others and encircled himself with a small clique of key people. He and his clique isolated themselves in the executive office that was made out of bounds to others in the company. Decisions were made without much consultation beyond this clique. When

Compaq acquired DEC, other members of senior management only knew about it through the media. The acquisition turned out to be disaster and hurt both companies. Pfeiffer was ousted from Compaq in 1999. Members of his clique also left the company or were forced to resign.

The third characteristic of declining organisations is cultural rigidity. These organisations start developing certain ways of doing things that were considered unchangeable. The superstitious learning that arise as a result of the self-deception and hierarchical orientation leads the organisation to treat certain habits and practices as sacred and unquestionable. This restricts thinking and the options the organisation is willing to consider when dealing with challenges. The organisation becomes like a ship with a damaged rudder that is heading straight towards an iceberg. Louis Gerstner relates that one the practices that is a part of IBM culture was the right for members of a team to object to a new idea or initiative. In the early days of IBM, this ensured that there was buy-in and commitment to decisions. However, when IBM was facing challenges to its survival, it became a dysfunctional aspect of the company's culture. New ideas were shot down simply because a team member disagreed with them. As a result, it became difficult to introduce new ideas and initiative. One of the things Gerstner did when he became the CEO of IBM was to dismantle the dysfunctional aspects of IBM's culture such as this right to object.

The fourth characteristic is the desire for conformity. As a result of cultural rigidities that make certain things sacred, people feel compelled to conform. The cultural rigidities that developed in the organisation become a strait-jacket and cannot be changed. The organisation loses adaptiveness and goes through a downward spiral. And finally, the fifth characteristic mentioned by Lorange and Nelson is decision-making in the organisation is marked by too much consensus and compromise. When an organisation is facing a strategic challenge, it is not always possible to reach consensus. The leader has to make the call. He or she should consult and involve others in decision-making but should not let it drag or remain indecisive under the guise of seeking consensus. In declining organisations, consensus and compromise are sought because no one wants to change. Everybody wants to protect the status quo and their immediate interests. The acceptable decision is the one that is least disruptive to everyone. In such a situation, seeking consensus is less about developing shared meaning and common destiny. Instead, it is more about procrastinating and resisting change.

Healthy companies are able to recognise the signs of failure and respond to them. They are able to learn from their mistakes, accept ownership of the problems, and do not let their egos get in the way. However, sick organisations are in a perpetual state of failure. These failures are rooted in many dysfunctional attitudes, norms, behaviours, and practices that prevent the organisation from adapting to the environment. Unfortunately, even successful organisations can fail to avoid failure.

Success Leads to Failure

It is baffling to see successful companies fail. How can they fail to see the cliff ahead of them? Surely their success had been due to capable leadership and a good system. How could such leaders go wrong? Shouldn't the smart leaders who led the organisations to success also prevent them from failing? Danny Miller provides an insightful analysis of how successful organisations end up failing. At the centre of his analysis is that successful organisations have the tendency to oversimplify. This then impedes their abilities to cope with complexities and changes in the environment.

According to Miller, oversimplification usually happens when organisations start translating the lessons from their experiences into "formulas for success". This formula for success starts shaping a mindset that causes people to begin to treat it like a creed. It becomes the template that is used repeatedly, even when it is no longer valid.

The institutionalisation of the formula for success leads to certain products and projects enjoying a special status. Certain functions may emerge as having more status and influence in the organisation. Leaders involved in the functions, projects, and products become the elite of the organisation. They are given the most and the best resources. They are the untouchables. The resources and internal capabilities are all configured to support this formula for success. The formula for success becomes self-perpetuating.

For a while, this formula for success works. It enhances the organisation's ability to do what it is currently doing. But this limits its capacity for change. When the external environment changes, the organisation is unable to respond to the changes. The core competencies that led the organisation to its success start to become a competency trap. Members of the organisation only know how to do what they have always been doing. The existing elite retreat into a defensive mode and try to protect the status quo and its formula for success. Leaders' perceptions of the environment are skewed by their perceptual biases. They see what they believe in. They start rationalizing and filtering information to fit their perceptions.

Instead of responding to change, they sometime escalate further their commitment to current decisions and investments. Over time, they become more misaligned with the realities of the external environment. Louis Gerstner's account of his effort to turnaround IBM in his book *Who Says Elephants Can't Dance? Leading a Great Enterprise through Dramatic Change* provides an interesting account of a company that showed some of the symptoms mentioned above. For a long time, IBM's success was due to its mainframe computer; that is, the IBM 360 machine. When the market started to change in the 1990s towards PC-based networks, IBM was slow to accept the change. Its own salespeople knew the change was taking place. But others higher in the hierarchy continued to believe that the future was going to be a continuation of their past successes. They could not let go of their current investments. The company suffered losses in the 1990s and had to bring in Gerstner to turn around the company. It was a courageous decision by IBM's board given that Gerstner was an outsider to the IT industry. In fact, Gerstner used to be an IBM customer who didn't find the experience of dealing with IBM then very pleasing.

IBM managed to rejuvenate itself and continues to be a strong company. Others in the computing industry were not so lucky. Computer firm Wang Laboratories filed for bankruptcy twenty years after it was established. Amstrad, Commodore, and Gateway are also casualties in the computing industry. Novell and Netscape were acquired by other companies. There are still more lessons to be learned from the decline of these companies.

A good strategist recognises that the route to success is equifinal. Competitors can find new ways to overtake a leading company. No formula for success is competition proof. Leaders start deceiving themselves when they start believing that their formula for success is eternal. They cease to learn and are unable to adapt. In the end, these organisations become sick organisations that can no longer compete effectively.

Folly of Best Practices

The view that the successes of leading companies can be imitated has led some management gurus to develop the notion of best practices. Yet, best practices do not immunise companies from failure. There are a number of reasons best practices are not always the best ones to emulate.

First, best practices are the products of history and learning in an organisation. This learning creates new procedures that become best practices. The insights that led to the development of the practice are often just as important, if not more important, than the practice. The insights enable us to understand why a practice was developed and its purpose. It also enables us to understand the limitations of a practice. The insights also constitute a part of organisational knowledge that enables it to continuously improve its practice. Without this knowledge, imitators of best practice could not understand the purpose and limitations of the adopted best practice. Even if another organisation can imitate a best practice, the source of the best practice would have improved its practice, making it even better. Thus, the imitator will always be playing a catch-up game.

Take the example of the LPS which was initiated by Toyota (known in Toyota as the Toyota Production System). Accounts of the LPS had evolved over time. In the early 1980s, the understanding of Toyota's practice in most MBA textbooks was that it was about just-in-time inventory management. However, by the 1990s, the discussion on LPS also focused on waste reduction. Achieving waste reduction requires implementing other practices such as total quality management, total preventive maintenance, and continuous improvement. All these have to be supported by the organisation's HRM practice. More recent studies on the LPS reveal that the strength of the system is also a product of how employees are trained. Toyota employees are trained to engage in critical thinking. Their superiors challenge them to question existing practices. This creates a climate where people feel that questioning is a part of the job. Some organisations fail in their attempts to implement the LPS simply because leaders are not comfortable with getting their subordinates involved in making decisions.

Even members of the organisations that own the best practices may not necessarily understand what makes a practice work. One senior Toyota manager admitted that even they in Toyota are not so sure how to explain the

LPS. It has become so embedded in the company's way of working that it is just a natural part of its habit. It takes outsiders to study and explain what the LPS is all about.

Second, best practices are developed with a context. The context includes the culture and existing practices in an organisation. Szulanski uses the term "barren context" to refer to internal conditions that are not conducive for the adoption of new knowledge. Adopting best practices of another organisation without understanding the context that supports the practice is bound to fail. It is akin to planting seeds in infertile soil. An interesting example is the adoption of QCC. Many Japanese companies use QCC for quality improvement, and the QCC movement is nationwide. However, attempts by organisations outside Japan to adopt the QCC have not been equally successful. Evidence shows that the success rate of the QCC initiative outside Japan was only around 20 percent. Many QCC initiatives fizzled out after the QCC convention.

Third, a problem that is usually present in trying to imitate the best practices of another organisation is imperfect knowledge. Imitators are not necessarily able to understand the broad range of capabilities that support the use of a good practice. For instance, what makes an airline successful? Is the success due to the type of aircraft that it uses? Is it the service that it provides? What about the role of culture and leadership? Is selecting the right people for the airline also important? An organisation is a complex configuration of capabilities. The strength of an organisation is never about one particular capability. Instead, it the synergistic combination of this complex set of capabilities. Quite often, even insiders are not sure how these capabilities interact to create the strengths of the organisation.

A strategist seeks to learn from the best practices of others. However, he or she also tries to understand the limitations of these practices. A strategist will assess the transferability of these practices to his or her organisation by looking at the internal capabilities in that organisation. More importantly, the strategist will seek to stimulate learning in his or her organisation to develop good practices that are compatible.

Early Signs of Decline

A good strategist has to be mindful of all these pitfalls and the causes of decline. It will help her or him see the future direction of the organisation without succumbing to the temptations to simply rely on the known and old formula for success. The strategist also needs to be wary of signs of internal decay that will lead to complacency and inability to learn and adapt. Lorange and Nelson identified a number of early warning signs of decline.

a. Excess personnel

When an organisation loses its focus and discipline, it starts having more people than it needs. As a result, it becomes inefficient, and the excess personnel start getting in the way of productive work. Excess personnel tend to have a negative multiplier effect. Not only do they raise the cost of the organisation, they also tend to have an impact on the processes of the organisation. An additional manager has to have subordinates and aides. Providing the manager with staff adds further to the cost. In addition, the new manager also becomes a conduit in any flow of information. This merely increases the possibility of distortion in the flow of information. In addition, it makes communication and decision-making slower. A strategist need to monitor simple metrics such as revenue per employee and net income per employee to see when these figures start to decline. That's the point where there are too much personnel and an early sign of decline.

b. Disproportionate staff power

When an organisation has more people than it needs, these people will start looking for something to do. It becomes particularly problematic when they are in staff functions. They do not directly impact the bottom line, yet they can make life difficult for others, especially line managers. The managers in these staff functions start interfering in the decisions and activities of line managers. Instead of supporting line functions, they try to dominate their line counterparts. This is especially the case when these staff managers have vague but powerful positions. One can see this happening especially when organisations start having many advisers, including senior advisers to the CEO or chairperson. This becomes especially problematic when the CEO or chairperson listens to these advisers more than they listen to their line managers. These advisers and senior advisers start overruling and interfering with decisions made by line managers.

c. Scarcity of clear goals

The lack of clear goals can manifest itself in a number of ways. One manifestation is the reliance on goals that are not grounded in reality. The goals do not address the problems faced by the organisation. Another manifestation is the tendency to develop goals that reflect the fad of the day. Before the 1997 Asian financial crisis, it was considered trendy to embrace globalisation. But not that many knew what it meant to be global. Related to this is the tendency to develop goals that sound sexy but are ambiguous to most people in the organisation. Most people in the organisation are unsure what the goals mean and what they need to do to achieve it. As a result, people in the organisation become inward looking. They become less concerned with their impact and just focus on executing routines and procedures. People in the organisation can be hardworking and committed, but they are not sure what they are working for. As a result, their effort does not have an impact on the overall performance of the organization.

d. Tolerance of incompetence

Related to the first three problems is tolerance of incompetence. Once organisations achieve success, some leaders start feeling complacent. They start to enjoy the wealth created by the success. They begin to assume that the success is self-sustaining. This is when they stop setting high standards and expectations. Instead, they begin to tolerate incompetence and mediocrity. In some cases, leaders start valuing those who make them feel good. These are followers who will only tell them the good news and avoid any mention of problems. The organisation starts believing that it is at the peak when in reality it is about to fall down the slippery slope. Leaders start living in their worlds of make believe.

e. Cumbersome administrative procedures

As organisations grow bigger, it increases the need to coordinate and control. It is no longer possible to monitor and coordinate through direct interaction. A typical response to this problem is to introduce rules and procedures. Over time, organisations tend to overdo and end up creating more rules and procedures that are counterproductive. People start spending more time filling forms and generating all kinds of low-value-added reports to comply with these rules and procedures. Along with all these rules and procedures is the creation of administrative units to enforce these rules and procedures. More often than not, they make life difficult for others without having any substantial impact on organisational performance. They slowly suffocate the organisation.

Insight Box 9.1

Looking Good at Olympus and Toshiba

In 2011, a scandal involving the Japanese company Olympus became public. It was involved in an attempt to hide investment losses estimated to be around USD1.5 billion. The concealment came to the attention of British-born Michael Woodfard, who was appointed president of the company. A report on the matter in a Japanese financial magazine caught his attention six months after he took office, and it raised his suspicion. He was then fired after exposing the matter.

Olympus finally admitted to having relied on inappropriate accounting practices to hide losses. Eleven people were arrested in Japan and the United States. The scandal wiped off more than 70 percent of the company's stock market value. Olympus had to terminate 2,700 employees to cut costs. Woodfard was paid GBP10 million as compensation for wrongful dismissal by Olympus.

Four years later, another scandal hit Japan when Toshiba was found to had also concealed its losses. The company had concealed losses of USD1.9 billion by inflating the company's profit since 2009. If in 2011 the Olympus scandal was considered the biggest corporate scandal in Japan, by 2015, Toshiba had overtaken Olympus in becoming Japan's biggest corporate fraud scandal.

In both cases, the leaders of the companies failed to deal with the problems in the company. Instead, they tried to create the impressions everything was well by hiding their losses.

---

f. Form replaces substance

A consequence of the above development is that leaders start being more concerned with appearance than substance. Managing impression becomes a form of self-assurance that things are okay. At the most extreme level, managing impression includes doctoring financial statements to hide problems. The public is misled into believing that everything is fine in spite of the fact that the company is imploding. The Olympus scandal in 2011 and the Toshiba scandal in 2015 in Japan are examples of such improprieties that result from a concern with form.

g. Fear of conflict and embarrassment

Dealing with problems means accepting that mistakes were made and dealing with them in a systematic and rational manner. However, in reality, this is not always easily done. Leaders sometimes make psychological investments in their decisions. They are not always willing to let go of bad decisions. Instead, they sometimes escalate their commitments to failed initiatives with the hope that things will get better. When such a decision is made by a senior leader, no one is prepared to be the messenger who brings bad news. As such, there is no debate or assessment of options. Everybody wants to avoid open conflict and embarrassing the leader. Instead, people either keep their opinions to themselves or only say what they think their leaders want to hear.

h. Loss of effective communication

The above developments converge to make communication more difficult in declining organisations. Cumbersome administrative procedures obstruct communication by creating elaborate steps and keeping people occupied with low-value-add activities instead of focusing on high-impact activities. Excess personnel create many levels that slow communication. Information gets filtered and sometimes even blocked. Fear of conflict and embarrassment makes people shun discussing problems in an honest and rational manner. The concern for form instead of substance makes leaders delusional and more concerned with looking good than taking actions that matter. In such a climate, communication tends to become distorted and more towards maintaining the delusion. People do not feel comfortable giving an honest opinion.

i. Outdated structure

The above developments also create a mindset where people are less concerned with being competitive. As such, the organisational structure is less oriented toward making the organisation more responsive to challenges in the environment. Instead, the organisation grows and creates a structure that insulates leaders from the realities of the external environment. This becomes a vicious cycle where the outdated structure creates an insular outlook that impedes leaders' abilities to adapt the structure to external realities. As a result, the organisation slides into decline.

Avoiding Decline

Decline is usually a gradual process. It is different from catastrophic failure where an event causes an organisation to collapse. Decline is more akin to the proverbial frog in a frying pan. Leaders may not realise they are experiencing decline. By the time they realise it, the situation may already be too late to avert a crash.

The ability to avoid and overcome decline is as much a strategic issue as the search for new markets and growths. Once an organisation has started to decline, it alienates some customers. If the decline is prolonged, it will also lead to job cuts and retrenchment. Jobs will be eliminated, and people will suffer. Even if the organisation recovers from decline, the stock of human capital that it still has will not be the same. The best people in the organisation may have already left.

a. Act proactively.

Chirantran Basu argues that leaders need to identify signs of decline early. This includes challenging lower and middle managers to identify areas of decline and the steps to rectify them. Create a climate where people are encouraged to be proactive in identifying issues and problems.

b. Create entities with clear accountabilities.

Lorange and Nelson propose that organisations should only create entities, new units, or departments or subsidiaries that have clearly defined purposes and are accountable for clear results. Avoid creating entities with vague roles. Since the role of such an entity is vague, the boundaries of their authority are difficult to define. If such a venture is led by unmotivated leaders, they'll end up doing little, and it becomes a cost and burden to the organisation. If the leader is someone ambitious, he or she may try to expand authority by doing many things that may be redundant and waste resources. Either way, nothing good will be achieved. Create only ventures that have a clearly defined outcome to be delivered.

c. Tie job definition to work.

For every position created in an organisation, there must be clearly defined purposes, roles, and performance targets. Avoid creating advisory positions that put people in high places with no defined limits to their authority. These individuals may end up interfering in the work of others. They have to justify their existence, and some do it by expanding their roles and intrude into the job responsibilities of other managers.

d. Benchmark against the toughest competitors.

Leaders have to be mindful of the complacency success can create. One way to push people to keep on improving is by benchmarking against toughest competitors. When a company is focused on overtaking the leader, it is less likely to be content with its current achievements. It provides people in the organisation with a specific goal to achieve. It galvanises their efforts and provides a sense of purpose. Companies that are already leaders in their market – like GE, Colgate Palmolive, and Proctor and Gamble – set the high target of being either number one or number two wherever they compete. Such a target motivates people in the organisation to work harder to please the customer to keep their positions.

e. Promote diversity.

Promote learning and improvement by encouraging people to express their views and debate the options available. Senior managers must be willing to stand back and let those below them express their views and even criticise current practices. This will help bring out the diverse range of opinions in the organisation. Organisations can also promote diversity by bringing in people from outside to the board and management team. This can help prevent the stereotype thinking that prevails when organisations are insular. A diverse set of people at various levels of the organisation will help bring fresh insights. They do not have emotional attachments to past decisions and initiatives, are not constrained in their thinking, and are less likely to simply take for granted current practices in the organisation.

f. Strengthen participation.

The ability to avoid decline depends on the ability to learn. Learning starts at the individual level. Crossan points out that individuals sense problems and opportunities. However, this learning will not translate into organisational learning if the insights gained by the individual are not shared, subjected to scrutiny, and assessed by others. The process of evaluating learning and debating the merits of an idea helps refine it and determine its viability. Once there is agreement on the merits of an idea, it can then be adopted and institutionalised in the organisation. This involves adapting the organisation by changing its procedures and policies. For this process to take place, the organisation must be willing to create room for people to participate in decision-making and sharing their experiences with others. Strengthening participation helps support continuous learning that is a prerequisite to adaptation and avoiding decline.

Capacity for Change

For organisations competing in fast-changing environments, change is a constant, and they often need to initiate frequent changes. These companies can also invest in developing their capacities for change. Organisations with high capacity for change find undergoing change much easier and less traumatic.

The capacity to change is something that should be built even before a change initiative is started. This includes building the foundations to make people receptive to change. Among the things that can be done to achieve this is developing absorptive capacity and psychological resilience.

Absorptive capacity

Cohen Levinthal defines absorptive capacity as an organisation's ability to recognise the value of new knowledge and assimilate it and use it successfully for commercial application. Absorptive capacity is necessary for sustaining innovation. Likewise, strategic change requires that organisations have the ability to absorb new knowledge in order to develop new capabilities. Organisations that have low absorptive capacity have greater difficult understanding the value of new knowledge and assimilating it. They are slow to recognise the benefits that can be gained from new knowledge. When they do try to assimilate new knowledge, it is because they noticed others doing it and are trying to play catch-up with what others do.

For instance, look at the diffusion of management techniques. Organisations that have high absorptive capacities tend to recognise the value of new management techniques and, when suitable, seek to adopt them. Low absorptive capacity organisations tend to adopt them much later because they tend to be slow to recognise the value of new ideas, tend to have high inertia, and will jump on the bandwagon only when many others have done so. In fact, high absorptive capacity organisations are able to generate and sustain continuous learning. They are able to generate and accept the flow of new knowledge as a natural part of their learning cultures.

Organisations that have high absorptive capacity are faster learners. During a change initiative, high absorptive capacity organisation are faster in learning and adopting new approaches, technologies, and techniques. For low absorptive capacity organisations, it is not uncommon for them to start an initiative to adopt a new management technique because of instructions from the top. Sometimes they do so with a superficial understanding of what it is all about.

Cohen and Levinthal point out that the ability to understand the value of and assimilate new knowledge is typically the product of prior learning. Those who have done more learning have a broader knowledge base. This broad knowledge base enables them to see the connection between ideas. It helps us see the value of new knowledge.

Developing absorptive capacity requires long-term investment. It cannot be developed by just organizing a workshop or having a launching ceremony on absorptive capacity. Instead, absorptive capacity is the product of long-term learning and organisational arrangements that facilitate learning. Absorptive capacity exists at the individual and organisational levels. Organisations need to ensure that learning at the individual level is captured and diffused at the organisational level. Organisational knowledge is always less than the aggregated knowledge of the members of the organisation. Organisations have different levels of ability to capture the learning of its members. Some are more effective, and some are simply ineffective. The effective ones are able to create the mechanisms to enhance absorptive capacity at both levels.

Individual-level absorptive capacity is the product of the individual's prior learning. This includes not only the amount of learning but also the breadth of learning. Individuals who accumulate experience and learn knowledge in multiple areas develop a higher level of absorptive capacity. For instance, an engineering researcher who spent all his or her career in a university lab will naturally have a lot of knowledge about an area of specialisation. However, an engineer who had worked in industry, performed managerial duties in addition to engineering work, had been involved in product design and launching it in the market, and attended training programs to develop managerial and leadership skills will naturally have a broader knowledge base. The engineering researcher knows a lot but about a little because of a narrow specialisation and limited work exposure. However, compared to the other engineer, the research engineer's ability to value knowledge outside his or her area of expertise and ability to assimilate new knowledge will be low.

Organisational-level absorptive capacity is created through knowledge-sharing structures and processes. In these organisations, knowledge from one location of the organisation is shared with and transferred to other locations in the organisation. This is done through the use of cross-functional teams, boundary-spanning roles, and gatekeepers. Cross-functional teams create the ability to share different functional perspectives when dealing with problems. Cross-functional teams are akin to bridges that connect islands. The team members who come from different functional backgrounds are able to enrich the understanding of other team members. In addition, individual learning is refined and amplified as a result of this experience.

Boundary spanners are individuals who act to connect various teams and functional areas. They help to connect people and bring ideas from one part of the organisation to other parts of the organisation. Typically, they are individuals who are quite high up in the organisation, are respected by others, and are able to assess the value and potential of ideas. Gatekeepers serve to manage the flow of ideas. Having too much information can also be overwhelming. The gatekeepers help to prioritise and manage the flow of information. Quite often they also liaise with top management so that team members can focus on their jobs. The gatekeeper keeps top management updated on progress and sometimes secures needed resources for the team.

On the other hand, organisations that work as silos and where people cannot see beyond their immediate work units or functional areas tend to share little knowledge and have low absorptive capacity. In fact, knowledge generated in one part of the organisation is often unnoticed by others. These organisations also suffer from organisational amnesia because of their inabilities to learn from each other and from their past experiences. Even when these organisations have many smart and knowledgeable people inside it, the organisation itself can still be dumb.

Organisations that have processes and structures that support knowledge sharing will find learning new ideas, critically examining current practices and knowledge, and adapting to these insights much easier. Strategic change will be easier to affect in these organisations. On the other hand, organisations that do not have processes and structures that support organisational learning will find change more difficult and awkward.

The level of absorptive capacity an organisation has will affect the speed of organisational learning that can take place. This subsequently affects its ability to adapt. Organisations that invest in developing their absorptive capacities will be better able to deal with changes in the external environment.

Psychological resilience

Psychological resilience is the ability to recover from setbacks and hardship, and the adaptability to adjust to shifting demands. Shin, Taylor, and Seo argue that employees' commitments to change can be developed by building up their personal abilities to overcome the strains and stresses experienced during a change process. It is created by providing support to create a positive work experience among organisational members. When this becomes a part of their regular experiences, they become more confident of their abilities to deal with uncertainties during change. In fact, such resilience is more likely to generate optimistic thinking and experience positive emotion during change. Shin, Taylor, and Seo argue that it helps members prepare for the hardships and stresses expected during change. They also point out that individuals with high psychological resilience tend to develop positive attitudes and high commitment levels.

Leaders will experience difficulties mobilizing the members of their organisations if their members' prior experiences in the organisation make them cynical and they have a negative attitude. Studies on psychological resilience show that it exists at the individual as well as collective levels. Individual psychological resilience (IPR) is a personal attribute that creates a positive attitude when facing stress, hardship, and uncertainty. Collective psychological resilience (CPR) is a collective attribute that enables individuals to come together, provide mutual support and assistance, and deal with the challenges before them.

IPR is the product of prior positive experiences. IPR develops from the experience of being treated fairly, having trust and a good relationship between members of the organisation and their leaders. Prior negative experiences will undermine psychological resilience. Most, if not all, individuals join organisations with the expectations that they will be treated fairly. When this expectation is violated, it erodes trust in the organisation. One of the responses to this erosion of trust is that people retreat and refocus their loyalties. A study done by this author found that a negative experience, such as downsizing, can lead to a perception of unfairness. When this happens, employees who remain in the organisation become more distrusting towards management. Instead, they shift their trust and commitment to their peers. Krasikova, Green, and LeBreton point out that this can also happen when leaders are seen as abusive or tyrannical and create stress and negative experiences among their followers. On the other hand, employees who are treated fairly are more likely to exhibit favourable attitudes towards change. They are more likely to be trusting towards their leaders and the motive for the change initiative. As such, they are more willing to commit themselves to the change process.

The theory on CPR is developed from research on behaviour during emergencies and disasters. Drury points out that contrary to popular stereotypes, people tend to be self-organizing during emergencies and disasters. Instead of becoming chaotic and panicked, they get together and figure out how to deal with the situation. They rely on their network of family members and close friends to help one another. This highlights the importance of social relationships in developing CPR. Helping members of an organisation develop social bonding can help them rely on each other when confronted with crises and uncertainties. Drury also points out that even complete strangers can develop this bond when they perceive themselves as sharing a common fate. Evidence on the behaviour of passengers trapped in underground trains during the London bombing of 2007 shows that complete strangers can get together to support one another during the incident. CPR can also develop when individuals perceive themselves as facing a common threat to survival.

Developing strategic leaders involves developing leaders who are mindful of how their behaviours affect their followers and their abilities to mobilise them during change. Strategic leaders need to be aware that developing IPR and CPR involves developing a climate that creates a positive experience and a sense of common destiny. Open and frequent dialogue is important in fostering mutual understanding and trust. This includes being open to criticism and feedback. Leaders need to overcome – in fact, dismantle – the barriers to direct communication and interaction. The use of cross-functional teams, job rotation, and even social activities can help develop the bonding that enhances the level of CPR.

Organisations that consciously invest in developing IPR and CPR will find it easier to win over support and commitment during change. As mentioned earlier, among the barriers to developing IPR and CPR are unfairness, politicking, silo mentality, and a hierarchical orientation where leaders tend to maintain as much distance from their followers as possible. Unfairness will undermine IPR. The divisive nature of political behaviour undermines positive feelings and divides people, thus reducing IPR and CPR. A silo mentality prevents people from working together across functional boundaries and undermines CPR. It causes people to retreat into their personal shells and not work with others. Perhaps this is why Christoph Mueller considers overcoming the silo mentality at Malaysia Airlines important.

It takes a lot of sincerity and commitment to create a climate that can nurture IPR and CPR. Followers will judge their leaders by their actions. No amount of impression management can overcome insincere and abusive behaviours. Some leaders say all the right things but act in a different manner. This author once complemented a physician for the "open door leadership" announced by his hospital's director. The physician smiled cynically and commented, "Well, there is not much use in having an open door policy if the mind remains closed."

Developing absorptive capacity enhances an organisation's ability to learn and willingness to adapt. Inevitably, this adaptation can cause uncertainty and stress. Psychological resilience provides the strength and energy to face uncertainty, adversity, and stress during change. As such, both are important resources to enable change to happen. The ability to adapt to change should be an enduring capability for organisations competing in dynamic environments. Strategic leaders need to invest in developing this enduring capability to ensure sustained performance.

Closing

A strategic leader has to be able to understand changes in the external environment. At the same time, the strategic leader must be mindful of the organisation's internal capabilities. The leader must assess when these capabilities are assets and when they become liabilities. A strategic leader has to be able to realign and reconfigure an organisation's internal capabilities to remain competitive. He or she must be slightly paranoid and accept the possibility that failure is just around the corner. The strategic leader must be alert to threats and opportunities from the external environment and vigilant about liabilities from within the organisation. Understand these must be a part of the strategic thinking process. Taking steps to avert disaster by initiating the necessary changes is also the strategic leader's responsibility. All of these must be done by using her or his influence and persuasion skills to get others to commit to the needed changes.

CONCLUSION

Starting the Journey

The pathway to strategic leadership is a journey of personal transformation. The strategic leadership role requires leaders who can think beyond operational issues. Strategic leaders need to be able to adapt to a different role when they assume a top management position. However, this transition is not always smooth and easy.

Not all organisations differentiate between leadership development programs for lower and middle managers from leadership development programs for strategic leadership programs. This limits the effectiveness of strategic leadership development programs. Leaders may become better at what they are currently doing, but this does not make them ready for advancement to a senior leadership position.

This book proposes a model of strategic leadership competencies. The model consists of basic competencies needed to be an effective strategic leader. This model is general enough that it can address the strategic leadership competencies needed by most organisations. Management can adapt this model to their unique conditions. For some organisations with a global presence, developing leaders with cross-cultural leadership abilities will be important. Likewise, organisations that rely on technology to compete may find the competency to manage technology a strategic competency that its strategic leaders should have. All these can be incorporated into the strategic leadership competency model for such organisations.

The Learning Journey

It should be highlighted that the strategic leadership competency model shown in this book does not negate the need to develop basic leadership competencies. Leaders need to develop their abilities to lead teams, maintain a high level of motivation among their followers, manage performances, plan task executions, and monitor operations. While the success of strategic leadership in businesses is often measured in terms of financial performance, getting there is about leading people. These competencies will continue to be important and will complement the strategic leadership competencies.

A point highlighted in this book is that developing strategic leadership competencies is more than just providing additional knowledge on strategy or strategic leadership skills. Instead, it will involve changing thinking habits and developing new insights and experiences. This includes the experience of working outside one's functional area. Since this typically involves getting out of one's comfort zone, this form of learning is as much about overcoming the psychological barrier and changing old habits formed by past work experience as it is about assessing the business landscape. It also involves developing the resilience to deal with ambiguities and the stress in dealing with the unfamiliar.

Affecting these changes in our mindsets and habits often requires an experience that stretches our imaginations and forces us to want to search for new ideas. This will require exposing leaders to demanding situations that will force them to use their creativity. Leaders also have to accept the possibility that they will make mistakes as they undergo this learning experience. They have to be willing to repeat their efforts and reflect on their mistakes. Insight can only be gained by those seeking it. Quite often this requires others to help provide insights on a person's shortcomings. As such, the learning process will benefit from have a mentor.

The learning a strategic leader has to undergo is like a journey with many junctions. He or she has a compass to enable to find one's bearings and a crude map to indicate the approximate route to take to reach the desired destination. A strategic leader has to create his or her own map as different routes are tried, and a better understanding of the terrain is achieved. The strategic leader's journey is a journey of discovery and continuous learning.

Those responsible for developing strategic leadership talent need to prepare a comprehensive learning plan. In addition to training programs, the learning plan should include work-based learning and relationship-based learning. They also have to sell this learning plan to line managers and top management. Line managers and top management have to be committed and support the many activities that will be implemented. Above all, those who are groomed to become strategic leaders must be motivated to learn and develop themselves.

Personal Motivation

The preceding discussion also highlights that only those who are self-motivated will benefit from strategic leadership development programs. Those who have to be spoon-fed knowledge will gain only a little from the learning experience. They will know what they are told without ever developing insights about the knowledge gained. They gain knowledge but not necessarily wisdom.

Only someone who is motivated to learn will be motivated to question what she or he knows. Those lacking the motivation to learn are usually content with whatever is given to them. The wise leader becomes wiser because of a questioning attitude. Passive learners do not become wiser and are less likely to become good strategists.

Many large organisations have talent development programs that seek to develop strategic leadership competencies. Those selected to join these programs should find the experience challenging and enriching. Typically, these programs are designed to go in tandem with career and succession planning. They demand a lot of time and effort from managers. Participants need to have the energy and drive to undergo this program.

Managers working in small and medium-size organisations can also develop their strategic leadership competencies. However, small and medium-size organisations usually do not have the resources and sophistication to develop talent management programs. Managers in such organisations can make their efforts to develop their leadership competencies. Among the key steps they have to take are

1. Seek a diverse work experiences.

    Managers should seek experiences beyond their functional areas to gain an understanding of the complexity in running an organisation and the synergy that should be created across functional areas. This will help them develop a system perspective of the organisation.

2. Volunteer to join cross-functional teams.

The organisation may establish cross-functional teams to deal with specific problems such as the launching of new products. Joining such a team will provide a rich experience in dealing with business problems and coordinating actions across functions. This would typically involve initiating and managing change. It will also help develop networks and influence in the organisation.

3. Find opportunities to gain experience in dealing with customers.

There is no substitute for dealing with customers when it comes to understanding the market. Certain functions, like sales and marketing, have more contact with customers. But functions such as finance, HR, and production can be insulated from customers. Managers in functions such as these should offer to participate in activities involving customers. They participate in customer focus-group discussions, visit customers, and help assess customer feedback.

4. Participate in dealing with crises.

Organisations deal with crises from time to time. A problem becomes a crisis simply because it is novel, unprecedented, threatens the organization, and there are no clear procedures on how to solve it. Getting involved in dealing with crises can provide experience density to managers. The complexity and novelty presence in a crisis also requires creative thinking.

5. Get feedback from others.

It is typical for us to not see some qualities that we have. This includes both strengths and weaknesses. Some of these qualities only surface when we are under stress, deal with crises, and are pushed outside our comfort zones. It is therefore important to seek feedback from others to enable us to understand these qualities and use the information to plan our improvement.

It should be evident from the discussion in this book that developing strategic leadership competencies is not a short journey. It will take time and commitment. The HR function has an important role to play in designing and implementing a sound strategic leadership development program. In most organisations, it is the key focus of their talent management program. It is hoped that this book has made a contribution to our understanding of the key elements in designing such a program.

As a concluding point, it should be noted that strategic leaders can make the world a better place or a much worse place. It is typical for the effectiveness of strategic leaders to be assessed based on financial performances. Some leaders create profit in the short term but destroy value in the long term.

Strategic leaders need to recognise that they are citizens of the world. The actions and decisions strategic leaders take can affect the environment, social justice, and well-being of others. It is important that we instil conscience as a key quality for those occupying strategic leadership positions. Organisations need to develop strategic leaders who are driven by a cause bigger than just making money. Profit should be a reward for doing greater good. Professionals such as physicians, pilots, and research scientists earn their rewards for serving a greater good. Physicians are supposed to diligently treat their patients. Pilots are supposed to fly their planes and reach their destinations safely. Researchers are supposed to contribute to knowledge and develop something useful for humankind. Why should strategic leaders in business be any different? Leading with conscience is not a trade-off for running a profitable business. It is a sine qua non in ensuring we are clear of our priorities in pursuing profit. The primary role of all strategic leaders is to make this world a better place.

GLOSSARY

Absorptive capacity: An organisation's ability to recognise the value of new knowledge, assimilate it, and use it successfully for commercial application.

Behavioural momentum: The tendency for people to continue behaving the way they always did because of the influence and habits formed through past behaviours and experiences.

Benefit realisation: The benefits that an organisation intends to create during a change process.

Capacity for change: An organisation's versatility and ability to accept and undergo change.

Causal ambiguity: The lack of clarity on the cause-effect relationship, affecting an outcome or an organisation's performance.

Causal thinking: The ability to assess and understand a problem by identifying the outcomes and the causes that create the outcome.

Change impact assessment: An assessment of what has to change in order to create the benefits the organisation intends to realise.

Change readiness assessment: An assessment of the extent an organisation's members are ready to support and implement change.

Dato/Dato Seri: An honorary title awarded by Malaysia's king or by one of the sultans in Malaysian states.

Deliberate practice: A learning approach that involves creating the opportunity to try the skills being taught, make mistakes, learn from the mistakes, and make repeated attempts in order to gain mastery.

Emphatic emotion: The ability to be aware of and understand the emotions of others.

Equifinality: The understanding that a given outcome or goal can be potentially reached through many different ways.

Experience density: The process of drawing out a learner's creativity and enriching his or her experience by exposing the learner to stress and challenges.

Inhibitive motivation: The desire to avoid causing harm to others and accepting responsibility for one's actions.

Knowledge brokering: Process of identifying what knowledge is needed in an organisation, where this knowledge is located, and connecting the types of knowledge with those needing the knowledge.

Learning mix: The combination of learning methods used in a learning program. Typically, this involves the combination of formal learning, experience-based learning, and relationship-based learning.

Leadership competency model: A model of the competencies of an effective leader.

Moral boundary: A boundary set by one's moral and ethical standards that defines what is appropriate and what is not appropriate.

Moral courage: The courage and persistence to behave according to one's moral standards.

Motivation to lead: An individual's willingness to assume leadership.

Need for cognition: A person's tendency to engage and enjoy thinking efforts.

Proactive motivation: The desire and motivation to do good on one's own initiative.

Psychological resilience: The ability to face uncertainty, adversity, and stress.

Reflective learning: The process of rationally examining and exploring an issue encountered during a learning experience to gain insight about how the learner dealt with the issue.

Stakeholder engagement: The process of engaging stakeholders at the beginning of a change initiative to understand the case for change and the benefit the organisation is seeking to realise from the initiative.

Talent pool: A select group of high-performance, high-potential managers who are chosen to undergo a systematic talent development program.

Talent sea: An approach that treats all managers as potential future leaders and involves all of them in the talent development process.

REFERENCES

Chapter 1

Beatty, Katherine, and Richard Hughes. "Strategic aims: Making the right moves in leadership." *Leadership in Action* 25 No. 4 (2005): 3–6.

Miles, Raymond, Charles Snow, Alan Meyer, and Henry Coleman. "Organisational strategy, structure, and process." *The Academy of Management Review* 3 No. 3(1978): 546–562.

Mintzberg, Henry."The rise and fall of strategic planning." *Harvard Business Review,* Jan–Feb (1994): 107–114.

Ohmae, Kenichi. *The Mind of the Strategist: The Art of Japanese Business.* New York: McGraw-Hill, 1982.

Sidhu, Bala. "Tough turnaround for Malaysia Airlines." *Asiaone Business.* http://business.asiaone.com/news/tough-turnaround-malaysia-airlines#sthash.wXggBGfZ.dpuf (accessed 7 May 2015).

Chapter 2

Beatty, Katherine, and Richard Hughes. "Strategic aims: Making the right moves in leadership." *Leadership in Action* 25 No. 4 (2005): 3–6.

Beatty, Katherine, and Richard Hughes. "Reformulating strategic leadership." *European Business Forum* 21 (2005): 14–17.

Byrne, John. *World Changers: Entrepreneurs Who Changed Business as We Knew It.* New York: Penguin, 2011.

Chen, Kim, and Fritz Drasgow. "Towards a theory of individual differences and leadership: Understanding the motivation to lead." *Journal of Applied Psychology* 86 No. (2001): 481–498.

Corson, Myles, and Tomohiro Miyagawa. "Global CFO: From scorekeeper to strategist." *FinancialExecutive* (November 2012): 20–23.

De Vries, Reinout, Robert Roe, and Thasi Tallieu. "Need for leadership as a moderator of the relationships between leadership and individual outcomes." *The Leadership Quarterly* 13 (2002): 121–137.

Gavetti, Giovanni. "The new pscyhology of strategic leadership." *Harvard Business Review* (January–April 2011): 118–125.

Graetz, Fiona. "Strategic thinking versus strategic planning; towards understanding the complementarities." *Management Decision* 40:5 (2012): 456–462.

Hughes, Richard, and Katherine Beatty. "Five steps to lead strategically." *Training and Development* (December 2005): 46–48.

Kaplan, Robert, and David Norton. *Strategy Focused Organisation.* Boston: Harvard Business School Press, 2001.

Liedtka, Jeanne. "Strategic thinking: Can it be taught?" *Long Range Planning* 31 No. 1 (1998): 120–129.

Mintzberg, Henry. "Patterns in strategy formation." *Management Science* 24 No. 9 (1978): 934–948.

Mintzberg, Henry. "The rise and fall of strategic planning." *Harvard Business Review* (Jan–Feb 1994): 107–114.

Moon, B. J. (2013). "Antecedents and outcomes of strategic thinking." *Journal of Business Research* 66 No. 10 (2013): 1698–1708.

Ohmae, Kenichi. *The Mind of the Strategist: The Art of Japanese Business.* New York: McGraw-Hill, 1982.

Schoemaker, Paul, Steve Krupp, and Samantha Howland. "Strategic leadership: The essential skills. *Harvard Business Review* (Jan–Feb 2013): 131–134.

"A history almost a century old." MMC. http://www.mmc.com.my/content.asp?menuid=100008&rootid=100000 (accessed on 1 December 2014).

"Twelve lessons from Jack Welch's leadership style," *Vietnamworks.* http://advice.vietnamworks.com/en/hiring/effective-management/twelve-lessons-jack-welch-s-leadership-style.html-0 (accessed on 23 March 2015).

"Jack Welch on how to manage employees." *Entrepreneur.* http://www.entrepreneur.com/article/224604 (accessed on 23 March 2015).

Chapter 3

Amabile, Teresa. "Motivating creativity in organisations: On doing what you love and loving what you do." *California Management Review* 40 No. 1 (1997): 39–58.

Byrne, John. *World Changers: Entrepreneurs Who Changed Business As We Knew It.* New York: Penguin, 2011.

Eisenhardt, Kathleen, and Donald Sull. "Strategy as simple rules." *Harvard Business Review* (January 2001): 107–116.

McGrath, Rita. "On the pitfalls of superstitious learning." *Harvard Business Review* (July 2011): 7–9.

Kogut, Bruce, and Udo Zander. "Knowledge of the firm, combinative capabilities and the replication of technology." *Organisation Science* 3 (1992): 383–397.

Liedtka, Jeanne. "Strategic thinking: Can it be taught?" *Long Range Planning* 31 No. 1 (1998): 120–129.

Miller, Danny. "The architecture of simplicity." *Academy of Management Review* 18 No. 1 (1993): 116–138.

Moon, Byeong-Joon. "Antecedents and outcomes of strategic thinking." *Journal of Business Research* 66 No. 10 (2013): 1698–1708.

Mumford, Michael, Samuel Hunter, Dawn Eubanks, Katrina Bedell, and Steen Murphy. "Developing leaders for creative efforts: A domain-based approach to leadership development." *Human Resource Management Review* 17 (2007): 402–417.

Ohmae, Kenichi. *The Mind of the Strategist: The Art of Japanese Business.* New York: McGraw-Hill.

Othman, Rozhan, and Rohayu Abd Ghani. "Supply chain management and suppliers' HRM practice." *Supply Chain Management: An International Journal*, 13 No. 4 (2008): 259–262.

Othman, Rozhan. "Balanced scorecard and causal model development: Preliminary findings." *Management Decision* 44 No. 5 (2006): 690–702.

Othman, Rozhan, Rasidah Arshad, Rosmah Md Isa, and Noor Azuan Hashim. "Psychological contract violation and organisational citizenship behaviour." *Gajah Mada International Journal of Business* 7 No. 3 (2005).

Schoemaker, Paul, Steve Krupp, and Samantha Howland. "Strategic leadership: The essential skills. *Harvard Business Review* (Jan–Feb (2013): 131–134.

Sirmon, David, Michael Hitt, and Duane Ireland. "Managing firm resources in dynamic environments to create value: Looking inside the black box." *Academy of Management Review* 32 (2007): 273–292.

Slywotzky, Adrian, and David Morrison. *The Profit Zone: How Strategic Business Design Will Lead You to Tomorrow's Profits.* New York: Three Rivers Press, 2002.

"Tony Fernandes on Driving ASEAN entrepreneurship." McKinsey. com. http://www.mckinsey.com/insights/public_sector/tony_fernandes_on_driving_asean_entrepreneurship (accessed 24 March 2015).

"Lesson #1: Take your market research to the streets." Evanmichael.com. http://www.evancarmichael.com/Famous-Entrepreneurs/1158/Lesson-1-Take-Your-Market-Research-to-the-Streets.html (accessed 25 March 2015).

"Xerox Was Actually First to Invent the PC, They Just Forgot to Do Anything with It." *Business Insider.* http://www.businessinsider.com/xerox-was-actually-first-to-invent-the-pc-they-just-forgot-to-do-anything-with-it-2012-2?IR=T& (accessed 15 May 2015).

Chapter 4

Battilana, Julie, Mattia Gilmartin, Matin Sengul, Anna-Claire Pache, and Jeffry Alexander. "Leadership competencies for implementing planned change." *The Leadership Quarterly* 21 (2010): 422–438.

Drury, John. "Collective resilience in mass emergencies and disasters: A social identity model." In Jetten, Jolanda, Catherine Haslam, and Alexander Haslam (eds.), *The Social Cure: Identity, Health and Well-being.* Hove: Psychology Press, 2012.

Greve, Henrich. "Microfoundations of management: Behavioural strategies and levels of rationality in organisational actions. *Academy of Management Perspective* 27 No. 2 (2013): 120–137.

Kahn, William. "Psychological conditions of personal engagement & disengagement at work." *Academy of Management Journal* 33 (1990): 692–724.

Krasikova, Dina, Stephens Green, and James LeBreton. "Refining and extending our understanding of destructive leadership." *Journal of Management* 39 (2013): 1308–1338.

Lewis, Laurie, Amy Schmissuer, Keri Stephens, and Kahtleen Weir. "Advice on communicating during organisational change." *Journal of Business Communication* 43 No. 2 (2006): 113–137.

Marino, Kenneth. "Developing consensus on competencies and capabilities." *Academy of Management Executive* 10 No. 3 (1996): 40–51.

Norzailan, Zumalia, Shazlinda Md Yusof, and Rozhan Othman. "Developing strategic leadership competencies." *Journal of Advances in Management Sciences* 4 No. 1 (2016): 66–71.

Othman, Rozhan, and Noor Azuan Hashim. "Typologizing organisational amnesia." *The Learning Organisation* 11 No. 3 (2004): 273–284.

Othman, Rozhan, Rasidah Arshad, Rosmah Md Isa, and Noor Azuan Hashim. "Psychological contract violation and organisational citizenship behaviour." *Gajah Mada International Journal of Business* 7 No. 3 (2005): 325–349.

Radzi, Nur Izzah, and Rozhan Othman. "Resistance to change: The moderating effects of leader-member exchange and role breadth self-efficacy." *Journal of Advances in Management Sciences* 4:1 (2016): 72–76.

Shin, Jiseon, Susan Taylor, and Myeong-Gyu Seo. "Resources for change: The relationships of organisational inducements and psychological resilience to employees' attitudes and behaviours towards organisational change." *Academy of Management Journal* 55 No. 3 (2012): 727–748.

Sidhu, Bala. "Tough turnaround for Malaysia Airlines." *Asiaone Business.* http://business.asiaone.com/news/tough-turnaround-malaysia-airlines#sthash.wXggBGfZ.dpuf (accessed 7 May 2015).

Van Dam, Karen, Shaul Oreg, and Brigit Schyns. "Daily work contexts and resistance to organisational change: The role of leader–member exchange, development climate, and change process characteristics." *Applied Psychology* 57 No. 2 (2008): 313–334.

Chapter 5

Ahlin, Johan, Eva Ericson-Lidman, Astrid Norberg, and Gunilla Strandberg. "Revalidation of the perception of conscience and the stress of conscience questionnaire." *Nursing Ethics* 19 No. 2 (2012): 220–232.

Ahlin, Johan, Eva Ericson-Lidman, Astrid Norberg, and Gunilla Strandberg. "Longitudinal relationships between stress of conscience and concepts of importance." *Nursing Ethics* 20 No. 8 (2013): 927–942.

Baker, Aryn, and Erik Stier. "The women at the head of Yemen's protest movement." *Time* February 16 (2011).

Boddy, Clive. "The dark side of management decisions: Organisational psychopaths." *Management Decision* 44 No 10 (2006): 461–475.

Byrne, John. *World Changers: Entrepreneurs Who Changed Business as We Knew It.* New York: Penguin, 2011.

Elshtain, Jean. "Is there such a thing as the female conscience?" *Virginia Quarterly Review* Fall (2012): 17–25.

Foss, Nicholai, and S. Siegwart Lindenberg. "Microfoundations for strategy: A goal-framing perspective on the drivers of value creation." *Academy of Management Perspective* 27 No. 2 (2013): 85–102.

Griffin, Beryl, and Barbara Hesketh. Counseling for work adjustment. In Brown, Steven, and Robert Lent (eds.), *Career Development and Counseling: Putting Theory and Research to Work* (pp. 483–505). Hoboken, New Jersey: Wiley, 2005.

Ho, Joann, and Zabid Abdul Rahman. "Perception of ethics in a multi-cultural community: The case of Malaysia." *Journal of Business Ethics* 43 (2003): 75–87.

Lim, W. H. "Something from nothing." *The Star*, 5 October 2015.

Mandela, Nelson. "Long Walk to Freedom." New York: Little Brown & Co., 1995.

Mintzberg, Henry. "Patterns in strategy formation." *Management Science* 24 No. 9 (1998): 934–948.

Musa, Bakri. *Liberating the Malay Mind.* Petaling Jaya; ZI Publications, 2013.

Sepper, Elizabeth. "Taking conscience seriously." *Virginia Quarterly Review* (16 October 2012): 1501–1575.

Svensson, Manfred. "Augustine on moral conscience." *The Heythrop Journal* 54 No. 1 (2013): 42–54.

Volling, B., A. Mahoney, and A. Rauer. "Sanctification of parenting, moral socialisation, and young children's conscience development." *Psychology of Religion and Spirituality* 1 No. 1 (2009): 53–68.

"Tawakkol Karman." *Wikipedia,* https://en.wikipedia.org/wiki/Tawakkol_Karman (accessed 18 April 2015).

Chapter 6

Aryee, Samuel, Pawan Budhawar, and Zhen Chen. "Trust as a mediator of the relationship between organisational justice and work outcomes: Test of a social exchange model." *Journal of Organisational Behaviour* 23 (2002): 267–285.

Claman, Priscilla. "6 ways to disagree with senior management." *Harvard Business Review* (June 2016).

Horton, Keith. "Strategy, practice and the dynamics of power." *Journal of Business Research* 56 (2003): 121–126.

Caldini, Robert. "Harnessing the science of persuasion." *Harvard Business Review* (October 2001): 72–79.

Hargadon, Anthony. *How Breakthrough Happens: The Surprising Truth about How Companies Innovate.* Boston: Harvard Business Press, 2003.

Uhl-Bien, Mary, and John Maslyn. "Reciprocity in manager-subordinate relationships: Components, configurations, and outcomes." *Journal of Management* 29 No. 4 (2003): 511–532.

Chapter 7

Alldredge, Margaret, and Kevin Nilan. "3M's leadership competency model: An internally developed solution." *Human Resouce Management* 39 No. 2–3 (2000): 133–145.

Avery, Derek, Scott Tonidandel, Kristin Griffith, and Miguel Quiñones. "The impact of multiple measures of leader experience on leader effectiveness. New insights for leader selection." *Journal of Business Research* 56 No. 8 (2003): 673–679.

Boehm, Virginia. "Using assessment centres for management development— Five applications." *Journal of Management Development* 4 No. 4 (1985): 40–53.

Breaugh, Jones. "Modeling the managerial promotion process." *Journal of Managerial Psychology* 26 No. 4 (2011): 264–277.

Chao, Georgia. "Mentoring phases and outcomes." *Journal of Vocational* 51 No. 1 (1997): 15–28.

Chiang, Fiora, and Thomas Birtch. "Appraising performance across borders: An empirical examination of the purposes and practices of performance appraisal in a multi-country context." *Journal of Management Studies* 47 No. 7 (2010): 1365–1393.

Collings, David. "Toward mature talent management: Beyond shareholder value." *Human Resource Development Quarterly* 25 No. 3 (2014): 301–319.

Collings, David, and Kamel Mellahi. "Strategic talent management: A review and research agenda." *Human Resource Management Review* 19 No. 4 (2009): 304–313.

Coughlan, Edward., Mark Williams, Allistair McRobert, and Paul Ford. "How experts practice: A novel test of deliberate practice theory." *Journal of Experimental Psychology:Learning, Memory, and Cognition* 40 No. 2 (2013): 449–458.

Crandell, Stuart. "Assessment centers in talent management: strategies, use and value." *Personnel Decisions International (PDI)* (2008): 4.

Cremer, Andreas, and Tom Bergin. "Fear and respect: VW's culture under Winterkorn." *Reuters.* http://www.reuters.com/article/2015/10/10/us-volkswagen- emissions-culture-idUSKCN0S40MT20151010 (accessed on 10 October 2015).

Dziczkowski, Jennifer. "Mentoring and leadership development." *The Educational Forum* 77 No. 3 (2013): 351–360.

Ericsson, Anders, Raif Krampe, and Clemens Tesch-Romer. "The role of deliberate practice in the acquisition of expert performance." *Psychological Review* 100 No. 3 (1993): 363–406.

Farndale, Ellain, Hugh Scullion, and Paul Sparrow. "The role of the corporate HR function in global talent management." *Journal of World Business* 45 No. 2 (2010): 161–168.

Fernandez-Araoz, Claudia, Boris Groysberg, and Nittin Nohria. "How to Hang on to your high potentials." *Harvard Business Review* October (2011): 76–83.

Garavan, Thomas, Ronan Carbery, and Andrew Rock. "Mapping talent development: Definition, scope and architecture." *European Journal of Training and Development* 36 No. 1 (2012): 5–24.

Gibson, Donald, and Diane Cordova. "Women's and men's role models: The importance of exemplars." In Murrell, Audrey, Faye Crosby, and Robin Ely (eds.). *Mentoring Dilemmas: Developmental Relationships within Multicultural Organisations.* Mahwah, NJ: Erlbaum, 1999.

Hambrick, David, Frederick Oswald, Erik Altmann, Elizabeth Meinz, Ferschund Gobet, and Guillermo Campitelli. "Deliberate practice: Is that all it takes to become an expert?" *Intelligence* (2013): 1–12.

Harvey, Michael, Ronald Buckley, Joyce Heames, Robert Zinko, Robyn Brouer, and Gerald Ferris. "A bully as an archetypal destructive leader." *Journal of Leadership and Organisational Studies* 14 No. 2 (2007): 117–129.

Haskins, Mark, and George Shaffer. "A talent development framework: tackling the puzzle." *Development and Learning in Organisations* 24 No. 1 (2010): 13–16.

Heinen, Stevens, and Colleen O'Neill. "Managing talent to maximize performance." *Employment Relations Today* 31 No. 2 (2004): 67–82.

Hotten, R. "Volkswagen: The scandal explained." *BBC News.* http://www.bbc.com/news/business-34324772 (accessed on 7 October 2012).

Høyrup, Steen. "Reflection as a core process in organisational learning." *The Journal of Workplace Learning* 16 No. 8 (2004): 442–454.

Lewis, Robert, and Robert Heckman. "Talent management: A critical review." *Human Resource Management Review* 16 No. 2 (2006): 139–154.

Newhall, Steve. "A global approach to talent management: High-quality leaders are the key to competitive advantage." *Human Resource Management International Digest* 20 No. 6 (2012): 31–34.

Othman, Rozhan, and Wardah Azimah Sumardi. "Talent management at Tenaga Nasional Berhad." *Asian Case Research Journal* 17 No. 2 (2013): 289–304.

Othman, Rozhan, and Wardah Azimah Sumardi. "Talent management at Steelcase Manufacturing, Malaysia: Managing high performance." *Emerald Emerging Markets Case Studies* 4 No. 6 (2014): 1–14.

Petronas Leadership Centre. "PLC case study talent assessment framework." *Petronas International Human Capital Summit,* 2013.

Pruis, Evert. "The five key principles for talent development." *Indusctrial and Commercial Training* 43 No. 4 (2011): 206–216.

Ready, Douglas, and Jay Conger, "Make your company a talent factory." *Harvard Business Review* 85 No. 6 (2007): 68–77.

Russell, Joyce, and Daniellle Adams. "The changing nature of mentoring in organisations: An introduction to the special issue on mentoring in organisations." *Journal of Vocational Behaviour* 51 No. 1 (1997): 1–14.

Sanchez, Ron. "Understanding competence-based management: Identifying and managing five modes of competence." *Journal of Business Research* 57 (2004): 518–532.

Sheehan, Maura. "Developing managerial talent: Exploring the link between management talent and perceived performance in multinational corporations (MNCs)." *European Journal of Training and Development* 36 (2012): 66–85.

Skogstad, Anders, Stale Einarsen, Torbjon Torsheim, Merethe Aasland, And Hilde Hetland. "The destructiveness of laissez-faire leadership behaviour." *Journal of Occupational Health Psychology* 12 No. 1 (2007): 80–92.

Stadler, Karien. (2011). "Talent reviews: The key to effective succession management." *Business Strategy Series* 12 No. 5 (2011): 264–271.

Sumardi, Wardah Azimah, and Rozhan Othman. Talent management at Telekom Malaysia Berhad. *Emerging Markets Case Studies Collection* 1 No. 1 (2011): 1–6.

Swailes, Stephens. "The ethics of talent management." *Business Ethics* 22 No. 1 (2013): 32–46.

Tesluk, Paul, and Rick Jacobs. "Toward an integrated model of work experience." *Personnel Psychology* 51 No. 2 (1998): 321–355.

Thunnissen, Marian, Paul Boselie, and Ben Fruytier. "A review of talent management: Infancy or adolescence?" *International Journal of Human Resource Management* 24 No. 9 (2013): 1744–1761.

Tichy, Noel, and Charan, R. "Speed, simplicity, self-confidence: An interview with Jack Welch." *Harvard Business Review.* (September–October 1989): 2–9.

Tichy, Noel, and Nancy Cardwell. *The Cycle of Leadership: How Great Leaders Teach Their Companies to Win.* New York: Harper, 2002.

Tierney, Thomas. "The leadership deficit." *Stanford Social Innovation Review* 4 No. 2 (2006): 26–35.

Ulrich, David, Jon Younger, Wayne Brockbank, and Michael Ulrich. "HR talent and the new HR competencies. *Strategic HR Review* 11 No 4 (2012): 217–222.

Yarnall, Jane. "Maximising the effectiveness of talent pools: A review of case study literature." *Leadership & Organisation Development Journal* 32 No. 5 (2011): 510–526.

"Petronas outlines six strategies to remain profitable." *The Star,* 12 October 2015.

Chapter 8

Buch, Robert, Ogvind Martinsen, and Bard Kuvaas. "The destructiveness of laissez-faire leadership behaviour: The mediating role of economic leader–member exchange relationships." *Journal of Leadership and Organizational Studies* 22 No. 1 (2015): 115–125.

Crossan, Mary, Henry Lane, and Roderick White. "An organisational learning framework: From intuition to institution." *The Academy of Management Review* 24 No. 3 (1999): 522–537.

Ekvall, Goran. "Organisational climate for creativity and Innovation." *European Journal of Work and Organisational Psychology* 5 No. 1 (1996): 105–123.

Maccoby, Michael. "Narcissistic leaders: Incredibale pros and inevitable cons." *Harvard Business Review* (January 2004): 92–101.

Othman, Rozhan, and Wardah Azimah Sumardi. Talent management at Tenaga Nasional Berhad. *Asian Case Research Journal* 17 No. 2 (2013): 289–304.

Padilla, Art, Robert Hogan, and Robert Kaiser. "The toxic triangle: Destructive leaders, susceptible followers, and conducive environments." *The Leadership Quarterly* 18 (2007): 176–194.

Paine, Lyn. "Managing for organisational integrity." *Harvard Business Review* (March–April 1994): 106–117.

Chapter 9

Basu, Chirantan. "How to prevent organisational decline." *Ehow.* http://www.ehow.com/how_7699127_prevent-organisational-decline.html (accessed on 10 September 2015).

Crossan, Mary, Henry Lane, and Roderick White. "An organisational learning framework: From intuition to institution." *The Academy of Management Review* 24 No. 3 (1999): 522–537.

Krasikova, Dina, Stephens Green, and James LeBreton. "Refining and extending our understanding of destructive leadership." *Journal of Management* 39 (2013): 1308–1338.

Krasikova, Dina, Stephens Green, and James LeBreton. "Destructive leadership: A theoretical review, integration, and future research agenda." *Journal of Management* 20 No. 10 (2013): 1–31.

Lorange, Peter, and Robert Nelson. "How to recognize – and avoid – organisational decline." *Sloan Management Review* 28 No. 3 (1987): 41–48.

Pretorius, Marian. "Defining business decline, failure and turnaround: A content analysis." *South African Journal of Entrepreneurship and Small Business Management* 2 No. 1 (2009): 1–16.

Randell, Gerry. "Organisational sicknesses and their treatment." *Management Decision* 36 No. 1 (1998): 14–18.

Shin, Jiseon, Susan Taylor, and Myeong-Gyu Seo. "Organisational inducements and resilience: Oft ignored, but effective resources for building commitment and support for change." *Academy of Management Journal* 55 No. 3 (2013): 727–748.